elevate science

SAVVAS
LEARNING COMPANY

You are an author!

This is your book to keep. Write and draw in it!
Record your data and discoveries in it! You are
an author of this book!

Print your name, school, town, and state below.

My Photo

Name _____

School _____

Town, State _____

SAVVAS Learning Company LLC, 15 East Midland Avenue, Paramus, NJ 07652

Cover: The cover photo shows a hot air balloon. FCVR: Anatol Pietryczuk/Shutterstock; BCVR: Marinello/DigitalVision Vectors/Getty Images.

Attributions of third party content appear on pages EM34–EM36, which constitute an extension of this copyright page.

Next Generation Science Standards is a registered trademark of Achieve. Neither Achieve nor the lead states and partners that developed the Next Generation Science Standards were involved in the production of this product, and do not endorse it. NGSS Lead States. 2013. Next Generation Science Standards: For States, By States. Washington, DC: The National Academies Press.

SAVVAS™ and **SAVVAS LEARNING COMPANY™** are the exclusive trademarks of SAVVAS Learning Company LLC in the US and other countries.

SAVVAS Learning Company publishes through its famous imprints **PRENTICE HALL®** and **SCOTT FORESMAN®** which are exclusive registered trademarks owned by SAVVAS Learning Company LLC in the U.S. and/or other countries.

SAVVAS REALIZE™ is the exclusive trademark of SAVVAS Learning Company LLC in the U.S. and/or in other countries.

littleBits, littleBits logo and Bits are trademarks of littleBits Electronics, Inc. All rights reserved.

Unless otherwise indicated herein, any third party trademarks that may appear in this work are the property of their respective owners and any references to third party trademarks, logos or other trade dress are for demonstrative or descriptive purposes only. Such references are not intended to imply any sponsorship, endorsement, authorization, or promotion of SAVVAS Learning Company products by the owners of such marks, or any relationship between the owner and SAVVAS Learning Company LLC or its authors, licensees or distributors.

SAVVAS
LEARNING COMPANY

ISBN-13: 978-0-328-94877-2
ISBN-10: 0-328-94877-2

7   20

Program Authors

ZIPPORAH MILLER, EdD

Coordinator for K-12 Science Programs, Anne Arundel County Public Schools.
Zipporah Miller currently serves as the Senior Manager for Organizational Learning with the Anne Arundel County Public School System. Prior to that she served as the K-12 Coordinator for science in Anne Arundel County. She conducts national training to science stakeholders on the Next Generation Science Standards. Dr. Miller also served as the Associate Executive Director for Professional Development Programs and conferences at the National Science Teachers Association (NSTA) and served as a reviewer during the development of Next Generation Science Standards. Dr. Miller holds a doctoral degree from University of Maryland College Park, a master's degree in school administration and supervision from Bowie State University, and a bachelor's degree from Chadron State College.

MICHAEL J. PADILLA, PhD

Professor Emeritus, Eugene P. Moore School of Education, Clemson University, Clemson, South Carolina
Michael J. Padilla taught science in middle and secondary schools, has more than 30 years of experience educating middle grades science teachers, and served as one of the writers of the 1996 U.S. National Science Education Standards. In recent years Mike has focused on teaching science to English Language Learners. His extensive leadership experience, serving as Principal Investigator on numerous National Science Foundation and U.S. Department of Education grants, resulted in more than $35 million in funding to improve science education. He served as president of the National Science Teachers Association, the world's largest science teaching organization, in 2005–2006.

MICHAEL E. WYSESSION, PhD

Professor of Earth and Planetary Sciences, Washington University, St. Louis, Missouri
An author on more than 100 science and science education publications, Dr. Wysession was awarded the prestigious National Science Foundation Presidential Faculty Fellowship and Packard Foundation Fellowship for his research in geophysics, primarily focused on using seismic tomography to determine the forces driving plate tectonics. Dr. Wysession is also a leader in geoscience literacy and education, including being chair of the *Earth Science Literacy Principles*, author of several popular geology *Great Courses* video lecture series, and a lead writer of the *Next Generation Science Standards**.

---

*Next Generation Science Standards is a registered trademark of Achieve. Neither Achieve nor the lead states and partners that developed the Next Generation Science Standards were involved in the production of this product, and do not endorse it. NGSS Lead States. 2013. Next Generation Science Standards: For States, By States. Washington, DC: The National Academies Press.

Program Consultants

Carol Baker
Science Curriculum

Dr. Carol K. Baker is superintendent for Lyons Elementary K-8 School District in Lyons, Illinois. Prior to that, she was Director of Curriculum for Science and Music in Oak Lawn, Illinois. Before that she taught Physics and Earth Science for 18 years. In the recent past, Dr. Baker also wrote assessment questions for ACT (EXPLORE and PLAN), was elected president of the Illinois Science Teachers Association from 2011-2013 and served as a member of the Museum of Science and Industry advisory boards in Chicago. Dr. Baker received her BS in Physics and a science teaching certification. She is a writer of the Next Generation Science Standards. She completed her Master of Educational Administration (K-12) and earned her doctorate in Educational Leadership.

Jim Cummins
ELL

Dr. Cummins's research focuses on literacy development in multilingual schools and the role technology plays in learning across the curriculum. *Elevate Science* incorporates research-based principles for integrating language with the teaching of academic content based on Dr. Cummins's work.

Elfrieda Hiebert
Literacy

Dr. Hiebert is the President and CEO of TextProject, a nonprofit aimed at providing open-access resources for instruction of beginning and struggling readers, and a former primary school teacher. She is also a research associate at the University of California Santa Cruz. Her research addresses how fluency, vocabulary, and knowledge can be fostered through appropriate texts, and her contributions have been recognized through awards, such as the Oscar Causey Award for Outstanding Contributions to Reading Research (Literacy Research Association, 2015), Research to Practice Award (American Educational Research Association, 2013), William S. Gray Citation of Merit Award for Outstanding Contributions to Reading Research (International Reading Association, 2008).

Content Reviewers

Alex Blom, Ph.D.
Associate Professor
Department Of Physical Sciences
Alverno College
Milwaukee, Wisconsin

Joy Branlund, Ph.D.
Department of Physical Science
Southwestern Illinois College
Granite City, Illinois

Judy Calhoun
Associate Professor
Physical Sciences
Alverno College
Milwaukee, Wisconsin

Stefan Debbert
Associate Professor of Chemistry
Lawrence University
Appleton, Wisconsin

Diane Doser
Professor
Department of Geological Sciences
University of Texas at El Paso
El Paso, Texas

Rick Duhrkopf, Ph. D.
Department of Biology
Baylor University
Waco, Texas

Jennifer Liang
University Of Minnesota Duluth
Duluth, Minnesota

Heather Mernitz, Ph.D.
Associate Professor of Physical Sciences
Alverno College
Milwaukee, Wisconsin

Joseph McCullough, Ph.D.
Cabrillo College
Aptos, California

Katie M. Nemeth, Ph.D.
Assistant Professor
College of Science and Engineering
University of Minnesota Duluth
Duluth, Minnesota

Maik Pertermann
Department of Geology
Western Wyoming Community College
Rock Springs, Wyoming

Scott Rochette
Department of the Earth Sciences
The College at Brockport
State University of New York
Brockport, New York

David Schuster
Washington University in St Louis
St. Louis, Missouri

Shannon Stevenson
Department of Biology
University of Minnesota Duluth
Duluth, Minnesota

Paul Stoddard, Ph.D.
Department of Geology and Environmental Geosciences
Northern Illinois University
DeKalb, Illinois

Nancy Taylor
American Public University
Charles Town, West Virginia

Safety Reviewers

Douglas Mandt, M.S.
Science Education Consultant
Edgewood, Washington

Juliana Textley, Ph.D.
Author, NSTA books on school science safety
Adjunct Professor
Lesley University
Cambridge, Massachusetts

Teacher Reviewers

Jennifer Bennett, M.A.
Memorial Middle School
Tampa, Florida

Sonia Blackstone
Lake County Schools
Howey In the Hills, Florida

Teresa Bode
Roosevelt Elementary
Tampa, Florida

Tyler C. Britt, Ed.S.
Curriculum & Instructional
 Practice Coordinator
Raytown Quality Schools
Raytown, Missouri

A. Colleen Campos
Grandview High School
Aurora, Colorado

Ronald Davis
Riverview Elementary
Riverview, Florida

Coleen Doulk
Challenger School
Spring Hill, Florida

Mary D. Dube
Burnett Middle School
Seffner, Florida

Sandra Galpin
Adams Middle School
Tampa, Florida

Margaret Henry
Lebanon Junior High School
Lebanon, Ohio

Christina Hill
Beth Shields Middle School
Ruskin, Florida

Judy Johnis
Gorden Burnett Middle School
Seffner, Florida

Karen Y. Johnson
Beth Shields Middle School
Ruskin, Florida

Jane Kemp
Lockhart Elementary School
Tampa, Florida

Denise Kuhling
Adams Middle School
Tampa, Florida

Esther Leonard M.Ed. and L.M.T.
Gifted and Talented Implementation Specialist
San Antonio Independent School District
San Antonio, Texas

Kelly Maharaj
Science Department Chairperson
Challenger K8 School of Science and
 Mathematics
Elgin, Florida

Kevin J. Maser, Ed.D.
H. Frank Carey Jr/Sr High School
Franklin Square, New York

Angie L. Matamoros, Ph.D.
ALM Science Consultant
Weston, Florida

Corey Mayle
Brogden Middle School
Durham, North Carolina

Keith McCarthy
George Washington Middle School
Wayne, New Jersey

Yolanda O. Peña
John F. Kennedy Junior High School
West Valley City, Utah

Kathleen M. Poe
Jacksonville Beach Elementary School
Jacksonville Beach, Florida

Wendy Rauld
Monroe Middle School
Tampa, Florida

Bryna Selig
Gaithersburg Middle School
Gaithersburg, Maryland

Pat (Patricia) Shane, Ph.D.
STEM & ELA Education Consultant
Chapel Hill, North Carolina

Diana Shelton
Burnett Middle School
Seffner, Florida

Nakia Sturrup
Jennings Middle School
Seffner, Florida

Melissa Triebwasser
Walden Lake Elementary
Plant City, Florida

Michele Bubley Wiehagen
Science Coach
Miles Elementary School
Tampa, Florida

Pauline Wilcox
Instructional Science Coach
Fox Chapel Middle School
Spring Hill, Florida

Topic 1

Properties of Matter

Quest

In this Quest activity, you meet a robotics engineer who presents you with a design challenge. You must design a procedure for a robotic chef to use.

Like a robotics engineer, you complete activities and labs to learn how to identify substances. You use what you learn in the lessons to help design a robot that can identify ingredients.

Find your Quest activities on pages 2–3, 14, 23, 32–33, 34

Career Connection Robotics Engineer page 35

 VIDEO

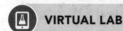 eTEXT

 INTERACTIVITY

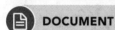 VIRTUAL LAB

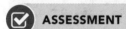 GAME

 DOCUMENT

ASSESSMENT

The Essential Question

HANDS-ON LAB

Changes in Matter

Quest

In this **STEM** Quest activity, you meet a materials scientist who presents you with a design challenge. You must design a model stepping stone for a school habitat.

Like a materials scientist, you complete activities and labs to learn how different combinations of material can make a design more useful. You use what you learn in the lessons to design a model for the stepping stone.

Find your Quest activities on pages 44–45, 55, 62, 74–75, 86–87, 88

Career Connection Materials Scientist page 35

- ▶ VIDEO
- 📖 eTEXT
- 👆 INTERACTIVITY
- 🔬 VIRTUAL LAB
- 🎮 GAME
- 📄 DOCUMENT
- ☑ ASSESSMENT

The Essential Question

HANDS-ON LAB

Topic 3

Earth's Systems

Quest

In this Quest activity, you meet an air pollution analyst who presents you with an acid rain problem. You need to develop an explanation about acid rain for the people of a city.

Like an air pollution analyst, you complete activities and labs to gather information about the effects of acid rain. You use what you learn in the lessons to help develop an explanation of how acid rain can affects Earth's four sphere.

Find your Quest activities on pages 98–99, 109, 116–117, 128, 130

Career Connection Air Pollution Analyist page 131

The Essential Question

HANDS-ON LAB

Icons legend

- ▶ VIDEO
- 📖 eTEXT
- 👆 INTERACTIVITY
- 🔲 VIRTUAL LAB
- 🎮 GAME
- 📄 DOCUMENT
- ✅ ASSESSMENT

Earth's Water

Quest

In this Quest activity, you meet a water quality specialist who wants your help to develop technology to provide safe drinking water to a community.

Like a water quality specialist, you complete activities and labs to evaluate different water sources. You use what you learn in the lessons to develop technology to make unsafe drinking water drinkable.

Find your Quest activities on pages 140–141, 151, 161, 170, 172

Career Connection Water Quality Specialist page 173

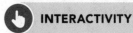 VIDEO

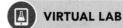 eTEXT

 INTERACTIVITY

 VIRTUAL LAB

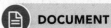 GAME

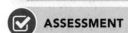 DOCUMENT

 ASSESSMENT

The Essential Question

HANDS-ON LAB

uConnect Lab
142

uInvestigate Lab
145, 155, 163

uDemonstrate Lab
178–179

Human Impacts on Earth's Systems

Quest

In this Quest activity, you meet an environmental scientist who presents you with a challenge to make your school more environmentally friendly.

Like an environmental scientist, you complete activities and labs to identify efficient and wasteful uses of resources in your school. You use what you learn in the lessons to write a plan of action that your school can use to conserve resources.

Find your Quest activities on pages 182–183, 193, 203, 210–211, 220, 222

Career Environmental Scientist page 223

 VIDEO

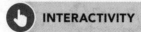 eTEXT

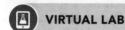 INTERACTIVITY

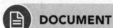 VIRTUAL LAB

 GAME

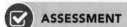 DOCUMENT

 ASSESSMENT

The Essential Question

HANDS-ON LAB

Topic 6

Solar System

Quest

In this **STEM** Quest activity, you meet an astronomical technician who presents you with a design problem. You must make a model of the solar system that fits in the lobby of your school.

Like an astronomical technician, you complete activities and labs to design and build your model solar system. You use what you learn in the lessons to make a model solar system that shows the correct size and placement of each planet.

Find your Quest activities on pages 232–233, 243, 252–253, 262, 264

Career Connection Astronomical Technician page 265

VIDEO

eTEXT

INTERACTIVITY

VIRTUAL LAB

GAME

DOCUMENT

ASSESSMENT

The Essential Question

HANDS-ON LAB

Patterns in Space

Quest

In this STEM Quest activity, you meet a planetarium curator who presents you with a museum task. You must make a brochure to explain space patterns.

Like a planetarium curator, you complete activities and labs to gather information for your brochure. You use what you learn in the lessons to make a brochure that the planetarium can use to teach others about patterns in space.

Find your Quest activities on pages 274–275, 283, 292, 303, 306

Career Connection Planetarium Curator page 307

- ▶ VIDEO
- 📖 eTEXT
- 👆 INTERACTIVITY
- 📱 VIRTUAL LAB
- 🎮 GAME
- 📄 DOCUMENT
- ☑ ASSESSMENT

The Essential Question

HANDS-ON LAB

uConnect Lab
276

uInvestigate Lab
279, 285, 295

uDemonstrate Lab
312–313

Topic 8

Energy and Food

Quest

In this Quest activity, you meet a nutritionist who presents you with a meal-planning challenge. You must plan a balanced menu for one day.

Like a nutritionist, you complete activities and labs to gather information about why animals need energy and how they get it. You use what you learn in the lessons to make a food plate for each meal a person eats in a day.

Find your Quest activities on pages 316–317, 327, 334–335, 344, 346

Career Connection Nutritionist page 347

VIDEO

eTEXT

INTERACTIVITY

VIRTUAL LAB

GAME

DOCUMENT

ASSESSMENT

The Essential Question

HANDS-ON LAB

Matter and Energy in Ecosystems

 VIDEO
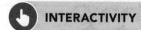 eTEXT
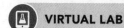 INTERACTIVITY
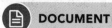 VIRTUAL LAB
GAME
DOCUMENT
ASSESSMENT

Quest

In this Quest activity, you meet a zoologist who presents you with a public relations challenge. You must make a video about an animal.

Like a zoologist, you complete activities and labs to gather information about a dangerous or creepy animal. You use what you learn in the lessons to make a video to improve the public opinion of the animal.

Find your Quest activities on pages 356–357, 367, 376, 384–385, 393, 396

Career Connection Zoologist page 397

The Essential Question

HANDS-ON LAB

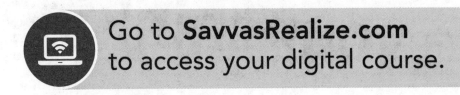

Go to **SavvasRealize.com** to access your digital course.

Elevate Science combines the best science writing with a robust online program. Throughout the lessons, look for digital support to increase your learning experience.

Online Resources

Savvas Realize™ is your online science class. It includes:

- Student eTEXT
- Teacher eTEXT
- Project-Based Learning
- Virtual Labs

- Interactivities
- Videos
- Assessments
- Study Tools
- and more!

Digital Features

VIDEO

INTERACTIVITY

VIRTUAL LAB

ASSESSMENT

eTEXT

GAME

Look for these **symbols**. They tell you that there are more things to do and learn online.

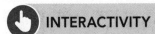

INTERACTIVITY

Complete an interactivity about chemical changes.

Elevate your thinking!

Elevate Science takes science to a whole new level and lets you take ownership of your learning. Explore science in the world around you. Investigate how things work. Think critically and solve problems! *Elevate Science* helps you think like a scientist, so you're ready for a world of discoveries.

Explore Your World

Explore real-life scenarios with engaging Quests that dig into science topics around the world. You can:

- Solve real-world problems
- Apply skills and knowledge
- Communicate solutions

Make Connections

Elevate Science connects science to other subjects and shows you how to better understand the world through:

- Mathematics
- Reading and Writing
- Literacy

Quest Kickoff

STEM Find the Right Mix— and Step on It!

How can we mix ingredients to make a model stepping stone?

Hi, I'm Alicia Gomez, a materials scientist! Suppose a school is setting up a prairie habitat. In this problem-based learning activity, you will build a model stepping stone so that students can observe the habitat without damaging the plants.

Like a materials scientist, you will evaluate your design and learn how different combinations of materials can make your design solution more useful. And you can decorate your model stepping stones, too!

Follow the path to learn how you will complete the Quest. The Quest activities in the lessons will help you complete the Quest! Check off your progress on the path when you com...

Visual Literacy Connection

What is the matter?

All matter is made up of smaller particles. How can you observe the magnification of matter?

If you were to look at a solid object, such as cotton shirt closely, describe what you might observe with your unaided eye?

Sample answers: I might be able to see strands of threads.

Properties of Matter

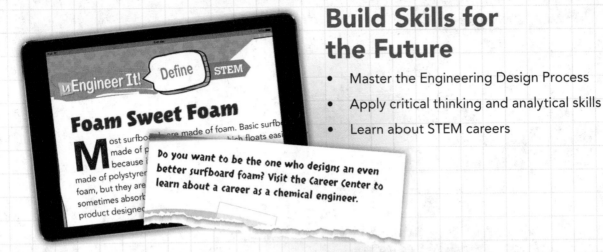

Build Skills for the Future

- Master the Engineering Design Process
- Apply critical thinking and analytical skills
- Learn about STEM careers

Do you want to be the one who designs an even better surfboard foam? Visit the Career Center to learn about a career as a chemical engineer.

Focus on Reading Skills

Elevate Science creates ongoing reading connections to help you develop the reading skills you need to succeed. Features include:

- Leveled Readers
- Literacy Connection Features
- Reading Checks

Literacy ▸ Toolbox 🔍

Use Evidence from Text
Water is formed by the combination of atoms of two different elements—hydrogen and ... smallest particl... atom or a mole... you think so?

✓ READING CHECK **Use Evidence from Text** Why d... you think aerogels could be used to clean up oil spills in... your community? Underline the important facts from th... text that support your claim with evidence.

Enter the Lab

Hands-on experiments and virtual labs help you test ideas and show what you know in performance-based assessments. Scaffolded labs include:

- STEM Labs
- Design Your Own
- Open-ended Labs

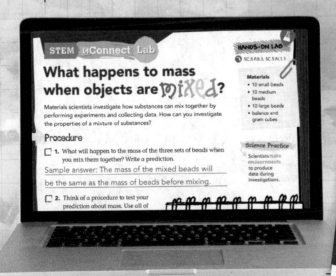

Properties of Matter

Next Generation Science Standards

5-PS1-1 Develop a model to describe that matter is made of particles too small to be seen.

5-PS1-3 Make observations and measurements to identify materials based on their properties.

The Essential Question

How do you describe properties of matter?

Show What You Know

Everything around you is made of matter. How can you tell one type of matter from another?

_____

_____

_____

Identify the Mystery Material

How can a robot identify materials?

Phenomenon Hi, I'm Maria Alvarez, a robotics engineer. My team is building a robotic chef that can prepare a meal while no one is at home.

In this problem-based learning activity, you will investigate ways that a robot can tell one substance from another. In the Quest, you will evaluate ways to identify substances. You will explore how kitchen ingredients are made of tiny particles. You will also compare substances based on their properties. Finally, you will design a procedure for the robot chef to use!

Follow the path to learn how you will complete the Quest. The Quest activities in the lessons will help you complete the Quest! Check off your progress on the path when you complete an activity with a QUEST CHECK ✓ OFF . Go online for more Quest activities.

Next Generation Science Standards
5-PS1-3. Make observations and measurements to identify materials based on their properties.

VIDEO

Watch a video about a robotics engineer.

Quest Check-In Lab 2

Lesson 2

Learn about the particles that make up matter as you explore materials the robot chef will use in recipes.

Quest Check-In Lab 3

Lesson 3

Use what you learn about the properties of matter to compare materials a robot chef might use in the kitchen.

Quest Check-In Lab 1

Lesson 1

Learn about the properties of matter and how a robot could tell one substance from another in a kitchen.

Quest Findings

Use your investigations to write a procedure to identify kitchen materials and tell one from another. You will make a chart to guide the robot.

HANDS-ON LAB

5-PS1-3, SEP.3

What's in the b☐x?

You can identify objects by using your senses. What clues help you identify an object?

Materials

• 3 boxes, each with an unknown object

Procedure

☐ **1.** Each box has a different object inside it. What tests could you use to gather information about the unknown objects?

_____

_____

_____

Science Practice

Scientists *make observations* to answer questions.

☐ **2.** **SEP Plan an Investigation** Write a plan. Show it to your teacher before you begin. Record your observations.

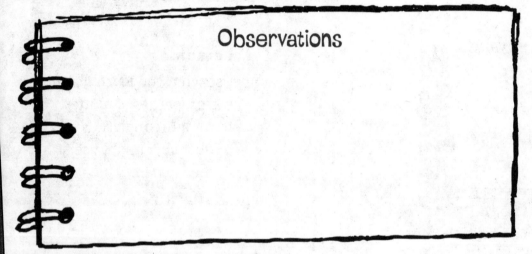

Observations

Analyze and Interpret Data

3. **SEP Use Evidence** Were you able to identify each object? What evidence did you use?

_____

_____

_____

_____

Use Evidence from Text

When you read, look for evidence that supports ideas. Several strategies can help you look for evidence.

GAME

Practice what you learn with the Mini Games.

- Think about what the text means.
- Read the text again and underline or record important points.

Read the text to find out why people might choose one building material instead of another.

Wood or Brick?

People use a variety of materials to build homes. Sometimes, people choose a certain material because of how it looks. There are other things to think about too.

Two common materials are wood and brick. Both materials can be used to make strong walls on a house. Brick walls will not burn. They do not need a layer of paint to protect them from weather. They are easy to take care of.

Some builders prefer wood. A brick home costs a lot more to build than a wood home, so it does not cost as much to buy a wood home. Wood is also easier to work with. The walls of a wood home are easier to change if the owner wants a different design. Wood is more flexible than brick, so it does not crack as a brick wall might. But wood also has some problems. Insects, such as termites, eat wood. Wood homes also have a greater chance of burning. Wood has to be painted to protect it from moisture and rot.

✓ **READING CHECK** **Use Evidence from Text** Circle Wood or Brick in the title to tell which building material you prefer. Underline the two sentences that support your claim with evidence.

Observe Matter

I can...

Observe and measure properties of materials.

5-PS1-3

Literacy Skill
Use Evidence from Text

Vocabulary
observe
measure
solubility

Academic Vocabulary
describe

▶ VIDEO

Watch a video about how measurements can show the differences between substances.

LOCAL-TO-GLOBAL ▷ Connection

When you buy fruit at the grocery store, how do you know how much to pay? Usually you see a sign that says the fruit costs a certain amount for one kilogram or one pound. Kilograms and pounds are units that we use to describe how heavy something is. At the grocery store, you might use pounds to say how much something weighs. In science, we describe the weight of something using the unit kilograms. People around the world use the same unit to tell about weight.

Different standard units describe the amounts of other properties, such as length and time. Because everyone agrees on the amount that each unit stands for, you always know what the unit means. Using standard units means that someone else—no matter where they live— will be able to know the exact amount you refer to.

Explain Why would it be hard to shop for food if there were no units to use to measure the amount of something?

_____

_____

_____

_____

uInvestigate Lab

How do we describe materials?

Scientists often use knowledge of different materials to identify what something is. How can you describe an object so that others can identify it?

Materials
- 4 objects

Suggested Materials
- ruler
- balance
- gram cubes

Procedure

☐ **1.** Choose three of the objects. Do not let others see them. Write the properties of each object in the Properties column of the table. Use the other materials to help you describe the properties. Do not write the name of the object.

Science Practice

Scientists make observations to produce data.

Object	Properties

☐ **2.** Trade notes with another group. Use that group's descriptions to identify each of the objects.

Analyze and Interpret Data

3. Evaluate What information helped you identify each object? What information would have made identifying the objects easier?

_____

_____

_____

Observing Properties

Every kind of material has properties. A property is a characteristic of a material, such as its color and odor. Some materials might have some properties that are the same as the properties of other materials. But no two materials have the exact same set of properties.

You can directly observe many of the properties of a material. When you **observe** something, you use your senses to gather information about it. For example, you use your eyes to observe the color and shape of the materials in the building in the photo. You use your ears to observe that a guitar string makes a specific sound. You observe the hardness and texture of a rock using your sense of touch. In the kitchen, you can observe the properties of foods by tasting or smelling them. When you observe something, you can use the information you gather to describe what you observed. When you **describe** something, you tell about its properties.

Apply Each material in the building has a unique set of properties. Circle the material that has these properties: white, hard, smooth, and in the shape of a rectangle.

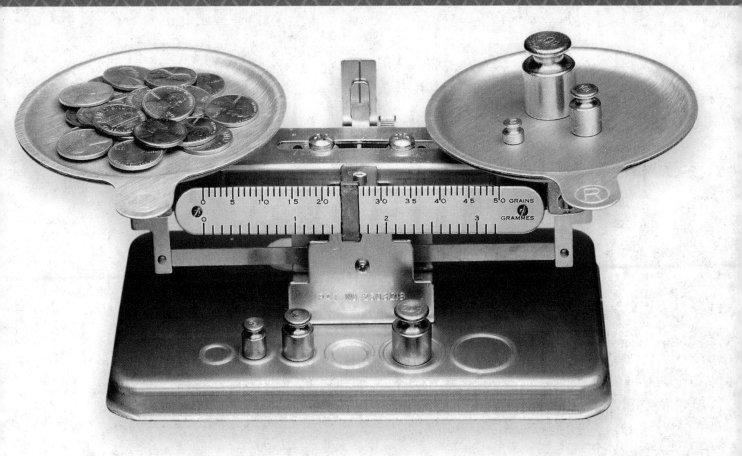

Measuring Properties

You observe some properties by using scientific tools. One way to use tools is to measure. When you **measure** a property, you compare it to a standard unit, or value, for that property. Each unit of measurement is recognized all over the world. For example, you might measure the length of an object using a meterstick. The unit of measurement for length is 1 meter. If the object is 3 meters long, then the measured length of the object is 3 times the length of 1 meter. The meter is the exact same length around the world.

When you measure the weight of an object, you use a balance or a scale. The balance compares the weight of the object to standard weights, such as the gram masses shown in the right pan in the photograph. Each gram mass is marked with a specific amount of grams or kilograms.

Another measurement is how much space a material takes up. This property is measured in liters and milliliters.

Compare Circle the gram mass on the balance pan that you think would measure the largest number of coins.

Science Practice
►Toolbox

Ask Questions Suppose you needed to find a material that would be a safe covering for a child's playroom. What questions would you ask about the properties of materials you are considering?

Can you TELL THEM APART?

Every material has physical properties that you can use to describe it. You can use these properties to tell one material from another. These two blocks have the same length, width, and height. One block is made of wood. The other block is made of steel. How can you tell them apart?

A

B

How do their masses compare?

A 500 g

B 7,500 g

How hard are they?

A   B

> Which block is made of wood and which block is made of steel? Shade in the block you think is made of steel. Describe how you can identify the material of the blocks.

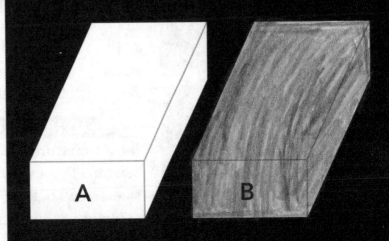

A   B

Conductors of Heat and Electricity

You can identify some properties directly by using your senses. Other times, you may need to observe how a material acts with other materials or with energy. If you stir a pot of soup with a metal spoon, the handle of the spoon gets hot. If you stir it with a wooden spoon, the handle does not get hot. A property of the metal is that it moves, or conducts, heat easily from the soup to your hand. A property of the wood is that it does not easily conduct heat.

Just as some materials transfer heat, some materials conduct electricity. When you connect a light to a battery to make it shine, you use wires. The wires are probably made of a metal called copper. One property of copper is that it conducts electricity. If you connect the battery and light with string instead of a copper wire, the light does not turn on. That is because a property of the string is that it does not easily conduct electricity.

Infer Why does the electric cord on a lamp have a layer of plastic around the copper wire?

_____

_____

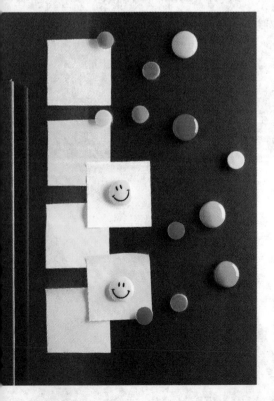

Magnetic Materials

Another property of materials is whether they are magnetic, or attracted to a magnet. Many people use magnets to hold notes on a refrigerator. Many refrigerator doors are made from magnetic steel. The magnets sticking to the door are also magnetic. If the refrigerator were made from brass, the magnets would not stick to the door. Brass is not magnetic.

✓ READING CHECK **Use Evidence from Text** If you have a mixture of steel screws and brass screws, you can separate them with a magnet. The magnet will pick up the steel screws but not the brass screws. Circle the text that explains why the screws can be separated this way.

Solubility

If you have ever gone swimming in the ocean, you probably know that seawater tastes salty. You cannot see the salt in the water, though, because salt dissolves in water. But if you put a bit of pepper into a glass of water, the pepper will not dissolve. The pepper does not appear to change at all. The solubilities of the two substances are different. **Solubility** is a property of material that refers to how well it dissolves in another material, such as water. Salt is soluble in water. Pepper is not. Some substances are more soluble than pepper but less soluble than salt.

Quest Connection

Some substances used in cooking dissolve in water. Others do not. The cooking oil and the water in the bottle form layers because oil is not soluble in water. How can solubility help the robot identify ingredients?

_____

_____

_____

☑ Lesson 1 Check

1. **Draw Conclusions** Two blocks of shiny, silver metal have the same width, length, and height. On a balance, one block weighs 1.5 kilograms. The other block weighs 2.3 kilograms. What can you conclude about the blocks of metal?

_____

_____

2. **Explain** What property of a thick cloth pad makes it useful for picking up a hot pan on the stove?

_____

How can you observe matter?

A robot chef would need a way to use properties to tell one ingredient from another. How can you learn about the properties of materials by making observations and doing investigations?

Procedure

☐ 1. Choose two materials. What are two properties of the materials that you could test?

_____

_____

☐ 2. Make a plan to test the properties. Show your plan to your teacher before you begin. Record your observations in the table.

Material	Property 1	Property 2

Materials
- safety goggles

Suggested Materials
- salt
- sugar
- baking soda
- flour
- white sand
- hand lens
- plastic cups
- water

 Wear safety goggles.

 Do not taste any of the materials.

Science Practice

Scientists make observations to produce data.

Analyze and Evaluate

3. **Compare** How could the robot use the properties to tell one substance from the other?

_____

_____

_____

Looking for Clues

Phenomenon Detectives on television often use evidence from a crime lab to solve a crime. This also happens in real life. Forensic scientists use clues from a crime scene to figure out what happened and who was responsible. These investigators pay close attention to details. The smallest clue, such as a single human hair, may be the key to solving a crime.

Crime scene technicians might pick up small pieces of dirt and soil that they find at the crime scene. Why would they do that? When you walk outside, bits of soil, sand, and even small pebbles stick to the bottoms of your shoes. Before going inside, you wipe your feet to avoid making a mess. Maybe someone at the crime scene was not so careful. Their tracks might solve the crime. Every kind of soil has particles with different properties—size, shape, and types of materials. By comparing the properties of soil at the scene to the properties of soil on a shoe, forensic scientists can tell where someone walked. That might be just the information that a detective needs.

What information could you obtain by observing a footprint?

_____

_____

Model Matter

I can...

Explain that matter is made of tiny particles too small to be seen.

5-PS1-1

Literacy Skill
Use Evidence from Text

Vocabulary
atom
atomic theory
compound
molecule

Academic Vocabulary
conclude

 VIDEO

Watch a video about how to model matter.

ENGINEERING Connection

Salt is a natural resource that people need in their diets. The salt that you use in your kitchen may come from a salt deposit. In these deposits, the salt is often a large, solid mass, like rock. People use tools to break it apart into smaller pieces. Even these small chunks are too big to use on your food. Sometimes the salt is crushed small enough to pour from a saltshaker. Another way to break the salt into smaller pieces is by using a salt grinder.

Predict What would happen if you could keep grinding the salt particles?

_____

_____

Divide Matter

When you grind salt, you divide chunks of salt into smaller pieces. These small pieces are still salt. The small grindings have a similar shape to the larger pieces. They taste the same on your food. You can crush them again with a spoon to make salt powder.

uInvestigate Lab

How can you detect matter without seeing it?

Materials scientists study all kinds of matter. How can you show evidence of matter that you cannot see?

Procedure

☐ **1.** Pull the plunger to the last mark on the syringe. Observe the syringe. Write a description of what you think is in the syringe.

_____

_____

_____

☐ **2.** Choose materials from the list to test whether matter is in the syringe. Write a procedure test whether the syringe contains matter. Show your procedure to your teacher before you start.

☐ **3.** Record your observations.

Analyze and Interpret Data

4. SEP Use Evidence How did your data provide evidence that the syringe contained matter?

_____

_____

_____

_____

_____

_____

Materials

- safety goggles
- 2 plastic syringes

Suggested Materials

- balloons
- rubber tubing
- cup of water
- plastic straw

Wear safety goggles.

Science Practice

Scientists **construct arguments** based on evidence.

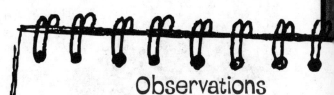
Observations

Atoms

From a distance, a sand castle on a beach looks like a solid object. If you look at it closely, you see that it is made of small particles of sand. The tiny sand grains combine to form the castle.

Explain What do you think is the smallest piece that you could break sand into? Why do you think so?

_____

_____

All matter is made of elements. An element is made up of only one kind of atom. The smallest part of an element that still has the properties of the element is called an **atom**. All substances are made of atoms. You cannot see atoms with a regular microscope because they are too small. However, special instruments can show how atoms are arranged in a particular substance.

The atoms of each element are different from the atoms of every other element. All the matter around you is made of atoms. The idea that everything is made of small particles is known as the **atomic theory**. The smallest piece of sand has many more atoms than the number of grains of sand in the whole sand castle.

Molecules

Most things around you are **compounds**, which are matter made of two or more elements. The atoms of different elements are joined together in a particular way to form each compound. Table salt is a compound that is made up of the elements sodium and chlorine.

The smallest particle of a compound that still has the properties of that compound is called a **molecule**. For example, carbon dioxide is a molecule that has only three atoms. Molecules can be made of many atoms.

Identify Circle the carbon dioxide molecule in the diagram.

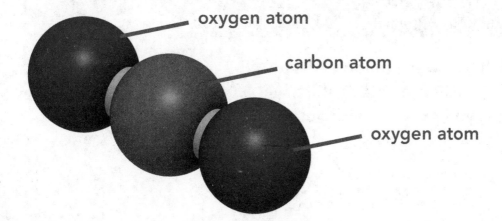

oxygen atom

carbon atom

oxygen atom

Quest Connection

Even when mixed, elements and molecules still keep their unique properties. Explain why.

_____

_____

_____

_____

What is the matter?

All matter is made up of smaller particles. How can you observe the magnification of matter?

! **Describe** If you were to look closely at a T-shirt, such as a cotton shirt, what might you observe with your unaided eye?

_____

_____

_____

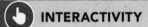
INTERACTIVITY

Complete an activity
about matter.

! **Infer** Why are you not able to see the loops holding the shirt together with just your eye?

_____

_____

_____

! **Compare** Scientists use magnification to help see fibers up close. How do the fibers in this image look different from the fibers without magnification?

_____

_____

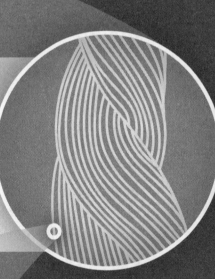

Infer Draw what you think the atoms of the shirt might look like if you could actually see them. Why are you not able to see them?

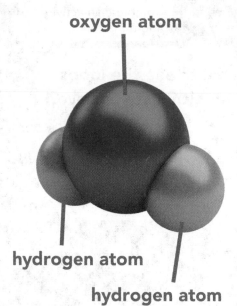

oxygen atom

hydrogen atom

hydrogen atom

Same Atoms, Different Matter

When the same kinds of atoms in a molecule combine in different amounts, different molecules form. For example, a water molecule has one atom of oxygen and two atoms of hydrogen. Another molecule is also made of hydrogen and oxygen atoms. However, it contains two hydrogen atoms and two oxygen atoms. Although this molecule also contains only hydrogen and oxygen, it is a substance different from water. It is hydrogen peroxide.

Changing the kinds of atoms in a molecule also results in a different molecule. Carbon dioxide is the gas you breathe out. Sulfur dioxide is a poisonous gas with an irritating smell. Because the properties of these two substances are different, you can conclude that their molecules are different. When you **conclude**, you use data and facts to make a statement.

☑ Lesson 2 Check

1. **Conclude** Table salt is a compound made of sodium and chlorine atoms. From the table, what can you conclude about the properties of compounds and the elements they are made of?

Some Properties of Three Substances			
Property	**Chlorine**	**Sodium**	**Table salt**
State (at room temperature)	gas	solid	solid
Color	green	silver	white
Toxicity	poisonous	poisonous	not poisonous

_____

_____

2. **☑ READING CHECK Use Evidence from Text** What makes up matter? Use the definition of *atomic theory* to answer.

_____

_____

How do you *know* that matter is still there?

When you mix two substances together, the appearance of the matter can change. Are the same atoms still there?

Materials
- safety goggles
- 3 plastic cups
- 3 small bowls
- 3 spoons
- salt
- sugar
- baking soda
- water
- wax marker

Procedure

☐ **1.** Label three plastic cups *Sugar*, *Salt*, and *Baking soda*. Pour the same amount of water into each cup.

☐ **2.** Use a spoon to add some sugar into the cup labeled *Sugar*. Stir until the sugar dissolves. Repeat with salt and baking soda. Use different spoons each time. Record your observations.

_____

_____

☐ **3.** How can you find out whether the original materials are still in each cup? Write a procedure. Show your plan to your teacher before you begin. Record your observations.

  Wear safety goggles.

⚠ Do not taste.

Science Practice

Scientists use evidence to support their conclusions.

Observations

Analyze and Interpret Data

4. SEP Use Evidence Did your observations present any evidence that matter is made up of small particles? Explain how.

_____

_____

uEngineer It! Define STEM

VIDEO

Watch a video about robots in the kitchen.

Robot Chef

Phenomenon What picture comes to your mind when you think of a robot? Many people "see" a robot that looks somewhat like a person. Some robots are designed that way. Others are very different. A robot can look like a snake, a crab, a tractor, or a human arm and hand. The shape of a robot depends on what the robot is intended to do.

A robot is a machine that uses one or more sensors to gather information about its surroundings. This is similar to the way people observe or measure. The robot records the information it gathers. Then it performs an action based on the information. People have placed information in the robot so that it is able to "decide" what to do. Some robots put parts together in factories or search for people after a disaster. Some robots even help doctors perform surgery.

Would you like to be the person who designs a robot chef?

Define It

Think about what a robot chef needs to do. What tools will it need to use to mix ingredients and cook a meal?

☐ Write the steps that a robot will follow to bake a loaf of bread.

☐ How will your robot know it has the right ingredients?

☐ Draw your robot and label the parts.

Properties of Matter

I can...

Identify materials based on their properties.

5-PS1-3

Literacy Skill
Use Evidence from Text

Vocabulary
temperature
mass
volume

Academic Vocabulary
organize

▶ VIDEO

Watch a video about properties of matter.

STEM ▶ Connection

Suppose that you are playing soccer on a winter evening. As it gets dark, you forget to take your ball inside. During the night, the air becomes very cold. In the morning, the ball seems different. It is not as round as it was. It feels soft and squishy. When you kick the ball, it does not go very far. It seems like some of the air is missing, but there is no leak. During the day, the ball gets warmer and goes back to the way it was yesterday.

The amount of air in the ball did not change during the night, but the volume of air did change. The air particles inside the ball put pressure on the inside of the ball. That is what causes the ball to inflate. As the air particles inside the ball cooled at night, the amount of pressure they put on the ball decreased. As a result, the ball shrank. When the particles warmed during the next day, they again put more pressure on the ball.

▤ Reflect Did you ever play a sport on a cold day? What did you like the best about playing in the cold?

uInvestigate Lab

How can you use properties to identify solids?

To identify an unknown substance, materials scientists compare its properties with the properties of known substances. How can you use properties to identify three substances?

Procedure

☐ **1.** You have three substances labeled A, B, and C. Use the table to plan an experiment to identify the three unknown substances. Show your procedure to your teacher before you begin.

☐ **2.** Identify each unknown substance by writing its letter beneath the name of each substance in the table.

Properties of Materials

Sugar	Salt	Cornstarch
white solid	white solid	white solid
irregular crystals	cube-shaped crystals	fine powder
dissolves in water	dissolves in water	does not dissolve in water
solution is not very conductive	solution is very conductive	does not form solution

Analyze and Interpret Data

3. SEP Use Evidence What evidence did you use to identify each unknown?

_____

_____

_____

Materials

- 3 substances labeled A, B, and C
- safety goggles
- 3 cups
- 3 spoons
- conductivity tester
- hand lens
- water
- wax marker

Wear safety goggles.

Do not taste.

Science Practice

Scientists *interpret data* when they analyze results of an investigation.

Food Coloring in Water

With an adult, fill one bowl with hot water and one bowl with cold water. Put one drop of food coloring in each bowl. What differences do you observe? How can you explain your observations?

States of Matter

Scientists organize all matter according to its state. When you **organize** something, you sort it. The three main states of matter are solid, liquid, and gas. Water is a solid when it is ice. It is a liquid when you drink it. The gas form of water is called water vapor. The state of a material is due to the motion of its atoms or molecules. A material can change from one state to another as the motion of its particles changes. Water is a solid when it is very cold and its particles vibrate in place. It turns into a liquid when it is heated and its particles move more. Water becomes a gas when it is very hot and its particles move very fast.

Solid

Liquid

Gas

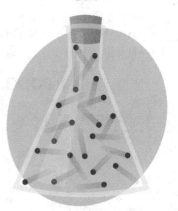

The particles of a solid do not slide easily past each other. They vibrate, or move back and forth, in place.

The particles of a liquid can move past each other.

The particles of a gas move very fast and spread out evenly to fill available space.

Model It! Suppose that you are a particle. With your classmates, act out how particles behave in a solid, liquid, and gas. How did you show each state of matter?

_____

_____

_____

Temperature

The **temperature** of an object is a measure of how fast its particles are moving. The higher the temperature, the faster the particles move. Different scales are used for measuring temperature. In science, you probably will find the temperature at which a substance melts given in degrees Celsius (°C). In a recipe, cooking temperature is most likely given in degrees Fahrenheit (°F). Both units are accurate measures of temperature.

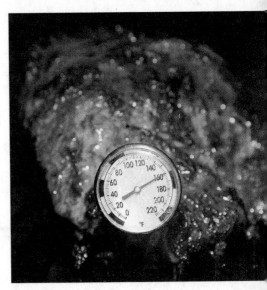

Collect Data This food thermometer shows the temperature of the meat. What is the temperature? Be sure to identify whether the temperature is given in Fahrenheit or Celsius.

_____

_____

Mass and Volume

The amount of matter in a substance is its **mass**. Scientists usually measure mass in units of grams (g) or kilograms (kg). To find the mass of an object, you can compare it to other objects that have a known mass. On a balance, the sides will be uneven, like those in the photo, when the masses are different.

The amount of space an object takes up is its **volume**. Volume can be measured in milliliters (mL). Solid and liquid materials have a definite volume. They take up a certain amount of space. Gases also have volume. The volume of a gas will change to fill all of the space available.

Infer Describe the relationship between mass and volume.

_____

_____

_____

_____

_____

_____

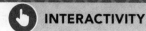
Crosscutting Concepts ▸ Toolbox

Stability and Change
One main goal of science is understanding how things change. Think about the properties discussed on these pages. How easily do you think these properties can change? Rank them from most changeable to least changeable.

Color

The physical properties of a material can be observed, measured, and described without changing the material. Color is a physical property of matter. Color is an easy property for identification because you can determine the color of something just by looking at it. You can often organize various types of matter based on similarities and differences in color.

Apply Give an example when using color to identify a substance would be important.

_____

_____

_____

Quest Connection

Do you think that color and texture are important properties of a stepping stone? Explain your answer.

_____

_____

_____

Texture and Hardness

When you touch a solid object, you can feel whether it is smooth, lumpy, grooved, spongy, or rough. This surface structure that you can feel by touching a material is its texture. Hardness is another property of a solid that you can feel. If something is hard, it tends to keep its shape when you push it or strike it. If it is soft, it tends to bend.

☑ READING CHECK **Use Evidence from Text**
What is texture? Describe the texture of the brick and copper.

_____

_____

_____

_____

_____

_____

_____

_____

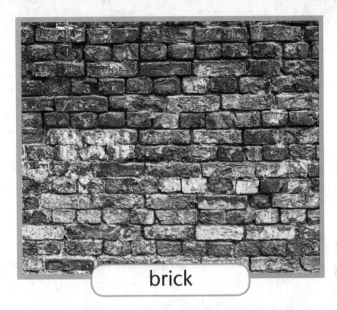

brick

copper

☑ Lesson 3 Check

1. **Analyze** A heavy brick weighs more than a fluffy cushion, but the cushion takes up more space. Which object has more matter? How do you know?

_____

_____

2. **Explain** Why does a solid fill only part of a closed jar while the same mass of a gas fills the whole jar?

_____

_____

How can you compare the properties of matter?

Before we can program the robot, we must understand the properties of the materials the robot will be sensing. How can you learn about the properties of familiar materials?

Suggested Materials
- cups
- water
- hand lens
- wooden block
- metal coin
- sugar
- salt
- flour
- baking soda
- white sand
- paper
- spoon

Procedure

☐ 1. Choose four objects from the list of materials. Record which objects you have chosen in the first column of the table.

☐ 2. Choose three different physical properties of the objects that you will test. Record the properties that you will test in the top row of the table.

☐ 3. **SEP Plan an Investigation** Plan how you will test the properties. Write your plan and have your teacher approve it.

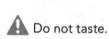
⚠ Do not taste.

Science Practice
Scientists use evidence to support explanations.

4. **SEP Conduct an Investigation** Test the three properties. Record your data and observations in the table.

Properties of Materials

Material	Property 1 _____	Property 2 _____	Property 3 _____
1			
2			
3			
4			

Analyze and Interpret Data

5. **Evaluate** Suppose you had an unknown sample and knew that it was one of the four materials you tested. How could you identify which material you had based on the properties you tested?

_____

_____

_____

_____

6. **Evaluate** What is another property that you could use to tell which of the four substances you have? Explain your answer.

_____

_____

_____

INTERACTIVITY

Organize data to support your Quest Findings.

STEM Identify the Mystery Material

How can a robot identify materials?

Design a Procedure

Phenomenon You have learned about the properties of matter. Now you will develop tests that a robot chef could use to be certain that it is using the right material in a recipe.

Several common ingredients in the kitchen are white solids. These include flour, salt, sugar, and baking soda. Write a procedure to test an unknown material and identify it as one of these white solids.

Procedures

_____

_____

_____

_____

_____

_____

_____

_____

Construct Explanations

Will your tests allow the robot to identify the material if it is one of the four ingredients listed above? How do you know?

_____

_____

_____

_____

_____

Robotics Engineer

Robotics engineers design and build new robots, program them to perform specific tasks, and find new things for robots to do. Many robots perform tasks in factories. Robotics engineers design these robots so they can handle tools. They also write computer programs that instruct the moving parts what to do.

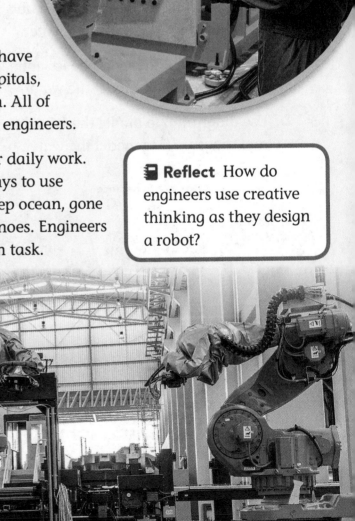

You might see a simple robot that vacuums the floor. Cars that carry passengers with no driver have been tested on roads. Robots help doctors in hospitals, run equipment on farms, and play with children. All of these robots were designed and built by robotics engineers.

Robotics engineers use math and science in their daily work. These engineers must be creative to find new ways to use robots to do tasks. Robots have traveled to the deep ocean, gone into burning buildings, and even explored volcanoes. Engineers figure out the best way to design a robot for each task.

Reflect How do engineers use creative thinking as they design a robot?

☑ Assessment

1. **Use Diagrams** Marisol wants to model the arrangement of the particles that make up an ice cube and the particles that make up liquid water. She finds the diagrams below in a library book.

   What is the best way for her to use these diagrams to model the particles of an ice cube and water?

   A. Use diagram A to model the ice cube and diagram B to model the water.

   B. Use diagram A to model the ice cube and diagram C to model the water.

   C. Use diagram B to model the ice cube and diagram A to model the water.

   D. Use diagram B to model the ice cube and diagram C to model the water.

   States of a Substance

   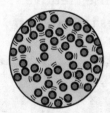 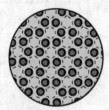 

   Diagram A   Diagram B   Diagram C

2. **Vocabulary** Which of these is always true of a compound?

   A. It is a solid material.

   B. It has more than one kind of atom.

   C. It melts when you heat it over a burner.

   D. It is part of a mixture of different substances.

3. **Summarize** What are three properties of a substance that you can determine just by looking at it?

   _____

   _____

   _____

   _____

   _____

   _____

4. **Predict** Potassium chloride is a compound that is very soluble in water. What will happen to the particles of potassium chloride if a spoonful of potassium chloride is stirred into a beaker of water?

   _____

   _____

   _____

   _____

   _____

   _____

   _____

5. Explain What happens to the molecules of water as you heat the water in a pan?

A. The molecules expand.

B. The molecules move faster.

C. The molecules move closer together.

D. The molecules break apart into separate atoms.

6. Interpret These cylinders are tools used to measure substances. What property of the liquids do they measure?

A. color

B. mass

C. reflectivity

D. volume

7. Differentiate How is a measurement of a property different from an observation that is not a measurement?

_____

_____

_____

_____

_____

The Essential Question *How do you describe properties of matter?*

Show What You Learned

Flour and baking soda are both white powders with very small particles. What test can you use to tell whether a sample is flour or baking soda?

_____

_____

_____

_____

_____

_____

_____

Read this scenario and answer questions 1–5.

A scientist in a manufacturing lab was given a substance to identify. The substance was known to be one of four possible chemicals. The chart shows some properties of four possible substances. Equipment for the investigation included beakers, water, vinegar, a hand lens, and a conductivity meter.

Properties of Substances				
Property	**calcium carbonate**	**calcium sulfate**	**sodium bicarbonate**	**fructose**
Solubility in water	not soluble	not soluble	soluble	soluble
Color	white	white	white	white
Particle appearance	powder	crystals	powder	crystals
Makes bubbles in vinegar	yes	no	yes	no
Is a solution conductive	does not form solution	does not form solution	yes	no

1. **Evaluate** The chart shows the scientist's tests and results. Someone in the lab suggested that an observation of the color of the substance would be important. Explain why color would or would not be a useful observation in this investigation.

_____

_____

2. **Evaluate** The scientist observed one unknown substance using a hand lens. It was made up of crystals. What conclusion could be made based on this observation?

   A. The substance is calcium carbonate.

   B. The substance is not fructose.

   C. The substance might be sodium bicarbonate

   D. The substance is either fructose or calcium sulfate.

3. **Collect Data** If the scientist thinks the substance is either sodium bicarbonate or fructose, what test could be used to decide which it is?

   A. Dissolve the substance in water.

   B. Observe the color of the substance.

   C. Measure the conductivity of a solution of the substance.

   D. Observe the substance with the hand lens to see whether it has a crystal form.

4. **Plan an Investigation** The scientist considered starting with tests that could identify the substance in one step. Could any of the tests make an identification in one test? If so, identify which substance or substances could be identified by that test.

   _____

   _____

   _____

   _____

5. **Evaluate** The scientist recorded these observations.

Property	Observation
Solubility in water	soluble
Color	white
Particle appearance	powder
Makes bubbles in vinegar	yes
Is a solution conductive	yes

What was the unknown substance?

   A. calcium carbonate

   B. calcium sulfate

   C. sodium bicarbonate

   D. fructose

How do you know what it is?

Phenomenon When scientists test substances, they make observations. Then they compare the substance to a substance with known properties. How can you identify unknown materials by comparing test results to known properties?

Procedure

☐ **1.** What tests will you perform to identify the unknown substances? You should use at least two different tests.

_____

_____

_____

_____

_____

☐ **2. SEP Plan an Investigation** Write a procedure for the tests of the unknown substances. Use all of the listed materials. Show your procedure to your teacher before you begin.

_____

_____

_____

_____

_____

Materials
- safety goggles
- 2 plastic cups
- 2 unknown substances
- hand lens
- water
- magnet
- spoon
- conductivity tester

 Do not taste any of the materials.

 Wear safety goggles.

Science Practice

Scientists make observations to answer questions.

3. Record your data.

Substance	Appearance	Magnetic	Soluble	Conductive
salt	white crystals	no	yes	yes
sugar	white crystals	no	yes	no
iron fillings	dark pieces	yes	no	no
activated carbon	dark pieces	no	no	no
unknown #1				
unknown #2				

Analyze and Interpret Data

4. Evaluate What were the properties of the substances that you used for identifying the unknown substances?

_____

_____

_____

5. CCC Structure and Function Was your test able to show differences among all of the four known materials? Provide evidence to support your answer.

_____

_____

_____

6. Draw Conclusions Were you able to identify the two unknown substances? Explain.

_____

_____

Changes in Matter

Next Generation Science Standards

5-PS1-2 Measure and graph quantities to provide evidence that regardless of the type of change that occurs when heating, cooling, or mixing substances, the total weight of matter is conserved.

5-PS1-4 Conduct an investigation to determine whether the mixing of two or more substances result in new substances.

Go online to access
your digital course.

▶ VIDEO

📖 eTEXT

👆 INTERACTIVITY

📱 VIRTUAL LAB

🎮 GAME

☑ ASSESSMENT

The Essential Question

What evidence do we have that matter changes?

Show What You Know

At one time the exteriors of these boats looked very different. What do you think happened to cause their appearance to change?

_____

_____

_____

STEM Find the Right Mix— and Step on It!

How can we mix ingredients to make a model stepping stone?

Phenomenon Hi, I'm Alicia Gomez, a materials scientist! Suppose a school is setting up a prairie habitat. In this problem-based learning activity, you will build a model stepping stone for the habitat so that students can observe the habitat without damaging the plants.

Like a materials scientist, you will evaluate your design and learn how different combinations of materials can make your design solution more useful. And you can decorate your model stepping stones, too!

Follow the path to learn how you will complete the Quest. The Quest activities in the lessons will help you complete the Quest! Check off your progress on the path when you complete an activity with a
QUEST CHECK ✔ OFF . Go online for more Quest activities.

Quest Check-In 1

Lesson 1

Learn about the states of matter and their properties to help you develop a list of criteria and constraints to guide the development of your model stepping stone.

Next Generation Science Standards
5-PS1-4 Conduct an investigation to determine whether the mixing of two or more substances result in new substances.

▶ **VIDEO**

Watch a video about a materials scientist.

Quest Check-In Lab 4

Lesson 4

Use what you learn about mixtures and solutions as you revise your "concrete" formula to get the best product. Then build your model stepping stone.

Quest Check-In Lab 3

Lesson 3

Find out about chemical changes and how they affect the model "concrete" you will make.

Quest Findings

Use your model to think about other important features of a concrete stepping stone. Suggest how you would change your model. Retest your model.

Quest Check-In 2

Lesson 2

Apply what you learn about physical changes in matter as you sketch a model for your stepping stone.

What happens to mass when objects are mixed?

Materials scientists investigate how substances can mix together by performing experiments and collecting data. How can you investigate the properties of a mixture of substances?

Materials
- 10 small beads
- 10 medium beads
- 10 large beads
- balance and gram cubes

Procedure

☐ **1.** What will happen to the mass of the three sets of beads when you mix them together? Write a prediction.

_____

_____

Science Practice

Scientists make measurements to produce data during investigations.

☐ **2.** Think of a procedure to test your prediction about mass. Use all of the listed materials. Share your procedure with your teacher before you begin.

☐ **3.** Make a bar graph to show your data. Label each bar on the x-axis. Label the units on the y-axis.

Analyze and Interpret Data

4. SEP Use Evidence What happens to the mass of objects when they are mixed?

_____

_____

_____

_____

_____

_____

Observations

Bead	Small	Medium	Large	Mixture
Mass (g)				

Mass (g) (y-axis)

Bead size (x-axis)

Use Evidence from Text

When you read carefully, you look for evidence. Use these strategies to help you look for evidence.

- Do a first read.
- Do a close read.
- Underline important facts.

Read the text to find out how materials scientists can help remove oil pollution from the environment.

Literacy Connection

🎮 **GAME**

Practice what you learn with the Mini Games.

Oil Spills and Aerogels

Small amounts of oil end up in streams and threaten the environment. One way to clean up this oil is with materials called aerogels. Aerogels are solids made from gels.

To make aerogels, materials scientists remove the liquid from the gel and replace it with gas. This process changes the physical properties of the gel. Aerogels are nicknamed "frozen smoke" because they are see-through and are the world's lightest solids. Some aerogels are very absorbent. Materials scientists tested the ability of these aerogels to clean up oil by mixing them with water and corn oil. In one investigation, the aerogel absorbed seven times its own weight in oil!

☑ **READING CHECK** **Use Evidence from Text** Why do you think aerogels could be used to clean up oil spills in your community? Underline the important facts from the text that support your claim with evidence.

_____

_____

_____

_____

States of Matter

I Can...
Identify the differences among the three states of matter.

5-PS1-2

Literacy Skill
Use Evidence from Text

Vocabulary
solid
liquid
gas

Academic Vocabulary
differentiate

▶ **VIDEO**

Watch a video about states of matter.

LOCAL-TO-GLOBAL ⟩ Connection

Think about the clothing that you wear when you go outside on a warm day. It is made of fairly thin fabric that protects you from too much sunlight or from biting bugs. If you were at the South Pole, though, you would dress very differently. There are no warm days at the South Pole. The temperature is always so cold that all of the water there is frozen. Vast plains of ice, or solid water, surround the pole. Explorers and researchers who travel near the South Pole need clothing that holds in warmth.

Relate Explain why it is necessary for travelers to the South Pole to wear clothing that protects them from the cold.

_____

_____

_____

uInvestigate Lab

Is goop solid or liquid?

Most of the materials around you are clearly solid, liquid, or gas. Could there be substances that are hard to classify?

Procedure

☐ 1. In the bowl, add one cup of cornstarch to 100 mL of water. Mix the substances with your hands or with the wooden spoon. If the mixture stirs easily, add a bit more cornstarch. If some of the cornstarch stays powdery, add a bit more water. You can also add a drop or two of food coloring.

☐ 2. When the cornstarch and water are thoroughly mixed, stir it slowly with the spoon. Then stir it very quickly. Record your observations.

☐ 3. Pick up some of the mixture in your hand. Try to roll it into a ball. Keep pushing on the mixture while rolling it. Then stop pushing on the mixture while you hold it over the bowl. Record your observations.

☐ 4. What are some other investigations that you can do with the mixture?

_____

_____

_____

Analyze and Interpret Data

5. **Classify** Can you classify the mixture as a liquid or a solid? Explain your answer.

_____

_____

_____

Materials
- water
- cornstarch
- spoon
- bowl
- safety goggles
- measuring cup
- graduated cylinder, 50mL

Suggested Materials
- food coloring

 Wear safety goggles.

 Do not taste.

Science Practice

Scientists use evidence to make explanations.

Observations

What states of matter do you see?

You are surrounded by different states of matter: solids, liquids, and gases. Study the different states of matter you see in this picture.

Solids are always around you.

! Identify two solids you see. Describe how you can identify that these objects are solids.

_____

_____

_____

_____

_____

Gases are always there but usually not visible.

! Identify two objects interacting with gases that you see. Describe how can you identify gases.

_____
_____

Liquids are often nearby.

! Identify three liquids you see. Describe how you can identify them as liquids.

_____
_____
_____
_____
_____

Solids

Solid, liquid, and gas are the three states of matter. Most substances can exist in any of these states, depending on temperature. A **solid** can be identified because it has a definite shape. When you place a solid object such as an ice cube in a cup, it does not spread to cover the bottom of the cup. An ice cube is solid and keeps its shape in the cup. As it becomes warmer, the ice cube may melt. Then it is no longer a solid.

Baking soda is a solid, and vinegar is a liquid. You may know already that those two substances react when they are mixed. In a large resealable plastic bag, mix one teaspoon of baking soda with four tablespoons of vinegar. Seal the bag right away. What did you observe about the bag? How can you explain this observation?

☑ **READING CHECK Use Evidence from Text** Ice is a solid that can come in many different shapes, such as crushed, cubed, or shaved. Explain how this can be. Support your answer with evidence from the text.

_____

_____

_____

_____

Liquids

When an ice cube melts, it forms water, which is a liquid. A **liquid** is a substance that has a definite volume but does not have a definite shape. If you pour liquid from a shallow, round bowl into a tall glass, its shape changes a lot. The new shape matches that of the inside of the glass, while the volume of the liquid in the bowl and in the glass are the same.

Liquids flow from one place to another unless something holds them in place. For example, the water in the waterfall rushes downward because nothing is stopping it.

Reflect What did you learn in this lesson that helped you understand something you observed in the past but could not explain? Write your thoughts in your science notebook.

INTERACTIVITY

Complete an activity about states of matter.

Quest Connection

Describe how the state of matter will affect the usefulness of materials used in a stepping stone.

_____

_____

_____

_____

Gas

Matter surrounds you all of the time. The air that you breathe is matter in the form of gas. If you move your hand back and forth quickly, you can feel the matter even though you cannot see it.

Gas is a form of matter that does not have a definite shape or a definite volume. You can **differentiate**, or tell the difference between, a gas, a liquid, and a solid because gases in a container always fill the entire volume of the container. Although some gases have color that you can see, most common gases are colorless. You can detect them by their effects on other objects. If you blow through a straw into a glass of water, you will see bubbles of gas coming up through the water. Moving air causes a wind turbine to turn.

Classify What is a characteristic of a gas?

_____

_____

_____

Science Practice
▶Toolbox

Designing Solutions
Engineers design solutions to problems by applying scientific knowledge. Suppose you must move a toy boat across a pond. How can you use your knowledge of gases to move the boat?

☑ Lesson 1 Check

1. **Compare and Contrast** An ice cube is placed in a jar and left on a table. The ice cube melts. The lid of the jar is placed on tightly. The jar sits on a sunny window sill, and all of the liquid water becomes a gas. Describe the differences in the three states of matter.

_____

_____

_____

2. **Explain** Mercury is a metal that is sometimes used in thermometers because it flows easily and takes the shape of the thermometer tube. Explain why mercury can be used in a thermometer but other metals cannot.

_____

_____

It's a Matter of Materials

Some types of matter may be useful for making a stepping stone. Other types of matter will not work as well. Answer the questions below to help decide some of the properties that materials for your stepping stone will need.

1. For your stepping stone project, describe the things that the stone must be able to do. List some of the criteria that will help you figure out what kind of design would work.

_____

_____

_____

2. Identify the state of matter that is most likely to meet your criteria. Will all materials in the state of matter that you identified meet the criteria for your design problem? Explain your answer.

_____

_____

_____

_____

3. What other characteristics are important in the materials you will use?

_____

_____

_____

Physical Changes

I can...

Use evidence to show that matter is conserved during a physical change. Explain how temperature can affect a physical change.

5-PS1-2

Literacy Skill
Use Evidence from Text

Vocabulary
physical change

Academic Vocabulary
establish

▶ **VIDEO**

Watch a video about physical changes.

STEM Connection

When a building is constructed, engineers and builders use different materials to put it together. Modern buildings over a few stories tall are often built using steel beams and concrete. These materials are strong and durable. Even if the materials are strong, people may want to remove a building. It may not be designed for modern uses. A taller or more modern building design may use the land better. When a building is knocked down using heavy equipment, the material it is made of does not change. The concrete is still concrete even though it is broken into small pieces. The beams are still made of steel even if they are bent and crumpled. The materials do not change, but their shape changes.

Infer How could you show that the building materials do not change when the building is knocked down?

_____

_____

_____

uInvestigate Lab

Which properties are affected by temperature?

When materials scientists develop new materials, they must consider how temperature affects the properties of a material. Which properties are affected by temperature?

Materials
- aluminum foil
- piece of thin rubber
- sugar cubes
- safety goggles
- water
- plastic cups
- spoon
- large dish of ice water
- large dish of warm water

Procedure

☐ 1. **SEP Plan an Investigation** Use all the materials. Think of a way to test how temperature affects solubility and flexibility, and how shiny a material appears. In the table, identify which substance you will use to test each property.

☐ 2. Write a procedure to test each property. Show your plan to your teacher before you start. Record your observations.

 Wear safety goggles.

 Do not taste.

Observations

	Sugar	Aluminum foil	Rubber
Property tested			
Observations			

Science Practice

Scientists *collect data* to answer questions.

Analyze and Interpret Data

3. **CCC Energy and Matter** Which physical changes were affected by the temperature difference and which were not affected by the temperature difference?

_____

_____

_____

_____

Changes in Shape

Matter often changes size and shape. A **physical change** is a change in some properties of matter that does not form a different kind of matter. A melted juice pop, torn paper, and broken glass are all examples of physical changes.

Some physical changes give matter a different shape. If you drop a cell phone, the glass screen might shatter. The glass has undergone a physical change. Some of its properties have changed, but the properties that make it glass are still there. It is still hard and clear. It still does not react with most substances. Cutting paper and stretching a rubber band are also physical changes. After breaking glass or stretching a rubber band, you still end up with glass or rubber. The mass of the parts of the broken phone screen is exactly the same as the mass of the unbroken screen.

Explain How can you tell that a physical change does not make a new substance?

_____

_____

Quest Connection

Why would you want to use a material that is not likely to undergo a physical change for your stepping stone?

_____

_____

_____

_____

_____

Changes in Temperature

The temperature of an object or material is one of its physical properties. A change in temperature is a physical change. A cold object feels different from how the same object feels when it is warm. When the temperature of an object changes, other physical properties might change at the same time. You can **establish**, or demonstrate, this concept with a balloon. If you put one of these inflated balloons in the freezer, it will shrink. That is because the volume of air will change when the air temperature changes. After you take the balloon out of the freezer, it will become warmer. It will then return to its original size.

The railroad tracks in the photograph appear to be warped and bent. That change in shape happened when the tracks became hot. The metal expanded. Sections of track could not stretch longer because they pushed against other sections. That caused the tracks to bend. In very hot climates, people must inspect the tracks often to keep them safe.

Cause and Effect Metal railroad tracks shrink when they get colder. Why do you think shrinking does not cause the tracks to warp?

_____

_____

_____

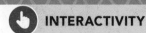
Science Practice
▶ Toolbox

Construct Explanations
Water melts at 0°C (32°F). At a lower temperature, water will be a solid. How can you use this information to predict the precipitation that will fall on a given day?

A Change of Physical State

Another physical change of a substance is a change of its physical state. As liquids get colder, their particles slow down. When the temperature gets cold enough, the particles can only vibrate in place. They cannot slide past each other, so the liquid becomes a solid. This change is called freezing. The opposite change can occur when a solid is heated. As its particles gain energy, they again move past one another. The solid melts to form a liquid.

Freezing and melting occur at the same temperature. When a liquid turns into a solid, this temperature is called the freezing point. It is called the melting point when a solid turns into a liquid. Each substance has its own melting point. The melting point can be used to help identify a material.

The melting point of water is 0°C (32°F). Below that temperature, water is solid ice. Above the melting point, water is a liquid.

Apply Concepts Label the liquid, solid, and gas in the photos. Predict the temperature for each state.

_____

_____

_____

Particle Changes

Evaporation takes place when particles leave a liquid and become a gas. Particles evaporate from a liquid when they are at the surface of the liquid and are moving upward with enough speed. This is how rain puddles and wet clothes become dry.

If the temperature of a liquid is high enough, particles will change to a gas not only at the surface but also throughout the liquid. As gas particles move quickly upward through a liquid, bubbles of gas form under the surface of the liquid. The boiling point of a liquid is the temperature at which this occurs. As with the melting point, each substance has its own boiling point. The boiling point can be used to help identify a substance. The boiling point of water is 100°C (212°F).

☑ READING CHECK **Use Evidence from Text** How can you use the melting point or boiling point to help identify a substance?

_____

_____

_____

_____

··········uBe a Scientist··········

Saltwater Ice Cubes
With an adult, fill an ice cube tray with water. In half of the spaces, use salt water. Use fresh water in the others. Make sure to keep track of which are which. Put the ice cube tray in a freezer. Check your tray one hour later. What can you infer from your observations about the properties of water and salt water?

☑ Lesson 2 Check

1. **Infer** Melting is a physical change. How does the mass of water formed by melting an ice cube compare to the mass of the ice cube?

_____

_____

2. **Explain** How can you tell that a change in a material is a physical change?

_____

_____

_____

Quest Check-In

Stepping Stone Properties

For your stepping stone, you might want to use a material that does not change easily. Draw a model of what your stepping stone will look like. Apply what you have learned about physical changes as you sketch your model stone. Consider the size, shape, and physical state of the stone. Label some of the physical properties of the stepping stone.

Design

QUEST CHECK ✓ OFF

Look Out for Flying Rocks!

Meteorites are small chunks of rock and metal that have traveled through space and fallen to Earth. In many ways, a meteorite is like other rocks on Earth. Still, finding a piece of matter that has traveled through space can be exciting. More than 50,000 meteorites have been found on Earth. Perhaps one is waiting for discovery in your backyard!

You can use the physical properties of a rock to figure out whether it is a meteorite. Almost all meteorites are made mostly of iron and nickel, so many times a magnet will stick to them. You can also look at the shape. If the rock is round like a smooth pebble, it is not a meteorite. Most often, as the meteorite falls through space, different parts of it melt or evaporate. This causes most meteorites to be unevenly shaped. They may even look like they have been burned. Meteorites are also much heavier than other rocks that are the same size. If your rock passes all these tests, it might be a meteorite. However, the only way to be sure is to have a lab test its true properties.

Connect What makes this meteorite different from the rocks that originated on Earth?

_____

_____

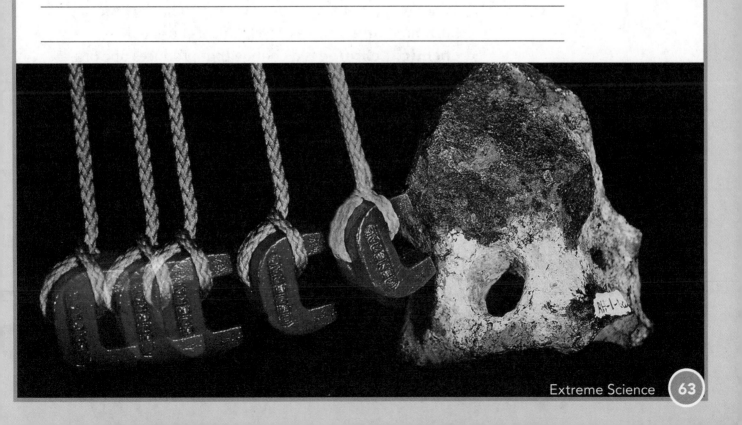

Chemical Changes

I can...
Use evidence to show that matter is conserved during a chemical change.

5-PS1-2, 5-PS1-4

Literacy Skill
Use Evidence from Text

Vocabulary
chemical change
conservation of matter
chemical reaction

Academic Vocabulary
support

 VIDEO

Watch a video about chemical changes

STEM Connection

Charcoal can be made from materials such as scraps and grass clippings. Materials scientists can determine how much of each material to use. Manufacturing engineers change this matter into charcoal, water and other liquids, and gases. They put the matter into a large metal container and heat it. After about 2–3 hours, charcoal is formed.

Describe Explain how matter is changed when engineers make charcoal.

_____

_____

New Substances

If you take a piece of charcoal and break it into pieces, the smaller pieces will still be charcoal. However, something different happens when you burn charcoal. Burning is an example of a chemical change. A **chemical change** is a change that produces one or more new substances. When charcoal burns, a chemical change occurs in which charcoal and oxygen form new substances. These new substances are ashes and gases that you cannot see.

How can you identify chemical changes?

Materials scientists conduct investigations to provide evidence that their product does what it is supposed to do. What evidence can you look for to show that a chemical change has occurred when substances are mixed?

Procedure

☐ **1.** Write a hypothesis about chemical change when substances are mixed.

_____

_____

☐ **2. SEP Plan, Conduct, and Investigate** Choose at least one liquid and one dry material. Write a procedure to test your hypothesis about chemical change. Remember to think about your variables. Show your procedure to your teacher before you start.

☐ **3.** Record your observations.

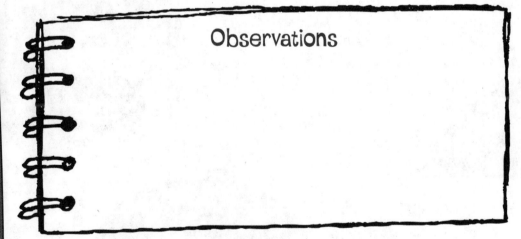

Observations

Analyze and Interpret Data

4. Use Evidence How does your data support your hypothesis?

_____

_____

Materials
- safety goggles
- plastic cups
- spoons
- graduated cylinder, 50 mL

Suggested Materials

Dry materials
- sugar
- baking soda
- salt

Wet materials
- vinegar
- water
- lemon juice

 Wear safety goggles.

⚠ Do not taste.

Science Practice

Scientists *collect data* when they investigate a scientific question.

Let's look at the changes that take place in another familiar example—baking a cake.

☑ READING CHECK **Use Evidence from Text** Circle the evidence that baking a cake involves a chemical change.

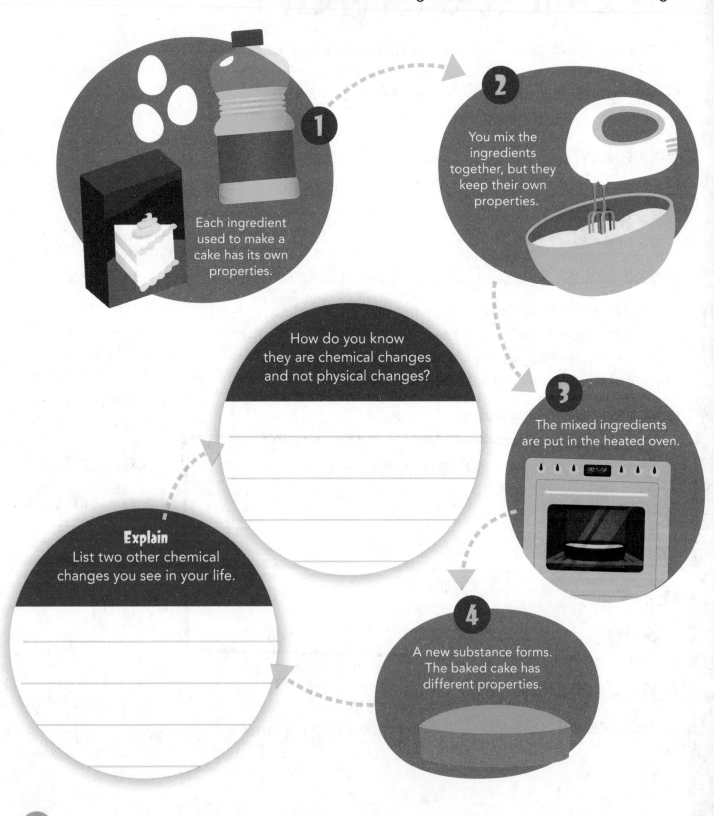

1 Each ingredient used to make a cake has its own properties.

2 You mix the ingredients together, but they keep their own properties.

How do you know they are chemical changes and not physical changes?

3 The mixed ingredients are put in the heated oven.

Explain
List two other chemical changes you see in your life.

4 A new substance forms. The baked cake has different properties.

Particles and Chemical Changes

When a chemical change occurs, the particles that make up the original substances rearrange to form new substances. It is not always easy to tell whether a substance has changed chemically. Evidence of chemical change may include the release of heat or light, a change in color, a new smell, gas bubbles, or the formation of a solid.

You can use building blocks to model a chemical change. In the picture, the blocks represent particles of matter. They are connected to form two substances. You can connect them in other ways to form different substances.

Model It! The blocks are combined to show two different substances. Draw how you could rearrange the blocks to make two other substances. Use all six blocks.

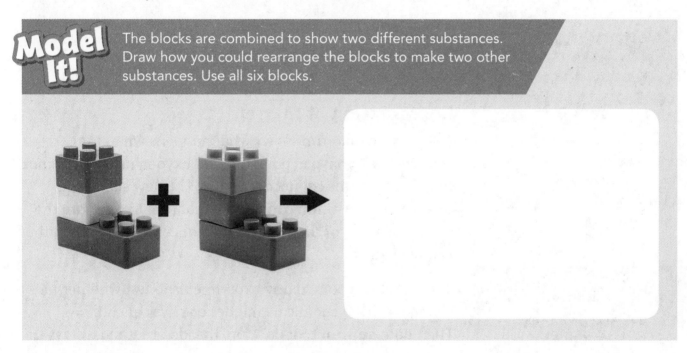

Like the building blocks, the particles that make up matter rearrange during a chemical change. In the example below, the balls each represent a different kind of particle in the two substances. After a chemical change happens, the same particles are in the two new substances, but they are arranged differently.

original substances   new substances

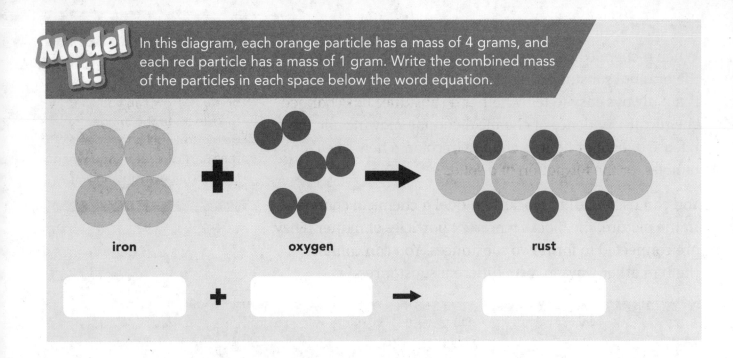

iron + oxygen → rust

[ ] + [ ] → [ ]

Conservation of Matter

The particle diagram shows what happens when iron combines with oxygen gas. Iron and oxygen are the original substances in this chemical change. The new substance that forms is rust. You can use the diagram to compare the combined mass of the original substances to the mass of the new substance.

Scientists have done many experiments to test whether mass changes during chemical changes or physical changes. Their data **support**, or back up, the idea that mass stays the same before and after any change—no matter what. From this evidence, scientists developed the law of **conservation of matter**. The law states that in any chemical change or physical change, the total mass of the matter does not change.

In a chemical change, all the particles that make up the original substances end up in the new substances. So, the combined mass of the substances before a chemical change is the same as the combined mass of the substances after the chemical change.

Literacy ▶ Toolbox

Use Evidence from Text
Scientists use evidence to support a claim. You can observe rust on a nail. The new substance, rust, is evidence of a chemical change. Read about the law of conservation of matter on these pages. Find and use evidence to support the claims of this law.

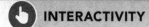
Look at the nails. The shiny new nails are made of iron. Over time, the nails can rust. Rusting is a chemical change. The change occurs when the iron on the surface of a nail combines with oxygen gas in the air to form rust.

When you observe one or more substances change into one or more new substances, you observe a **chemical reaction**. The nails rust as a result of a chemical reaction. The iron in the nails and oxygen gas from the air react to form rust.

☑ **READING CHECK** **Use Evidence from Text** If you measure the mass of nails before and after they rust, will the masses be the same? Explain your reasoning.

_____

_____

_____

_____

_____

_____

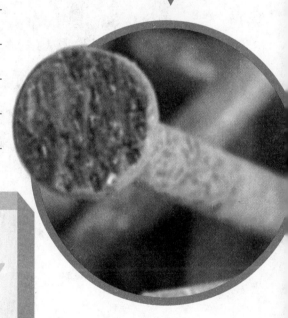

Quest Connection

▼▼▼▼▼▼▼▼▼▼▼▼▼▼▼▼▼▼▼▼▼▼▼▼▼▼▼▼▼▼

Use the law of conservation of matter to explain what you think will happen to the substances you will mix to make modeling dough.

_____

_____

_____

_____

_____

Is matter conserved?

Read the information for each step to see what happens during the chemical reaction. Write a math equation to model how the masses of the original substances and the new substances compare.

1

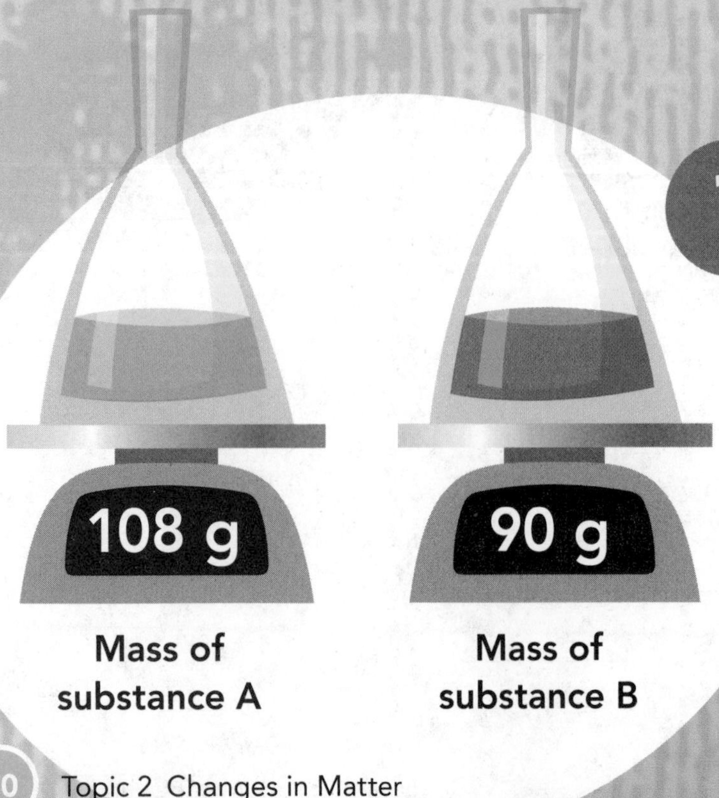

108 g

Mass of substance A

90 g

Mass of substance B

Each flask holds a different substance. Read the mass on each scale. The mass seen on each scale is the mass of the substance. The mass of the flask has been subtracted.

Two new substances

The color of the liquid substance is different from the colors of substances A and B. A new solid substance is visible, too. These observations provide evidence of a chemical change.

3

Write the total mass of the two new substances. (Ignore the mass of the beaker.) Hint: Use the information in step 1.

_____

2

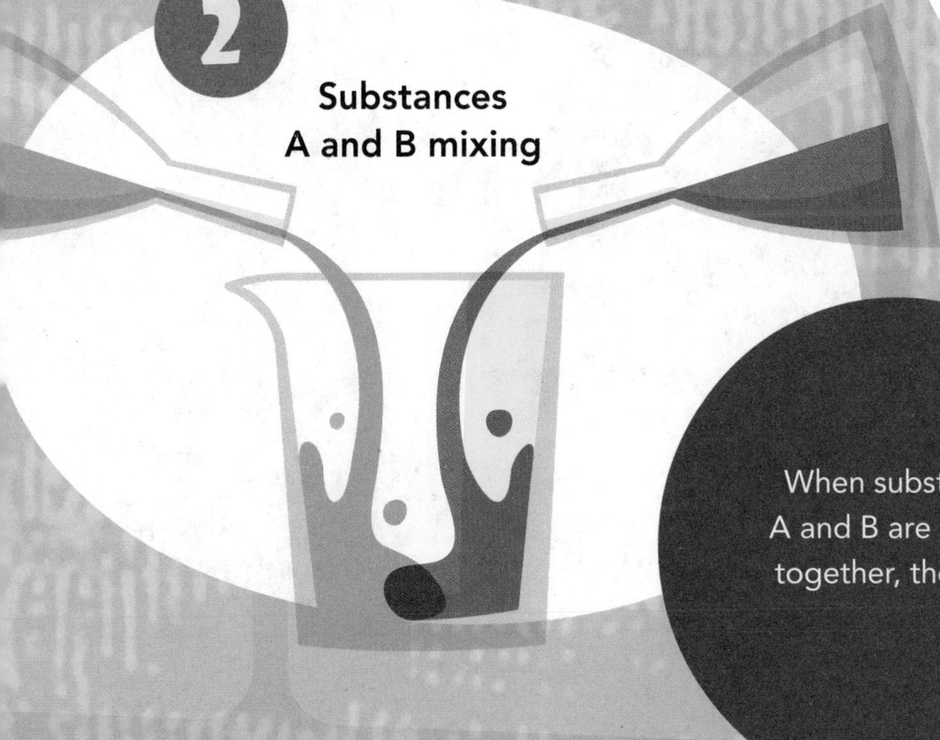

Substances A and B mixing

When substances A and B are poured together, they mix.

Mass and Plant Growth
Chemical changes happen in living things, too. Try this! Put a wet paper towel in a sealable bag. Put a seed in the paper towel and seal the bag. Find the mass of the prepared bag. Wait until the seedling grows and has a few leaves. Find the mass again. You will see that the masses are the same. The plant's mass increases as it grows because it uses matter from the water and the trapped air. The water and air decrease in mass as the plant grows.

Examples of Chemical Changes

Chemical changes happen in the kitchen all the time. A chemical change occurs when a chef makes fresh cheese. To make fresh cheese, the chef adds lemon juice to whole milk. Once the two liquid ingredients are mixed, solid pieces start to form. The solid pieces, called curds, are chunks of the fresh cheese. They form as a result of a chemical change. To prepare the cheese to eat, the chef separates the curd from the liquid.

Different kinds of cheeses are produced by further processing the curds. For example, to make soft, stringy cheese like mozzarella, the curds are kneaded. Many cheeses are "aged." During aging—which can take months—bacteria in the cheese chemically change the cheese. Gouda is an example of an aged cheese.

Write About It Do a close read on the paragraph above. Identify the main idea. In your science notebook, explain how the author uses key details to help support the main idea.

You may have noticed another chemical change. Over time, some pennies change color from copper to green. This color change happens because of a chemical change. The copper metal that makes up a penny combines with oxygen in the air to form a green substance. The green substance is copper oxide.

Identify What two substances is copper oxide made of?

_____ **+** _____ ➡ **copper oxide**

Explain Do you think the old penny will have the same mass as the new penny? Explain your reasoning.

_____

_____

_____

_____

☑ Lesson 3 Check

Kolab recorded the properties of two liquid substances, A and B. He then mixed them together in a beaker, and the liquid changed colors. He recorded the properties of the mixed substances.

Substance	Color	Odor	Mass
A	colorless	none	3.6 grams
B	colorless	foul	2.1 grams
A + B	yellow	none	?

1. ☑ **READING CHECK** **Use Evidence from Text** Is this a chemical change? How do you know?

_____

_____

2. **Analyze** Write the mass of the mixture of substances A and B. How can this mass be used as evidence of the conservation of matter?

_____

_____

How can you make modeling dough?

It's time to make the dough you will use to build your model stepping stone. Look at the list of suggested materials and decide which materials to use and the quantities of each. How will using different quantities of materials affect the dough?

Materials
- bowl
- sealable bags
- balance and weights
- spoon
- plastic gloves

Suggested Materials
- water
- flour
- cooking oil
- salt
- sand
- glitter
- food coloring

 Do not taste.

 Wear plastic gloves.

Design Your Model

☐ **1. SEP Develop a Model** Make a list of criteria your stepping stone needs to meet.

_____

_____

_____

Engineering Practice

Engineers develop models to test that a design meets specific criteria.

My Formula

_____

_____

_____

_____

_____

_____

_____

2. Choose your materials and list them on the formula card.

3. **SEP Design Solutions** Make two different formulas by changing the quantities of materials.

4. Measure each material and record the amount on the card.

5. Share your formula card with your teacher before you start.

6. Make your different formulas.

7. **SEP Interpret Data** Conduct an investigation to produce data to serve as the basis of evidence about which formula works best. Use fair tests in which variables are controlled. Consider how many trials you should do for each formula.

Evaluate Your Model

8. **Use Evidence** Do your results show whether a chemical change occurred? Provide evidence to support your answer.

_____

_____

_____

_____

9. **Evaluate** Which formula met your criteria for a model stepping stone? Provide evidence to support your answer.

_____

_____

_____

10. **Use Models** How does your modeling dough compare to concrete that is used to make stepping stones?

_____

_____

_____

_____

uEngineer It! **Define** STEM

INTERACTIVITY

Go online to evaluate and compare competing designs.

Foam Sweet Foam

Phenomenon Most surfboards are made of foam. Basic surfboards are often made of polyurethane foam, which floats easily in the water because it is very light. It is also strong. Other boards are often made of polystyrene foams. These foams are lighter than polyurethane foam, but they are not as strong. Besides, some polystyrene foams can sometimes absorb water. That, of course, is not a good quality for a product designed to float!

Recently, a group of chemists and engineers designed a new type of foam for surfboards. This new foam is not only lighter than any other surfboard foam. It also lasts longer and floats better.

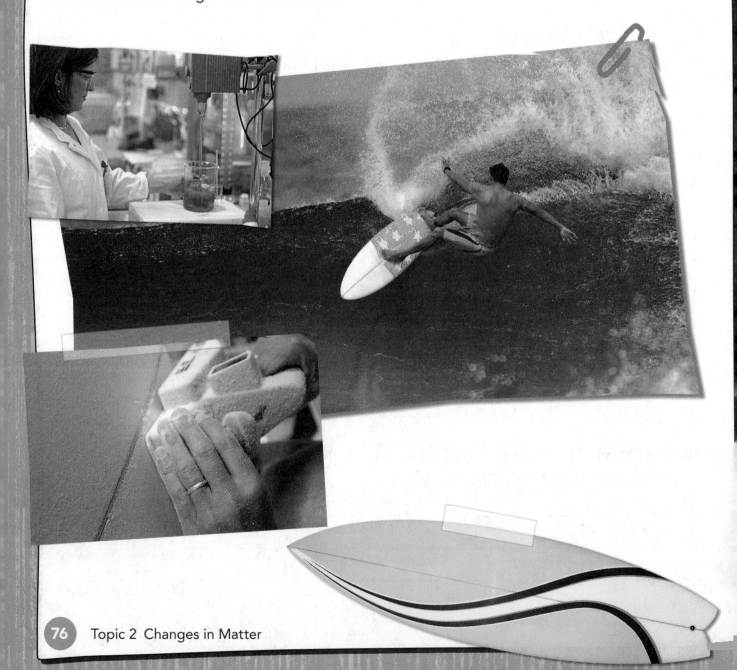

Define It

Foams are made using a series of chemical and physical changes. They are used in the design of many products, including automobiles, helmets, pillows, and food containers. There are many types of foam, and they each have different properties. Suppose you work for a company that builds playground equipment. The company wants to build a new piece of equipment for small children.

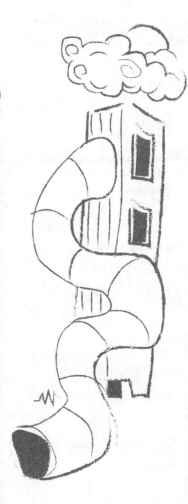

☐ Choose one piece of equipment that can be built using foam or that you think should include foam.

☐ Define the purpose of the foam in the product you choose.

☐ Brainstorm some **criteria** that could help you judge which foam is best for your product.

It should...	It should not...

☐ Draw your piece of equipment.

Mixtures and Solutions

I can...

Explain what happens when different substances are mixed. Explain how to slow down or speed up the dissolving process when mixing materials in water. Demonstrate that mixtures of solids can be separated.

5-PS1-2, 5-PS1-4

Literacy Skill
Use Evidence from Text

Vocabulary
mixture
solution

Academic Vocabulary
component

▶ **VIDEO**

Watch a video about mixtures and solutions.

CURRICULUM ▶ Connection

When you look at an oil painting from a distance, it might seem to have large areas of a single color. For most paintings, a closer look tells a different story. There are many different colors side by side, often in very small patches of color. How do artists have so many colors to work with? Do they have to buy hundreds of different colors and shades so that they can always have the one they need? No, artists start with a few basic colors of paint. Then they mix them together to get just the right color for a particular place on the canvas. By combining these basic colors in different groupings and amounts, the artist can make any color that you can imagine.

Apply Most packages of food coloring have only four bottles of food dye. How could you make different colors of icing for a cake?

_____

_____

uInvestigate Lab

How can you separate a mixture?

Knowing physical properties of matter can help scientists separate individual substances from a material. How can you use physical properties to separate the parts of the mystery mixture?

Materials
- mixture
- plastic cups
- water
- sieve
- magnet inside a plastic sealable bag
- safety goggles
- spoon

Procedure

☐ **1.** Observe the mixture. What parts of the mixture can you identify?

_____

_____

_____

Wear safety goggles.

Do not taste.

Science Practice

Scientists **conduct investigations** to provide evidence.

☐ **2.** **SEP Plan an Investigation** Plan a way to separate the components from one another. Use all of the materials. Show your procedure to your teacher before you start.

☐ **3.** **SEP Conduct an Investigation** Separate the components of the mixture and record your observations.

Analyze and Interpret Data

4. **Use Tools** How did the magnet help you separate the components of the mixture?

_____

_____

_____

_____

_____

_____

Observations

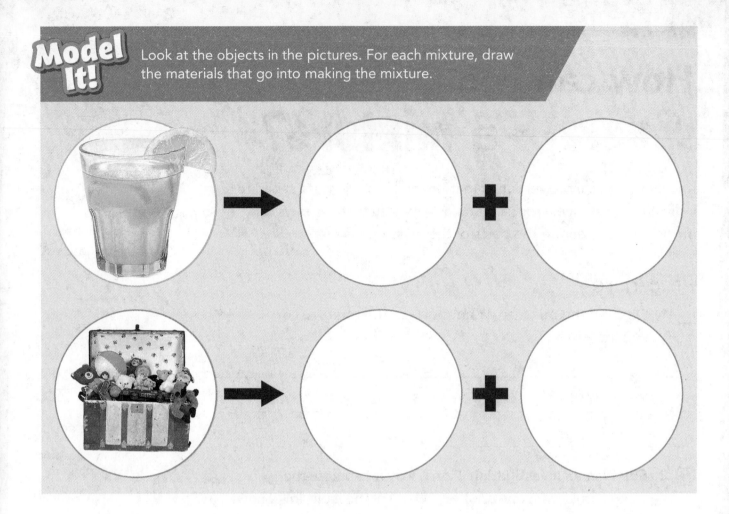

Mixtures

If you mix peanuts and raisins, each of the substances keeps its own properties. In a **mixture**, different materials are placed together, but each material in the mixture keeps its own properties. In the nut and raisin mixture, you can easily separate the nuts from the raisins. Different parts of a mixture can be separated from the rest of the mixture. When sand and blocks are mixed, you could separate the blocks from the mixture by picking them out. You could also use a strainer to separate the parts.

Some mixtures cannot be separated as easily as the nuts and raisins. For example, iron ore is a rock that is a mixture of different substances. One of these substances is iron. Large factories separate the iron from the other **components**, or parts, of the mixture. To do this, they use a lot of energy to make the iron liquid and separate it from the other components.

Solutions

If you place salt in water, the salt and water form a mixture. But the salt seems to disappear. That is because the salt water is a solution. A **solution** is a mixture in which substances are spread out evenly and do not settle to the bottom of the container. The substance that is dissolved in a solution is called the solute. The substance in which the solute is being dissolved is called the solvent. When the salt dissolves in the water, individual salt particles separate from the solid and spread evenly throughout the water. Ocean water is a familiar example of a salt and water solution. The water has a salty taste because salt is dissolved in the water. You can make solids dissolve in a liquid faster by stirring or heating the solution. Grinding a solid into smaller pieces will also help it dissolve faster.

Not all solutions are made by dissolving a solid in a liquid. Two liquids can make a solution. For example, vegetable oils used in cooking might be a solution of soybean oil and sunflower oil. A gas can also dissolve in a liquid. For example, water can contain dissolved oxygen and carbon dioxide gases.

☑ READING CHECK **Cite Evidence from Text** Circle the words or phrases on this page that support the explanation of how to change the speed of the dissolving process.

Engineering Practice ▸ Toolbox

Construct Explanations
Although it is not always an easy process, the components of a mixture can be separated, and they keep their properties. How can you know that something is a mixture?

Quest Connection

When you make your stepping stone, you may want to include pebbles or coarse sand as a component. How could you tell if these are part of a mixture or a solution?

_____

_____

_____

when is a mixture also a solution?

Some mixtures have parts that can be easily separated.

Draw the parts that make up the mixture.

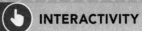
In a solution, the parts mix evenly and cannot be easily separated.

Draw the parts that make up the solution.

Separating Solutions

The components of a solution keep their own properties, but they usually cannot be separated as easily as other mixtures. That is because the components of a solution are evenly mixed. You cannot pick out chunks of one material from the mixture. You cannot remove a solid component with a filter paper. Its particles are spread out and become part of the liquid. However, the parts of a solution can be separated. To separate the parts of the solution, you use physical properties of the substances in the solution.

Plan It!

How can you separate the salt and the water in a saltwater solution? Identify the properties you can use. Then write a plan to separate the materials.

_____

_____

_____

_____

_____

_____

_____

_____

Mixtures and Solutions

Remember that all solutions are mixtures, but not all mixtures are solutions. You can tell the difference by observing the mixture closely. A solution is the same in all parts. For example, clear apple juice is a solution. Any samples of the juice are just alike, and there are no separate particles in the mixture. Fresh squeezed orange juice is not a solution. You can see chunks of orange in the mixture. If you let the orange juice pass through a filter paper into a glass, it will separate. The glass will contain a clear liquid, and the filter paper will have solid orange pulp. You cannot separate a solution by filtering it. To separate a solution, you have to cause a physical change to one or more of its components.

Infer If you separate orange juice by filtering it, is the liquid in the glass a solution? Why or why not?

_____

_____

📖 **Make Meaning** Mixtures and solutions are important to people in their everyday lives. In your science notebook, identify mixtures or solutions that you use every day. Why are they important to you?

.... ⓤ **Be a Scientist** ....

Kitchen Science
Mix common kitchen substances, such as salt, pepper, sugar, and cinnamon with water. Observe the mixtures to determine which substances form solutions and which do not form solutions.

☑ Lesson 4 Check

1. **☑ READING CHECK Use Evidence from Text** Sugar consists of fine white crystals. Salt also consists of fine white crystals. A mixture of salt and sugar consists of fine white crystals. If they are mixed well, do the sugar and salt form a solution? How do you know?

   _____

   _____

2. **Explain** Can a solution consist of more than two components? Explain your answer.

   _____

   _____

How can you make a new and improved formula?

Consider how well your stepping stone model met the criteria and constraints of your engineering problem. How will using different materials or quantities of materials affect the model?

Materials
- bowl
- sealable bags
- balance and weights
- spoon
- plastic gloves

Suggested Materials
- water
- flour
- cooking oil
- salt
- sand
- glitter
- food coloring
- pebbles
- copper wire

Design Your Model

☐ **1.** Write any criteria that your model did not address well.

_____

_____

☐ **2.** Choose your materials and list them on the formula card.

 Do not taste.

 Wear plastic gloves.

Engineering Practice

Engineers redesign a solution after testing to find a solution that meets specific criteria.

My New Formula

_____

_____

_____

_____

_____

_____

☐ **3.** Write a new formula by changing the materials or quantities that you use in the model. Measure each material and record the amount on the card.

☐ **4.** Share your formula card with your teacher before you start.

☐ **5.** Make your new formula.

Evaluate Your Model

6. Test Decide how to test your new model in order to determine whether it meets the criteria and constraints better. Write down your test.

_____

_____

_____

_____

7. Evaluate Did the new formula improve the model? Provide evidence to support your answer.

_____

_____

_____

_____

8. SEP Use Models How does your new model compare to concrete that is used to make stepping stones?

_____

_____

_____

_____

_____

INTERACTIVITY

Organize data to support your Quest Findings.

STEM Find the Right Mix— and Step on It!

How can we mix ingredients to make a model stepping stone?

Identify Factors and Retest

Phenomenon When you made the dough, you provided criteria. With a group, discuss if your model stepping stone met the criteria you set.

Discuss how you would change your model to improve it. Write a procedure for testing your improved model. Retest your model.

Construct Explanations

Did the change to your model improve it? How do you know?

_____

_____

_____

Do you think the same change to the concrete stepping stone would result in a better product? Why or why not?

_____

_____

Procedure to Retest

_____

_____

_____

_____

_____

Materials Scientist

Materials scientists develop many of the products we use. These individuals develop new kinds of materials and find ways to improve existing materials. They consider ways that products can be made better, lighter, or stronger. For example, a materials scientist might develop a helmet that is lighter and that can hold up under greater forces. Many of the materials used to build bikes and skateboards were developed by a materials scientist to improve their ability to move fast and to withstand the rigors of their tasks.

Materials scientists usually work in labs. They identify needs or problems and think of possible solutions. They design products, test prototypes, and identify improvements that need to be made. They also communicate with other scientists as they work.

Reflect In your science notebook, write ways you acted like a materials scientist as you developed your model stepping stone.

☑ Assessment

1. **Differentiate** How is a solid different from a liquid? How are a solid and a liquid different from a gas?

_____

_____

_____

_____

_____

_____

_____

_____

_____

_____

_____

_____

_____

2. **Vocabulary** Which process is an example of a chemical change?

   A. Bread is toasted.

   B. Oil soaks through a shirt.

   C. A girl forms a soap bubble.

   D. Red food coloring spreads out in water.

3. **Summarize** What happens to the particles of substances when a chemical change occurs?

_____

_____

_____

4. **Describe** Which statement describes something that occurs only during a physical change?

   A. New substances form.

   B. Chemical properties change.

   C. The substances gain or lose mass.

   D. The properties of substances stay the same.

5. **Explain** Which statement describes what happens when sugar dissolves in water?

   A. Sugar particles attach to the water particles.

   B. A new substance with new properties forms.

   C. The sugar particles change into a different kind of particle.

   D. The particles of both substances become evenly spread apart.

6. Interpret Which picture shows evidence of both a chemical change and a physical change?

A.

B.

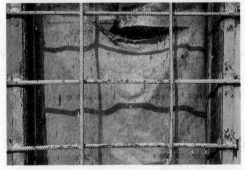

C.

D.

7. Describe How do you know that a chemical change has occurred?

_____

_____

_____

_____

_____

_____

_____

_____

_____

The Essential Question

What evidence do we have that matter changes?

Show What You Learned

Several changes occurred when you mixed the ingredients to make modeling dough. Based on the evidence you saw, what kind of changes took place?

_____

_____

_____

_____

_____

_____

_____

Read this scenario and answer questions 1–5.

A young scientist found 2 liters of an unlabeled solution of white liquid in a glass jar. She wanted to find out what some of the properties of the substance were. So, she tested the substance. Her results are in the table.

Mystery Substance Property	Observation
Color	white
Odor	slightly sweet
Boiling point	100.5°C (212.9°F)
Reaction with acid	solution separated into clear liquid and white solid matter, sour smell produced.

1. **Use Math** The scientist added 0.5 grams of a solid to 2 grams of the liquid. Can you predict the total weight of the substances after the materials were mixed? Explain your answer and give the weight if possible.

_____

_____

_____

_____

2. **Cause and Effect** Which conclusion can you draw about what has happened to the solution when it was mixed with an acid?

   A. The solution was separated by a physical change only.

   B. The solution was broken down into its smallest particles.

   C. The solution was changed chemically into new substances.

   D. The solution was changed physically.

3. **Collect Data** What evidence supports your answer to question 2?

   A. Liquid is left behind when matter is broken down.

   B. New substances with new properties were observed.

   C. The sour odor produced is evidence of waste products.

   D. Part of the liquid solution changed state to become solid.

4. **Cause and Effect** The scientist noticed a gas rising from the solution while boiling it. Afterwards, she noticed that there was less mass remaining than when she started. How can this phenomenon be explained?

   A. Boiling destroyed some of the matter in the solution.

   B. Boiling resulted in a chemical change that altered the solution's properties.

   C. Boiling resulted in a state change from liquid to gas.

   D. Boiling caused the solution to clump together, increasing the total density of the solution.

5. **Evaluate** Which of the following is evidence of a chemical change having taken place?

   A. New substances appeared when substances were mixed together.

   B. The solution became solid as the temperature was lowered to −5°C (23°F).

   C. The volume of the solution increased when the solution was heated.

   D. Gas could be observed escaping from the solution when it was heated.

uDemonstrate Lab

How does mass change when you make glop?

Phenomenon When materials scientists mix ingredients, they produce data that shows what happens to mass. They make observations about any changes that occur when ingredients are mixed. What do you think will happen when you mix glue, water, and borax solution?

Procedure

☐ **1.** Make glop using 30 mL of glue, 15 mL of colored water, and 15 mL of borax solution. What will happen to the mass of the ingredients after they become glop? Write a hypothesis.

_____

_____

_____

_____

_____

☐ **2.** Write a procedure to test your hypothesis about mass. Use all of the listed materials. Show your procedure to your teacher before you begin.

_____

_____

_____

_____

_____

_____

_____

Materials

- 3 measuring cups
- white glue
- balance
- gram cubes
- food coloring
- water
- borax solution
- spoon
- safety goggles

 Wear safety goggles.

 Do not taste.

 Wash your hands when finished.

Science Practice

Scientists make measurements to produce data during investigations.

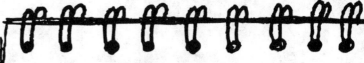

☐ **3.** Make a table to show your data. Your table should display evidence that relates to your hypothesis.

Analyze and Interpret Data

4. Calculate Add together the masses of the glue, water, and borax solution. How does this combined mass compare to the mass of the glop?

_____

_____

_____

_____

Observations

Substance	Mass of substance and cup (g)	Mass of substance (g)
Glue		
Colored water		
Borax solution		
Glop		

5. Use Evidence Did a chemical reaction occur? Provide evidence to support your answer.

_____

_____

_____

_____

6. Draw Conclusions Is your hypothesis supported by your data? Explain.

_____

_____

_____

_____

Earth's Systems

Lesson 1 Geosphere and Biosphere

Lesson 2 Hydrosphere and Atmosphere

Lesson 3 Interactions Among Earth's Systems

Next Generation Science Standards

5-ESS2-1 Develop a model using an example to describe ways the geosphere, biosphere, hydrosphere, and/or atmosphere interact.
3-5-ETS-1 Define a simple design problem reflecting a need or want that includes specified criteria for success and constraints on materials, time, or costs.

Go online to access
your digital course.

▶ VIDEO

📖 eTEXT

👆 INTERACTIVITY

📱 VIRTUAL LAB

🎮 GAME

☑ ASSESSMENT

The Essential Question

How can you model interactions among Earth's systems?

Show What You Know

Systems on our planet work together. What do living things need in order to survive?

_____

_____

_____

Connect the Spheres

How can acid rain affect Earth's spheres?

Phenomenon Hi, my name is Logan Reynolds. I am an air pollution analyst. Recently, acid rain has been reported near our city. The city's people need to understand effects of acid rain.

I will be collecting data to confirm the acid rain report. In the meantime, I need you to educate the people in our city about acid rain. In this problem-based learning activity, you will develop an explanation of how acid rain can affect Earth's four spheres.

Follow the path to learn how you will complete the Quest. The Quest activities in the lesson will help you complete the Quest! Check off your progress on the path when you complete an activity with a **QUEST CHECK ✓ OFF**. Go online for more Quest activities.

Quest Check-In 1

Lesson 1

Explore the characteristics of acid rain. Explain its effects on soil and plants.

Next Generation Science Standards

5-ESS2-1 Develop a model using an example to describe ways the geosphere, biosphere, hydrosphere, and/or atmosphere interact.

▶ VIDEO

Watch a video about pollution.

Quest Check-In 3

Lesson 3

Investigate natural processes in different spheres. Predict how these processes may change.

Quest Check-In Lab 2

Lesson 2

Make a physical model of Earth's four spheres.

Quest Findings

Complete the Quest! Use what you have learned to explain the effects of acid rain on all four spheres. Describe interactions between spheres to inform your city.

How can you model Earth?

Scientists use models to understand the composition of Earth.
How can you model what Earth looks like?

Procedure

☐ 1. Based on what you know about Earth, design a model of it.
Use any of the materials to build your model.

☐ 2. Show your plan to your teacher before you build your model.

_____

_____

_____

Analyze and Interpret Data

3. **SEP Use Models** How can you use your model to explain what
Earth is like?

_____

_____

_____

4. **Compare and Contrast** Exchange your model with another
group. What were some similarities and differences you notice
between your model and other models?

_____

_____

_____

5. **CCC Systems and System Models** What characteristics make a
model of Earth look most Earth-like?

_____

_____

Suggested Materials

- colored paper
- scissors
- glue
- markers
- colored pencils
- crayons
- clay

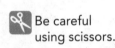
Be careful using scissors.

Science Practice

Scientists use models to help study very large objects.

Cause and Effect

Scientists look for cause and effect relationships to help them understand why things happen. They explore what happens in certain situations.

GAME

Practice what you learn with the Mini Games.

- A cause is why something happens.
- An effect is what happens.

Read the text about water on Earth.

Population and Water Availability

All living things on Earth, including humans, need freshwater. Freshwater is a renewable resource because rain can replace what we use. But the amount of water is limited, and in some places we use it faster than it gets replaced. About 7,400,000,000 people live on Earth. That number is getting larger quickly. As the human population gets larger, the need for water also grows.

Some places on Earth have plenty of water. Other places have very little water. All water on Earth is connected, though. Everyone can help conserve water—even if they have plenty. If everyone helps save water, there will be more water to go around.

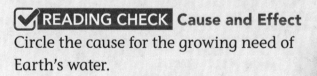
READING CHECK Cause and Effect
Circle the cause for the growing need of Earth's water.

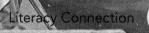

Geosphere and Biosphere

I can...

Describe what makes up the geosphere. Describe what makes up the biosphere.

5-ESS2-1

Literacy Skill
Cause and Effect

Vocabulary
biosphere
geosphere
lithosphere

Academic Vocabulary
system

▶ **VIDEO**

Watch a video about the geosphere and the biosphere.

CURRICULUM ▶ Connection

The plow is one of the most important farming developments in history. Farmers use plows to till, or turn over, the soil. Before the invention of the plow farmers used digging sticks to remove weeds and break up the layer of topsoil. Plows make turning and breaking up the soil easier. Most plants grow better in soil that has been plowed. Plants can get water and nutrients more easily from soil that has been plowed. When plants grow better, they produce more food. The invention of the plow has made a big impact on human life.

Summarize How does plowing help plants grow better?

_____

_____

How does water move through soil?

Scientists can use models to investigate the natural world in a controlled setting. How can you model how land and water interact?

Materials
- 2 paper cups
- 2 samples of different soils
- graduated cylinder
- water
- 2 small bowls

Procedure

☐ **1.** Observe the soil samples. How are the samples different?

_____

_____

_____

 Wash your hands.

☐ **2.** Write a plan to find out whether water flows through both soil samples in the same way. Use all the materials. Show your plan to your teacher before you begin. Make sure you change only one variable at a time. Record your observations.

Science Practice

Scientists use models to investigate the natural world.

Observations

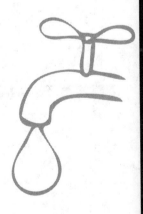

Analyze and Interpret Data

3. SEP Construct Explanations How did differences in soil affect the movement of water? Use your results.

_____

_____

_____

Earth's Systems

Earth is made of four major systems—the geosphere, biosphere, hydrosphere, and atmosphere. Each **system** is a collection of parts that work together. Different processes move Earth's materials within the systems and from one system to another. If a part of a system is damaged or missing, the system will not work as well—or may not work at all. As a result, other systems may be affected.

Earth is the only planet in our solar system that has these four systems. For example, seven of the planets have an atmosphere, or a layer of gases that surround the planet. But only Earth has a biosphere. The **biosphere** is an Earth system that incudes all living things, including humans.

Explain What are four different components of the biosphere?

_____

_____

Geosphere and Biosphere

Earth's biosphere includes the living things in the air and water and on land. The mountain lion in the photo is just one of the millions of kinds of living things that are part of the biosphere. The biosphere is able to support so many kinds of living things because of its interaction with other spheres.

The large rock in the photo is part of Earth's geosphere. The **geosphere** is the Earth system that includes rocks, soil, and sediments. Rocks on Earth's surface are easy to see, but rocks are also below the surface. Some of those rocks are molten, or melted. Rocks are present in all parts of Earth—from its surface to its very center.

☑ READING CHECK **Cause and Effect** Why can the biosphere support so many different kinds of living things? Underline the cause.

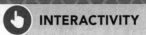
INTERACTIVITY

Complete an activity about the geosphere and biosphere.

Math ▸ Toolbox

Graphing Earth's geosphere is thousands of kilometers thick. The inner core is 1,220 km thick. The outer core is 2,260 km thick. The mantle is 2,866 km thick. And the continental crust is only about 25 km thick on average. Make a bar graph to show Earth's layers. Based on the graph, compare the thickness of the mantle and the thickness of the crust.

Quest Connection

How might the biosphere be affected if a harmful substance entered the geosphere?

_____

_____

_____

_____

What are parts of Earth's geosphere and biosphere?

The mantle makes up about **84%** of Earth's total volume.

Biosphere

All living things make up the biosphere. Most nonliving things are part of the geosphere. Air, water, and the sun are nonliving, but they are not part of the geosphere.

! **Describe** How do you think the geosphere and biosphere interact?

_____

_____

_____

_____

crust

1-100 km

mantle

2,866 km

outer core

liquid 2,260 km

inner core

solid 1,220 km

Geosphere

Lithosphere

An important part of the geosphere is the lithosphere. The **lithosphere** is made up of the outer, rocky parts of Earth and includes the crust and the outer, rigid part of the mantle. Below the lithosphere, the solid rock of the mantle can move and flow. The lithosphere is not only the outer layer of land. It also forms the bottom of the ocean. The lithosphere can be much thicker below a continent than below the ocean. The lithosphere can extend more than 200 kilometers (124 miles) below continents.

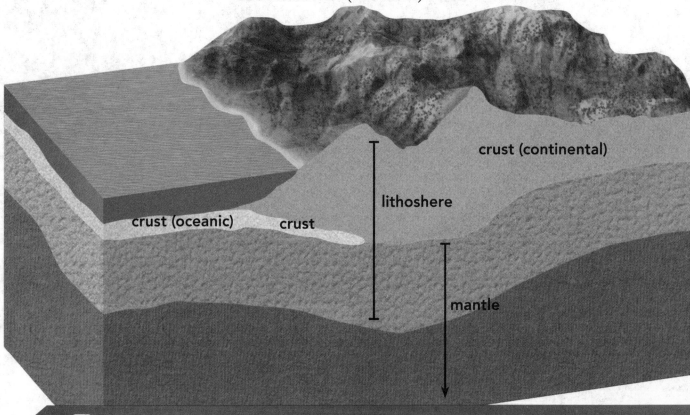

crust (continental)

lithoshere

crust (oceanic)   crust

mantle

☑ Lesson 1 Check

1. Describe Describe the lithosphere. Include how it is related to the geosphere.

_____

_____

_____

2. Identify What makes up the biosphere?

_____

Quest Check-In

Raining Acid

Rainfall is important for the health of all living things. Without water, no living thing could survive. However, precipitation can be harmful. Rainwater picks up particles when it falls through the air. If the air contains certain pollutants, the rain will become polluted too. When the amount of certain pollutants in the rain is high, the precipitation is called acid rain. Acid rain looks exactly like normal rain, but it can have harmful effects on Earth's systems.

Acid rain can affect all of Earth's spheres. Acid rain can enter streams, lakes, and other bodies of water. This makes the water more acidic. Acid rain can also strip minerals, such as aluminum, from soil as it flows toward bodies of water. Some aquatic organisms can survive in water that has been polluted by acid rain and minerals from the soil. Other organisms, however, cannot survive. Acid rain can also harm land organisms that drink the polluted water or eat organisms that live in the water. Organisms that need soil can also be harmed when acid rain strips minerals from it. Acid rain also affects the atmosphere because the same particles that are in acid rain can combine with other gases in the air. This changes the types of gases that are in the atmosphere.

How might the effect of acid rain on soil affect crops and other plants in a community?

_____

_____

_____

Hydrosphere and Atmosphere

I can...

Describe what makes up the atmosphere.
Describe what makes up the hydrosphere.

5-ESS2-1

Literacy Skill
Cause and Effect

Vocabulary
atmosphere
hydrosphere

Academic Vocabulary
distinguish

▶ VIDEO

Watch a video about the hydrosphere and atmosphere.

ENGINEERING ⟩ Connection

A greenhouse is a structure made of glass—and not just its walls. Its roof is also made of glass! People use greenhouses to grow plants because the greenhouse stays warm inside all year. The warmth comes from the sun's energy. Sunlight enters the greenhouse through the glass. Although sunlight can enter through the glass, the heat of the greenhouse cannot escape. This causes the greenhouse to warm. A similar process occurs in the blanket of air that surrounds Earth. People build greenhouses to get this effect on a small scale.

📓 **Write About It** In your science notebook, write about how you would use a greenhouse.

uInvestigate Lab

How does a greenhouse work?

Scientists carry out investigations with models to understand processes. How can you make a model to demonstrate how greenhouses stay warm inside all year?

Procedure

☐ **1.** Write a hypothesis about whether the air in a closed jar or an open jar will warm faster.

_____

_____

☐ **2.** Make a plan to test your hypothesis. Use all of the materials.

☐ **3.** Show your plan to your teacher before you begin. Record your observations.

Observations

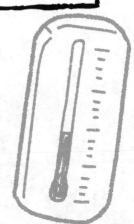

Analyze and Interpret Data

4. CCC Systems and System Models How does your model represent what happens to air that surrounds Earth?

_____

_____

_____

Visual Literacy Connection

What are parts of Earth's hydrosphere?

All the water on, under, or above Earth's surface makes up the **hydrosphere**. Most water on Earth is saltwater, and only a very small amount is freshwater. Humans and many other living things need freshwater to survive.

stream
precipitation
ocean

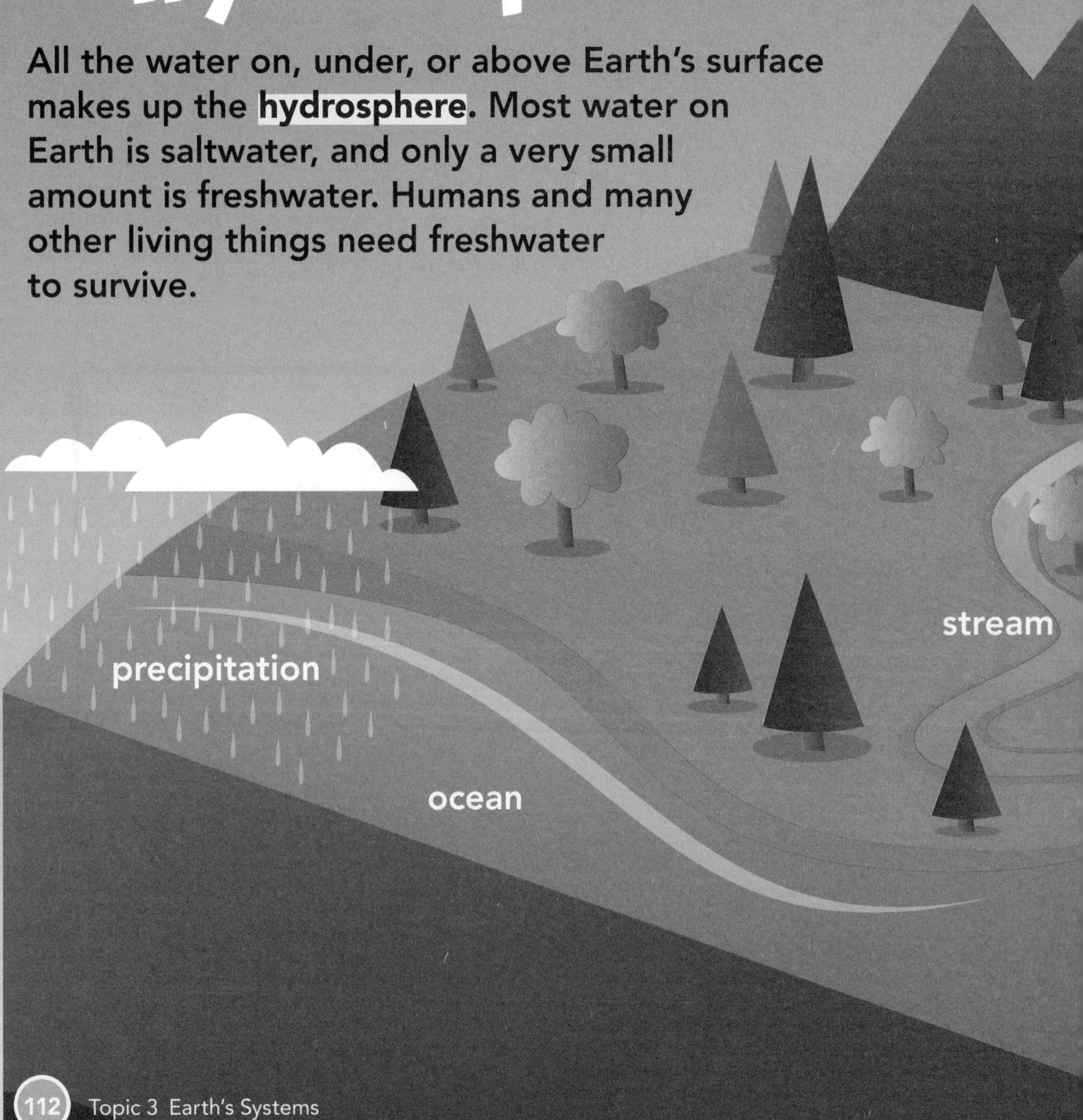

water vapor

ice and
snow

! **What other spheres on Earth interact with the hydrosphere?**

_____

_____

_____

lake

groundwater

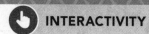
Atmosphere

The **atmosphere** is the layer of mixed gases that surrounds Earth. The most plentiful gases are nitrogen and oxygen. Other gases, such as argon, carbon dioxide, and water vapor, are also in the atmosphere.

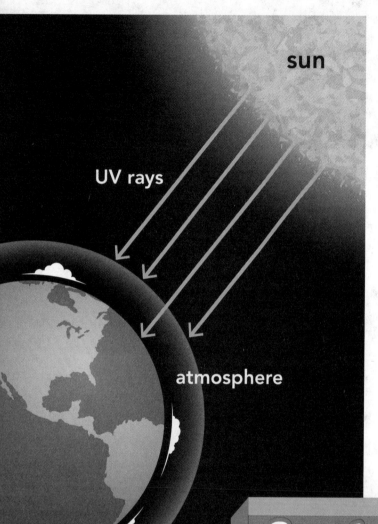

sun

UV rays

atmosphere

Look at the arrows in the diagram. They show that Earth's atmosphere absorbs most of the sun's UV rays. These rays are harmful to living things. Have you ever had a sunburn? UV rays cause this condition. The atmosphere allows most visible sunlight to pass through it, warming Earth's surface. The atmosphere also traps some of the heat that leaves Earth's surface. This keeps the atmosphere warm enough to support life.

☑ **READING CHECK** **Cause and Effect**
Suppose the atmosphere was only half as thick as it is now? What effect might this cause on Earth's biosphere?

_____

_____

_____

Quest Connection

How do the hydrosphere and atmosphere interact? How would you show that in a model?

_____

_____

_____

_____

Hydrosphere and Atmosphere Together

The hydrosphere and atmosphere constantly interact. For example, both rain and snow are common in many parts of the world. The temperature of the air affects the kind of precipitation that will fall.

Another example of the hydrosphere and atmosphere working together is a hurricane. A hurricane is a large, swirling tropical storm. Hurricanes bring damaging winds and a lot of rain. They form when a lot of water vapor enters the air due to evaporation of warm ocean water. If conditions are right, a tropical storm produces clouds that spiral like the clouds shown in the photo. The speed and pattern of the winds in the storm **distinguish**, or make a clear difference, between a storm and a hurricane.

Science Practice Toolbox

Analyze and Interpet Data Find out where major hurricanes occurred in the United States in the last 10 years. Identify any patterns you see. How did these hurricanes affect other Earth spheres?

☑ Lesson 2 Check

1. Identify What is one way in which the atmosphere interacts with the hydrosphere?

_____

_____

2. Make Connections What makes up Earth's atmosphere?

_____

_____

Lesson 2 Hydrosphere and Atmosphere (115)

Where are Earth's spheres?

It is time to start working on the models you will use in your Quest Findings activity. Make a model to show the four spheres of Earth. Remember to include important details for each sphere in your model.

Suggested Materials
- colored paper
- shoe box
- colored markers
- glue
- tape
- clay
- scissors

Procedure

☐ **1.** Develop a list of important details to include in your model.

_____

_____

 Be careful using scissors.

☐ **2.** Draw a design for your model. Label it with the materials you will use for each part.

Science Practice

Scientists develop models to show the parts of a system.

☐ **3.** **SEP Develop Models** Show your drawing to your teacher before you build your model.

My Design

Analyze and Interpret Data

4. SEP Explain Which spheres are in other spheres? Explain.

_____

_____

_____

_____

_____

_____

5. SEP Use Models Look at the models of other students. In what ways was your model better than their models? What did their models show better than your model?

_____

_____

_____

_____

_____

uEngineer It! Improve STEM

INTERACTIVITY

Go online to find out how changes to Earth spheres affect stability.

A New Home

Phenomenon Today, most zoos are built to educate people. They are important places where scientists can study animals. Many zoos also manage conservation projects to make sure that different kinds of animals do not disappear from Earth. The scientists, designers, and engineers that build zoos try to give animals habitats that are similar to their natural habitats.

One popular habitat at some zoos is the rain forest. The Lied Jungle in Omaha, Nebraska, was one of the first and largest indoor rain forest habitats in the world. It is as tall as an eight-story building. Inside are waterfalls and flowing streams. The temperature is always warm. The roof was specially designed to let in sunlight. This zoo exhibit is home to about 90 different kinds of animals and many types of plants.

Improve It

Suppose you are in charge of improving a zoo's rain forest habitat. The zoo wants to add a new kind of animal that naturally lives in a rain forest, but the zoo rain forest does not have everything the new animal needs. The current habitat was built mainly for rain forest birds. The focus was on having the right kinds of trees. The new animal lives on the rain forest floor. The zoo habitat is covered only with soil, a few rocks and plants. Your job is to change the rain forest habitat so that the new animal can live in it.

☐ Choose an animal that lives on the rain forest floor to add to the zoo's rain forest habitat. Identify the criteria that should be met in order for the animal to survive in the improved habitat. If you need help identifying criteria, brainstorm with another student or do research.

_____

_____

_____

_____

_____

_____

☐ Brainstorm some constraints that should be considered so that the improved habitat would meet the needs of all the zoo's rain forest animals. Discuss these questions as you brainstorm.

- What changes might be good for the new animal but harmful for the other animals?

- Would the change to the habitat also be good for the other animals?

☐ Draw a diagram showing how you would improve the rain forest habitat. Label the important changes you would make.

Interactions Among Earth's Systems

I can...

Describe how Earth's systems interact with each other.

5-ESS2-1

Literacy Skill
Cause and Effect

Vocabulary
greenhouse effect

Academic Vocabulary
interdependent

▶ **VIDEO**

Watch a video about interactions among Earth's systems.

SPORTS ⟩ Connection

Mountain climbing is the sport of climbing and hiking mountains—often to reach the highest part of the mountain. It is a challenging sport. Climbers must prepare carefully before they climb. They must think of the different weather conditions that they will pass through. As the climber goes higher, the air temperature will get colder. Also, the weather on one side of a mountain can be different from the weather on the opposite side. One side may have more wind than the other side. The weather on the windy side may be colder and wetter than the weather on the opposite side of the mountain.

Use Evidence from Text The mountain climbers shown are climbing during a storm. What side of the mountain are they climbing? Support your answer with evidence from the text.

_____

_____

_____

_____

How does the geosphere affect the hydrosphere?

Scientists use drawings and models to propose explanations of scientific phenomena. How can you explain changes in precipitation on mountain ranges?

Materials
- Precipitation Map

Science Practice

Scientists **construct explanations** to understand the natural world.

Procedure

☐ **1.** Study the Precipitation Map. Use the map key to help you.

☐ **2.** Identify patterns of precipitation on the map. Make and label a drawing to identify and explain any differences in precipitation on the two sides of the mountain.

Analyze and Interpret Data

3. SEP Construct an Explanation Explain how the geosphere and hydrosphere act together and make the pattern you observed.

_____

_____

_____

_____

_____

Interdependence of Earth's Systems

Earth is made up of four spheres—the geosphere, hydrosphere, atmosphere, and biosphere. None of the spheres acts all by itself, though. The spheres are always interacting. They have an **interdependent** relationship, which means that they depend on one another. When you see plants growing, observe rainfall, or watch waves move sand, you are observing relationships among Earth's spheres.

The balance among Earth's spheres makes life on the planet possible. Each sphere plays a part in making our home planet unique.

Explain On what spheres does the biosphere depend? How?

_____

_____

_____

Biosphere

Living things take in gases, such as carbon dioxide and oxygen, from the atmosphere. They use these gases for life processes, such as growing, making food, or getting energy. Living things also give off gases, such as carbon dioxide and oxygen, during life processes. These gases enter the atmosphere.

📓 **Write About It** In your science notebook, explain how you have an interdependent relationship with one of Earth's spheres.

Geosphere and Atmosphere

If you observe a rock in the open air for days, weeks, or even years, you might never see it change. If you could watch it for thousands of years, though, you might see it get smaller. The rock cliff in the photo was at one time much larger. Over time, gases from the atmosphere reacted with the rock, and chemical changes wore away the rock. The pieces were then carried away by water or wind. Today the rock has a unique shape.

✓ READING CHECK **Cause and Effect** Which of Earth's spheres causes rocks to have unique shapes?

_____

Air in the atmosphere is constantly moving. But its movement usually is not in a straight line. Air travels over flat land easily. But mountains can change the flow of air. When winds run into the side of a mountain, the air will flow up and over the mountain.

As the air rises and cools on one side of the mountain, water vapor in the atmosphere forms clouds. The water in the clouds falls as rain or snow. The other side of the mountain tends to be much drier because it gets little rainfall or snow.

Explain How are the geosphere, atmosphere, and hydrosphere interacting as air moves over a mountain?

_____

_____

_____

_____

_____

How does the ocean affect other systems on Earth?

Earth's ocean is the largest part of the hydrosphere and has a strong effect on Earth's systems.

Matter from the geosphere gets washed into the ocean. Ocean waves erode coastlines.

How might Earth's systems change if the ocean did not exist?

_____

_____

_____

The ocean causes winds to blow in certain patterns around the world.

The ocean supports Earth's biosphere. Living things may become part of the geosphere when they die. Some may become fossils.

Water from the ocean goes into the atmosphere. Wind carries the water to land where it falls as rain.

INTERACTIVITY

Complete an activity about interactions among Earth's spheres.

Disrupting the Balance

The balance among spheres can be disrupted. For example, Earth's atmosphere contains a mixture of gases. Organisms need some of these gases to stay alive. Certain gases in the atmosphere, called greenhouse gases, trap heat. This trapped heat causes temperatures on Earth to be warm enough to support living things. This warming of Earth's atmosphere, land, and water is called the **greenhouse effect**.

The amount of greenhouse gases in the atmosphere can change. As a result, the temperature of the atmosphere can also change. The more greenhouse gases that are in the atmosphere, the more heat is trapped. If the atmosphere has too much greenhouse gas, it may get too warm. Living things, such as these corn plants, may not be able to survive in the warmer temperatures. Various sources add greenhouse gases to the atmosphere. But the primary source is the burning of fossil fuels.

Explain On a separate sheet of paper, draw a picture to show how greenhouse gases affect Earth's spheres.

Quest Connection

Acid rain deposits nitrogen in the soil. Some scientists think this may increase the release of methane gas, a major contributor to the greenhouse effect. How might an increase in methane gas affect Earth's spheres?

_____

_____

_____

Natural Disruptions

Natural events can disrupt the balance in Earth's spheres. When volcanoes erupt, huge amounts of gases and dust particles are released into the atmosphere. These gases and dust can spread out over very large areas of the atmosphere. They can cause changes to local weather. Thunderstorms are common in areas near the eruption. Globally, volcanic eruptions cool Earth's atmosphere and surface for the first couple years or decades.

Identify Small particles released by volcanic eruptions block some sunlight from reaching Earth's surface for years. How would this affect the atmosphere, biosphere, and hydrosphere?

_____

_____

_____

_____

_____

_____

☑ Lesson 3 Check

1. **Apply Concepts** Describe one way that the hydrosphere and atmosphere interact.

_____

_____

_____

2. **Make Connections** Complete the sentences by writing the name of the correct sphere in each blank.

Rain from the _____ falls from clouds in the _____.

The rain gathers in streams that flow across the _____. Plants and

animals in the _____ rely on the rain to get water for survival.

Earth's Interactions

In your Quest Findings, you will pull together what you learned to teach people about acid rain and its effects on Earth's systems. In this Check-In, you will choose two natural processes and predict how they can affect Earth's spheres.

1. **Identify** Choose two processes that occur on Earth.

   • Process A _rainfall_____

   • Process B _____

2. **Identify** Which of Earth's spheres are involved in each process?

   • Process A _____

   • Process B _____

3. **Describe** Write a brief description of how the spheres interact in each process.

   • Process A _____

   _____

   • Process B _____

   _____

4. **Evaluate** How might a change in one of these processes affect Earth's spheres?

   _____

   _____

   _____

   _____

   _____

   _____

QUEST CHECK ✓ OFF

Interpret a Graph

A lot of corn is grown in the midwest region of the United States. The amount of corn produced can be very different from year to year. The conditions of the environment are a big reason why. The graph shows rainfall amounts and how much corn was produced in different years.

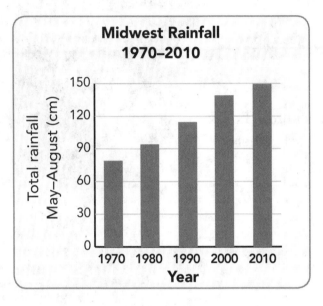

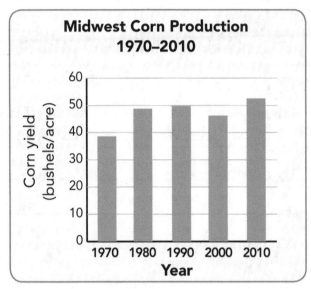

Use the graph to answer the questions.

1. **SEP Interpret Data**

   a. What was the total rainfall in 1990?_____

   b. What was the corn yield in 2010?_____

2. **Draw Conclusions** Based on the data, what can you conclude about the overall effect of rainfall on corn production in the Midwest?

   _____

   _____

   _____

INTERACTIVITY

Complete an activity to help with your Quest Findings.

Connect the Spheres

How can acid rain affect Earth's spheres?

Organize Information

Phenomenon Think of the different effects acid rain has on Earth's spheres. Write at least one effect on each sphere.

Hydrosphere _____

_____

Atmosphere _____

_____

Geosphere _____

_____

Biosphere _____

_____

_____

Construct an Explanation

Now you can make a presentation to inform your city about the potential effects of acid rain. Use the four spheres model you made earlier to show effects that can result from acid rain. Include a Venn diagram to describe ways that all four spheres interact. Show and describe how each sphere affects the other spheres, both with and without acid rain.

Air Pollution Analyst

Air pollution analysts research, inspect, and investigate levels of air pollution. They also use their research to ensure good air quality. They address any public health concerns. Air pollution analysts usually work in offices and laboratories. There they analyze data and develop solutions to air pollution problems.

Although air pollution analysts can be found in all parts of the country, most work in urban areas where industry and traffic are heaviest. They play a key role in evaluating and reducing the impact of air pollution on people and ecological systems.

📓 **Write About It**
In your science notebook, summarize the importance of air pollution analysts.

1. **Classify** The lithosphere is within the geosphere. What layers of Earth's geosphere make up the lithosphere?

    A. the crust and top of the mantle

    B. the inner core and the crust

    C. the outer core and the crust

    D. the mantle and the outer core

2. **Vocabulary** When you add certain gases to the atmosphere, more heat is trapped. This phenomenon is called

    _____.

3. **Infer** List the spheres that the biosphere relies on.

    _____

    _____

4. **Identify** What two gases are most abundant in the atmosphere?

    A. oxygen and carbon dioxide

    B. oxygen and nitrogen

    C. carbon dioxide and nitrogen

    D. carbon dioxide and hydrogen

5. **Apply Concepts** Which statement best describes the relationship between the geosphere and weather patterns?

    A. Clouds in the atmosphere interact with different rivers.

    B. Winds and clouds in the atmosphere interact with different landforms.

    C. Winds in the atmosphere interact with different parts of the ocean.

    D. Rain in the atmosphere interacts with different landforms.

6. **Summarize** Briefly describe the relationship between all four spheres. Support your response with examples.

    _____

    _____

    _____

    _____

    _____

7. **Identify** Which choice lists parts of Earth's hydrosphere?

    A. seaweed and fish

    B. glaciers and ice caps

    C. rain clouds and air masses

    D. riverbeds and ocean basins

8. Interpret Diagrams Which sphere is represented by the diagram?

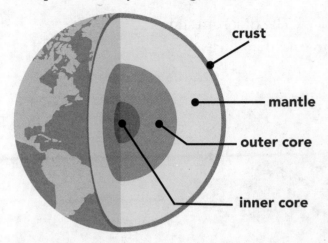

crust

mantle

outer core

inner core

A. biosphere

B. geosphere

C. lithosphere

D. hydrosphere

9. Apply Concepts Tell how matter from one sphere can move through at least two other spheres.

_____

_____

_____

_____

_____

_____

How can you model interactions among Earth's systems?

Show What You Learned

Our planet relies on a connection of systems in order to sustain life. How do these connections interact with one another?

_____

_____

_____

_____

_____

_____

_____

_____

_____

_____

_____

_____

_____

_____

_____

_____

_____

_____

Read this scenario and answer questions 1–6.

Jacques is developing a model for a research project. The diagram shows the model that he is making. Look at the diagram and then answer questions 1–6.

1. What do the white arrows in the model represent?

   A. movement of energy from the sun

   B. movement of energy in the atmosphere

   C. movement of matter from the biosphere

   D. movement of matter in the hydrosphere

2. The fish in the model are part of which Earth sphere?

   A. geosphere

   B. atmosphere

   C. biosphere

   D. hydrosphere

3. How do the biosphere and hydrosphere interact in Jacques's model?

_____

_____

_____

4. Describe one way that the two Earth systems you described in question 1 work together to affect Earth's surface features.

_____

_____

_____

5. Which statement describes an interaction between two of Earth's spheres shown by the arrows in the model?

  A. The hydrosphere and atmosphere interact because water from the ocean evaporates and forms clouds.

  B. The biosphere and hydrosphere interact because fish live in water.

  C. The lithosphere and atmosphere interact because without the lithosphere, the atmosphere could not exist.

  D. The biosphere and atmosphere interact because living things take oxygen from the atmosphere.

6. Which statement describes an interaction within one of Earth's spheres shown in the model?

  A. Rain clouds move to new locations as a result of wind.

  B. Freshwater and saltwater mix as rainwater runs back to the ocean.

  C. Some rainwater that falls gets stored in aquifers deep underground.

  D. Matter from decomposing plants eventually becomes part of the soil.

uDemonstrate Lab

How are the spheres represented in a terrarium?

Phenomenon Scientists use models to study things that are too big to investigate. How is each sphere represented in a closed terrarium?

Procedure

☐ **1.** Use the materials to build a closed terrarium. In the table, note which materials represents each sphere.

☐ **2.** Choose a variable you want to test. Predict what will happen in the terrarium.

_____

_____

_____

_____

_____

☐ **3.** Write a plan to test your predictions. Show your plan to your teacher before you begin. Record what happens to each sphere.

Materials
- glass container
- plastic wrap
- graduated cylinder
- pebbles
- rocks
- sheet moss
- soil
- water
- variety of plants
- planting tools

 Wear safety goggles.

 Do not taste.

 Use caution when handling glass

Science Practice

Scientists use models to study very large objects.

	Materials used to model before adding your variable	Observations after testing variable
Atmosphere		
Hydrosphere		
Geosphere		
Biosphere		

Analyze and Interpret Data

4. **Evaluate** How did your variable affect the part of your model that represents the biosphere? Provide evidence to support your answer.

_____

_____

_____

_____

5. **Make Connections** How is a terrarium similar to a greenhouse?

_____

_____

_____

6. **Form a Hypothesis** What factors would you need to consider if you were to plant your terrarium plant outside?

_____

_____

_____

_____

Earth's Water

Next Generation Science Standards

5-ESS2-2 Describe and graph the amounts and percentages of water and fresh water in various reservoirs to provide evidence about the distribution of water on Earth.

Go online to access
your digital course.

▶ VIDEO

📖 eTEXT

👆 INTERACTIVITY

🔬 VIRTUAL LAB

🎮 GAME

☑ ASSESSMENT

The Essential Question

How much water can be found in different places on Earth?

Show What You Know

This ice is slowly melting. A piece breaks off and falls into the ocean. If many more of these very large chunks of ice melt, how might this change where water is found on Earth?

_____

_____

_____

Water, Water Everywhere!

How can you make undrinkable water drinkable?

Phenomenon Hello! I am Chris Walker, a water quality specialist. I have been hired to help several towns that do not have fresh drinking water. I would like your help with this task. In this problem-based learning activity, you will develop solutions to make unsafe water safe for the people who live in these towns.

Like a water quality specialist, you will develop technology to make unsafe water drinkable. You will evaluate the challenges of getting drinking water from different sources.

Follow this path to learn how you will complete the Quest. The Quest activities will help you complete the Quest successfully. Check off your progress on the path when you complete an activity with a 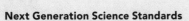 QUEST CHECK ✓ OFF . Go online for more Quest activities.

Quest Check-In 1

Lesson 1

Learn how rainfall moves over land and enters the ground.

Next Generation Science Standards
5-ESS2-2 Describe and graph the amounts and percentages of water and fresh water in various reservoirs to provide evidence about the distribution of water on Earth.

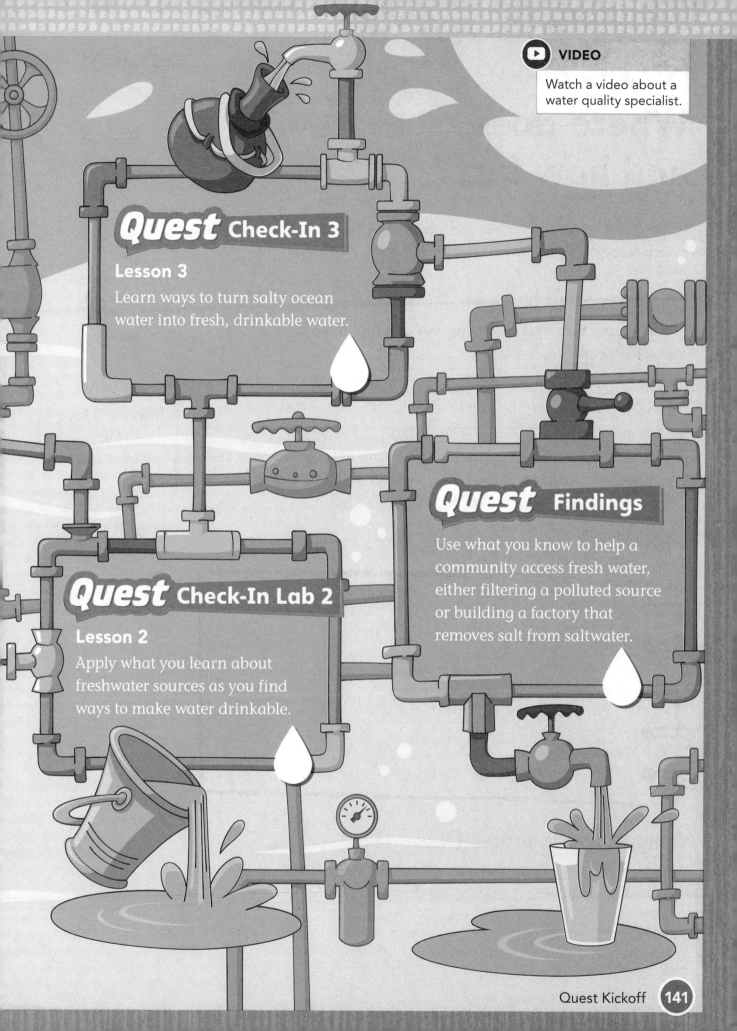

▶ VIDEO

Watch a video about a water quality specialist.

Quest Check-In 3

Lesson 3

Learn ways to turn salty ocean water into fresh, drinkable water.

Quest Findings

Use what you know to help a community access fresh water, either filtering a polluted source or building a factory that removes salt from saltwater.

Quest Check-In Lab 2

Lesson 2

Apply what you learn about freshwater sources as you find ways to make water drinkable.

STEM · uConnect Lab

Where does water flow... and how fast?

Water quality specialists often must determine how quickly water moves from a reservoir to the user. How can you make water move faster?

Design a Solution

☐ **1.** Predict how the height from which water flows affects its speed.

_____

_____

☐ **2. SEP Plan an Investigation** Make a plan to build a device to test your prediction on a measured amount of water. Show your plan to your teacher before you begin.

☐ **3.** Build your device and test your prediction. Record your results.

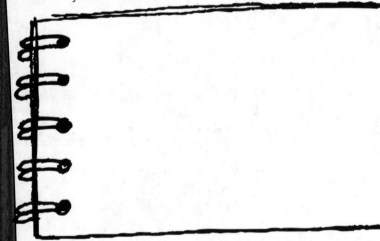

Analyze and Interpret Data

4. Use Math Based on the data you collected, how much faster were you able to move water with your device?

_____

_____

Materials

- safety goggles
- apron
- funnel, wide stem
- bucket
- PVC pipe
- stopwatch
- graduated cylinder
- protractor

 Wear safety goggles.

 Wear safety apron.

Engineering Practice

Engineers describe quantities to provide evidence.

Draw Conclusions

When you read, you must figure out what information is in the text. Use these strategies to draw conclusions from text.

- Look for facts, such as dates, places, names, or other data.
- Ask yourself what the facts mean when you put them together.

Read these paragraphs. Look for clues that will help you draw conclusions from the text.

🎮 **GAME**

Practice what you learn with the Mini Games.

The Mystery of the Shrinking Lake

In the past, Utah's Great Salt Lake was the largest natural lake west of the Mississippi River. The lake is fed by several freshwater rivers. Today, the lake is drying up. Its water volume is about half of the normal volume. The lake's water level has dropped 3.4 meters when compared to its height in 1847.

Recently, Utah has recorded higher temperatures than normal and has experienced a long-term drought. The areas surrounding the lake have a shortage of freshwater. To overcome the lack of freshwater, local residents now get 40 percent of their freshwater from the rivers that supply water to the lake. The rivers were once full of water, but today their water barely trickles into the lake.

✓ **READING CHECK** **Draw Conclusions** The pictures show the Great Salt Lake's Farmington Bay. Which picture is more recent? What makes you draw that conclusion?

_____

_____

_____

_____

Water Cycle

SPORTS ⟩ Connection

The site for the Winter Olympic Games is chosen years in advance. Outdoor events, such as skiing and snowboarding, must take place in snow. How can these events occur in places that do not have enough snow? The solution is making snow by machine. A snow machine blows tiny droplets of water into air that is cold enough to freeze the droplets to form snow. At the Sochi Olympics in Russia, snow machines made enough snow to cover 500 football fields with about 60 centimeters of snow. However, making snow reduces local freshwater levels. It also increases soil erosion and is expensive. But no snow means no skiers. At one California ski area, 38 people work full-time to make snow.

Use Evidence from Text How did Sochi use technology to support skiing and snowboarding at the Olympics? What evidence supports your ideas?

_____

_____

_____

_____

uInvestigate Lab

Where did that WATER come from?

HANDS-ON LAB

5-ESS2-2, SEP.6

A water quality specialist must understand the interactions of water with the environment. How can you investigate why water forms on the outside of a cup?

Suggested Materials
- 2 plastic cups
- water with ice cubes
- warm water

Procedure

☐ 1. Write a hypothesis to answer the question: Will water form on the outside of a cup with warm water or with ice water?

_____

_____

☐ 2. **SEP Plan and Carry Out an Investigation** Write a procedure to test your hypothesis. Show your procedure to your teacher before you start. Record your observations.

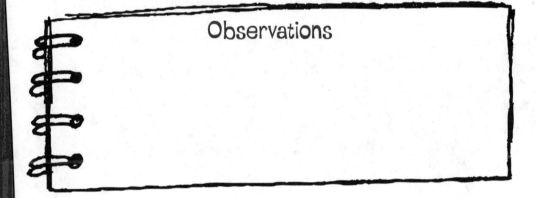

Observations

Science Practice

Scientists describe observations to construct explanations.

Analyze and Interpret Data

3. **Draw Conclusions** Was your hypothesis supported by evidence? What caused the difference between the cups?

_____

_____

_____

Water on Earth

Earth is called the water planet because water is everywhere on the planet. It surrounds you all the time, not just when you are bathing or swimming. Water also always surrounds you in your classroom, in your home—even in the desert. Where is the water in these dry places?

Water is in the air and underground. Much of the water you cannot see is an invisible gas called water vapor. It is in the air that surrounds you. Air always has some water vapor. Water vapor in the air changes to liquid water when it cools.

It is important to understand that water vapor and steam are not the same thing. Water vapor is usually at the same temperature as the air around it. Steam, however, is above the air's temperature. It is created when water boils. What you see as steam is actually tiny water droplets formed when the hot water vapor meets the cool air in the room.

☑ READING CHECK **Draw Conclusions** Early on a summer morning, the grass is wet. If it did not rain, where did the water come from? How did the grass get wet?

_____

_____

_____

Crosscutting Concepts ▸ Toolbox

Energy and Matter What is another example that you observed of water changing to water vapor?

Movement of Earth's Water

The water vapor in the air is only a very small part of all the water on Earth. Most of Earth's water near the surface is in its ocean, but ocean water can become water vapor in the air around you. This happens when water particles that make up the ocean become water vapor that moves above Earth's surface.

Water on Earth constantly moves in a **cycle**, or a series of events or processes that repeat. As it moves, water can change into any of its forms—water vapor, liquid water, and ice. The **water cycle** is the continuous movement of water on Earth. Two of the processes of the water cycle are evaporation and condensation. Ocean water changes to water vapor when the water heats. **Evaporation** is the process of changing liquid water into water vapor. Heat causes air to rise, carrying water vapor as part of it. At higher altitudes, air temperatures are lower, and water vapor cools and changes to a liquid. This change from water vapor to liquid water is called **condensation**. Clouds are drops of liquid formed from cooled water vapor.

📓 **Write About It** In your science notebook, write what you think would happen if water did not evaporate and condense.

……… иBe a Scientist ………

Solid, Liquid, Gas
Water changes state as it moves through the water cycle. At different times, water can be a gas, a liquid, or a solid. Make a model that helps you explain how water can change from one state to another and then back to the original state.

How does water cycle on Earth?

The processes of the water cycle have no start or finish. They are affected by air temperature, air pressure, wind, and landforms. Water does not always flow in the same path through the water cycle. It can take many paths.

Precipitation

Precipitation is water that falls from clouds in the form of rain, sleet, snow, or hail.

Snow

Rain

Runoff

Runoff is water moving downhill. When precipitation falls, water runs off into streams and rivers. From there, water flows to lakes or the ocean.

River

Groundwater

Some precipitation soaks into the ground and becomes groundwater.

INTERACTIVITY

Do an activity about the water cycle and plants.

Condensation

In cold air, water vapor condenses into liquid water or ice crystals. Droplets of water combine with other droplets and may form a cloud.

 Draw a picture of the water cycle in your community.

Evaporation

As water evaporates, liquid water changes into water vapor.

River

Lake

Energy and the Water Cycle

The sun provides the energy that makes the water cycle work. The sun's heat causes frozen water to melt and surface water to evaporate. Heat also causes winds to blow, and the wind moves clouds. Water in clouds falls as **precipitation**, which is water that falls as rain, snow, sleet, or hail, and the cycle continues. This cycle has been happening as long as Earth has had water—soon after its formation. The water that dinosaurs drank has been recycled millions of times through the processes of evaporation, condensation, and precipitation.

Quest Connection

How could you use the processes of the water cycle to make drinkable water?

_____

_____

☑ Lesson 1 Check

1. **Explain** Tran is doing an investigation about weather. He uses a rain gauge to collect precipitation. On Monday, the gauge collects 15 millimeters of rain. He fails to record the rainfall. On Friday, he remembers, but the gauge now holds 12 mm of rain. How did the water cycle directly affect Tran's experiment?

_____

_____

2. How is the ocean connected to the water cycle?

_____

_____

_____

Follow the Flow

groundwater

lake

To advise a town on how to get clean drinking water, you should know what happens to water on Earth's surface. When precipitation falls on land, it soaks into the soil, sand, and rocks. Some of it is taken up by plants or is lost to evaporation. However, some of it eventually seeps down into cracks and crevices underground. Where does it go from there?

The diagram shows surface water and groundwater in an environment. Some parts are missing from the diagram.

1. Draw blue arrows to show how runoff will flow on this diagram.

2. Draw green arrows to show where precipitation enters the ground.

3. Place yellow arrows to show the flow of underground water to the lake.

4. **Describe** How might knowing how freshwater flows on and below Earth's surface help you provide clean drinking water to a community?

_____

_____

_____

_____

_____

_____

иEngineer It! Define STEM

VIDEO
Go online to learn about freshwater depletion.

It's Melting!

Phenomenon In 1992, a giant piece of ice broke off from Antarctica's ice shelves. It broke in two, and one of the pieces was about the size of Rhode Island—39 kilometers wide and 78 kilometers long. Since then, several large ice sheets in Antarctica have broken into smaller parts and floated out to sea.

The Arctic is also losing ice. Arctic winter temperatures normally freeze seawater that is 1 to 5 meters thick. Some of this sea ice forms and melts each year. Now, though, the sea ice is thinner, freezes later, and breaks up much earlier in the year. The volume of Arctic sea ice in the summers is now less than a third of what it was in the 1980s. Ice that took centuries to form can melt in just a few years. In other words, Earth's ice is melting! The cause is warmer global temperatures.

The melting ice can have major effects. Sea levels rise, and ocean currents change. Living things are affected too. Polar bears hunt seals on sea ice packs. When the ice melts early, polar bears cannot find enough food for

Define It

Earth's temperatures have been getting warmer. Scientists are investigating to find out what is causing the climate to change. They think that the change can be slowed or possibly stopped. One way to do this is for people to reduce their carbon footprint. A carbon footprint is a measure of carbon dioxide that is produced by using fossil fuels. Increasing amounts of carbon dioxide cause Earth's atmosphere to become warmer.

Suppose you work for an organization that advises communities on how to reduce their carbon footprint. They want you to define the problem in your community.

☐ List five questions you would ask individuals and community leaders to help you define their carbon footprint.

1. _____

2. _____

3. _____

4. _____

5. _____

☐ What would you want individuals and communities to understand to help them avoid negatively affecting climate?

_____

_____

_____

_____

_____

_____

_____

_____

_____

Earth's Freshwater

Identify that most of Earth's freshwater is in glaciers, in ice caps, or underground.
Explain that some freshwater is found in lakes, rivers, wetlands, and the atmosphere.
5-ESS2-2

Literacy Skill
Draw Conclusions

Vocabulary
glacier
aquifer
reservoir

Academic Vocabulary
distribute

▶ **VIDEO**

Watch a video about Earth's freshwater.

LOCAL-TO-GLOBAL ▶ Connection

In the 1800s, Chicago's wastewater flowed through the Chicago River into Lake Michigan, which was the source of Chicago's drinking water. Over time, the river and the lake became polluted. To solve the problem, a canal called the Chicago Sanitary and Ship Canal opened in 1900. It changed the flow of the Chicago River so that it carried water away from Lake Michigan. Instead, the water flowed to the Mississippi river.

Chicago's problem was solved, but a new one developed. Today, invasive species, such as Asian carp, can be found in Lake Michigan. Some carp accessed Lake Michigan by swimming up the Mississippi River. The carp threaten the lake's fishing industry. People are now evaluating whether to close the canal.

✓ **READING CHECK** **Draw Conclusions** Why was it a problem that the Chicago River flowed into Lake Michigan?

_____

_____

STEM uInvestigate Lab

How can you find water

UNDERGROUND?

Water quality specialists must sometimes locate and test new sources of water. How can you use a model to find and test underground water?

Design and Build

☐ **1.** Soak a sponge with water and then put it somewhere on the bottom of the baking pan. Cover the sponge with soil, rocks, and sand to make a landscape in the pan. Exchange landscapes with another group.

☐ **2.** Design a tool to find the water in the new landscape. Your tool should change the landscape as little as possible. What other criteria should you consider when designing the tool?

_____

_____

☐ **3.** Show your design to your teacher before you begin. Record your observations.

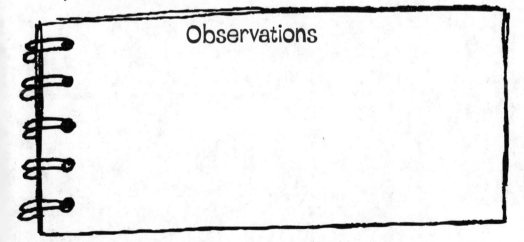

Observations

Materials

- safety goggles
- baking pan
- sponge
- sand
- soil
- pebbles
- water

Suggested Materials

- string
- piece of drinking straw
- turkey baster
- tape
- cardboard

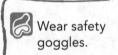 Wear safety goggles.

Engineering Practice

Engineers apply scientific ideas to design an object.

Evaluate Your Design

4. Did your tool help you find water? How could you improve your tool?

_____

_____

HOW IS freshwater distributed ACROSS EARTH?

Nearly three-fourths of Earth is covered by water. Only a very small amount of that water is freshwater. How is water distributed over Earth?

96.5% Ocean

Total Global Water

Water that is saline has large amounts of dissolved salts. The Mediterranean Sea is an example of a body of water that is made of saline water.

1.0% Other saline water

2.5% Freshwater

30.1% Groundwater

1.2% Surface/Other freshwater

A glacier is a slowly moving body of ice on land.

Freshwater

68.7% Glaciers and ice caps

0.2% Living things

0.5% Rivers

2.6% Swamps, marshes

3.0% Atmosphere

3.8% Soil moisture

20.9% Lakes

! List four freshwater sources that are included in surface water:

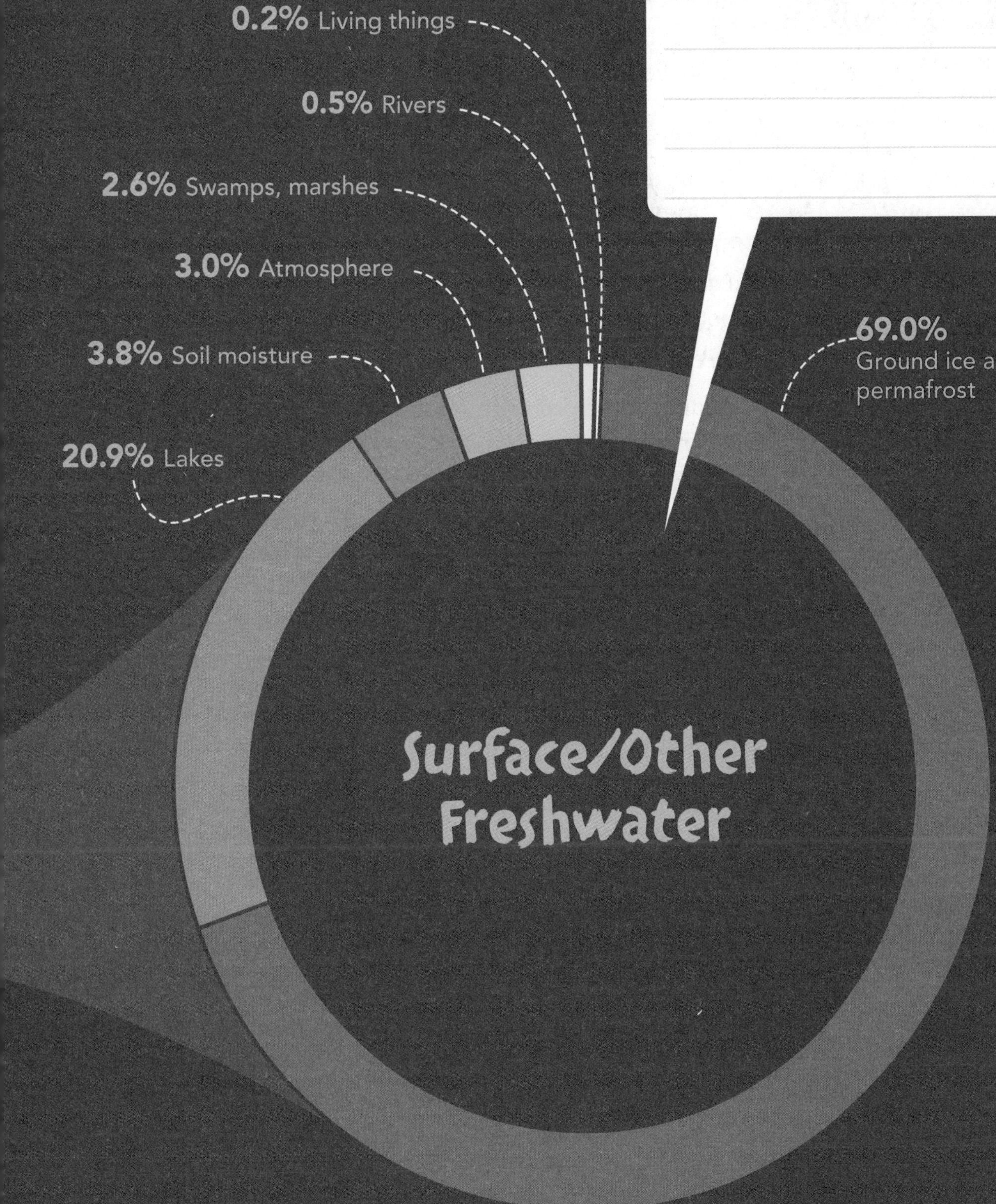

69.0%
Ground ice and permafrost

Surface/Other Freshwater

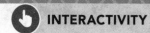
uBe a Scientist

Modeling Water Distribution

Using graph paper, mark off a grid 10 squares by 10 squares. With a pair of scissors, cut off 97.5 squares for the ocean and other saline water. You have 2.5 squares left. Cut off 1.75 squares of paper to represent water held in ice. The 100 original squares represent all of Earth's water near the surface. How much is left? That is the liquid freshwater for human use.

Freshwater Shortages

Earth's freshwater is not evenly **distributed**, or spread out. Some areas, such as Brazil's rainforests, get rain almost daily. Other areas, such as Chile's Atacama Desert, are dry all the time. In places like Nebraska, people rely on water pumped from **aquifers**, underground water supplies. Worldwide, about 1 billion people do not have access to clean water. Another 2.7 billion people do not have freshwater for at least one month a year. To help solve the problem, people build **reservoirs**, places to collect and store water. Scientists predict that about 75 percent of Earth's people will have water shortages by 2025 if we do not change the amount of water we use. Scenes such as the one in the photo will become more common.

Adding to the problem is water pollution and habitat destruction. More than half of the world's wetlands have disappeared. Wetlands are important ecosystems that can remove pollutants from the water. The Florida Everglades at one time covered 3 million acres, but in the last 100 years, people have dug canals and built dams there. They took water, built homes, and expanded agriculture. Today, the Everglades is less than half of its former size.

Reflect Why might someone who lives where freshwater is plentiful worry about water shortages elsewhere?

Quest Connection

Why is it important to find ways to make dirty, or polluted, water or saltwater drinkable in the future?

_____

_____

You can use math to compare the volume of a lake to the volume of a glacier.

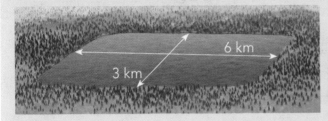
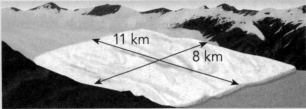

1. **Calculate** Find the surface area of the lake and the glacier using the formula.
   B (surface area) = $l \times w$

2. **Calculate** The depth of the lake is 0.1 km. The depth of the glacier is 0.2 km. Calculate the volume of each freshwater source using the formula. V (volume) = $l \times w \times h$

3. Round the volume of each up to the nearest round number. Estimate how many times more volume the glacier has compared to the lake.

✓ Lesson 2 Check

1. **Explain** If more than half of Earth is covered with water, why is freshwater so limited?

_____

2. **Explain** Surface water is found in lakes, rivers, swamps, marshes, the atmosphere, and ice- and snow-covered land. Why are people not always able to use water from all these sources?

_____

_____

How do we filter water?

It's time to figure out a way to filter drinkable water from a freshwater source. Water straight from a lake or stream can have dirt and harmful materials that need to be removed before people drink it. How can you filter the water to make it cleaner?

Design Your Model

☐ **1.** List the criteria for your water filter.

_____

_____

_____

☐ **2.** What materials will you use to filter the water?

_____

_____

☐ **3.** How will you test the water to see whether your filter is successful?

_____

_____

☐ **4. SEP Develop a Model** Draw your filter design.

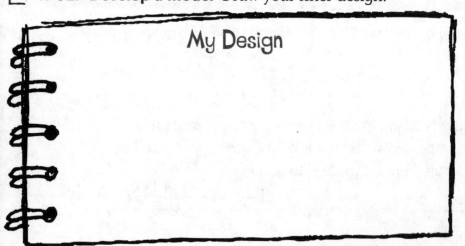

My Design

Materials
- cup to hold filtered water
- cup of nonfiltered water
- white plastic lid or container
- safety goggles

Suggested Materials
- water bottle
- water bottle cap with hole in center
- coffee filter
- cotton balls
- eyedropper
- hand lens
- gauze square
- sand
- charcoal
- scissors

 Wear safety goggles.

 Handle scissors carefully.

 Do not drink water used in the investigation.

Engineering Practice

Engineers use models to analyze a system.

5. Develop a procedure, and show it to your teacher before you test your filter design. Record your observations.

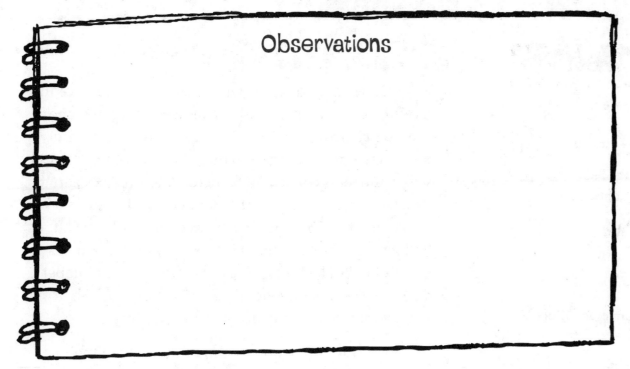

Observations

Evaluate Your Model

6. SEP Use Models Did the filter remove most of the particles from the water? How do you know?

_____

_____

_____

_____

7. Explain Is your water safe to drink now? Explain your answer.

_____

_____

_____

_____

_____

Earth's Ocean

I can...

Describe how most of Earth's water is in the ocean.
5-ESS2-2

Literacy Skill
Draw Conclusions

Vocabulary
circulation
tides
salinity

Academic Vocabulary
primary

▶ **VIDEO**

Watch a video about saltwater.

LOCAL-TO-GLOBAL ▶ Connection

In 1992, a shipping container fell into the Pacific Ocean. It dumped a load of 28,000 rubber ducks into the ocean. Eventually, nearly 26,000 of the ducks washed ashore. The ducks crossed the ocean and headed both north and south. Currents carried ducks across the Arctic Ocean to beaches in Canada, Scotland, and England. Some ducks also landed in Chile, South America, and in Australia. Rubber ducks were found most recently on Alaskan beaches in 2011. You can see the travels of these rubber ducks on the map. Rubber ducks, like other rubbish at sea, travel thousands of ocean miles.

Communicate What does the map show about the ocean? Explain.

_____

_____

LEGEND
X Location where ducks were found

STEM · uInvestigate Lab

How can you separate salt from water?

In places where water is scarce, engineers look for ways to get freshwater from saltwater. This process is called desalination. How can you get freshwater from saltwater?

Suggested Materials
- large bowl
- small plastic cup
- string
- cling wrap
- 2 stones
- saltwater
- beaker

Design and Build

☐ 1. How can you use what you know about the water cycle to help separate the salt and the water in saltwater? Use the materials and what you know about the water cycle to make a plan to separate the salt and the water in saltwater. Include how you will know that the salt and water have been separated.

☐ 2. Show your plan to your teacher before you begin. Record your observations.

 Do not drink or taste anything in the lab.

Observations

Engineering Practice

Engineers describe observations to address scientific questions.

Evaluate Your Design

3. **Explain** How could the results of this investigation be applied to providing freshwater to a coastal city?

_____

_____

_____

100%

Where Is Water?

No matter where Earth's water is located, it is in a system called the hydrosphere. The hydrosphere can be divided into two main sections—saltwater and freshwater. Saltwater makes up about 97.5 percent of Earth's water. Many plants and animals, including humans, cannot use saltwater. The other 2.5 percent of water on Earth is found mostly in glaciers, ice caps, and groundwater.

Although different sections of the ocean have specific names, they are all connected. **Circulation**, or a swirling motion, moves ocean water around the globe. The ocean is Earth's main water storage and the **primary**, or most important, source for water in the water cycle. The water cycle links the ocean to all freshwater bodies.

Graph Data Fill in the bar chart with labels and the correct percentages of saltwater and freshwater.

0%

Quest Connection

If Earth has so much water, why do people in some areas have none to drink? Explain.

_____

_____

_____

_____

_____

Ocean Temperatures

The sun's heat warms Earth's ocean water. Water temperatures change with latitude because of the angle of Earth's axis and its relation to the sun. Sunlight at Earth's poles is spread out more than at the equator. Water temperatures near the equator are about 30°C (86°F). Polar ocean water can be as cold as –2°C (28°F). Surface water around the equator evaporates more quickly than at the poles.

Water temperature also changes with ocean depth. Deep ocean water receives less sunlight and is colder than surface water, even at the equator. Wind and waves stir up ocean water. Currents move water along the surface and beneath it. Ocean water is also moved by **tides**, or rising and falling patterns caused by the pull of gravity.

✓ READING CHECK **Draw Conclusions** Using a ruler, make a dark line along the equator in the picture. Compare the temperature of the water north and south of the equator.

_____

_____

During which season in the north do you think this map was drawn? Why?

_____

_____

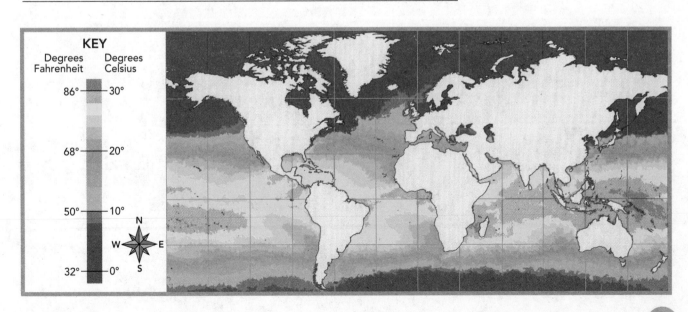

KEY

Degrees Fahrenheit | Degrees Celsius

86° — 30°

68° — 20°

50° — 10°

N
W — E
S

32° — 0°

What is the motion of the ocean?

The ocean's surface water moves in a consistent pattern in the form of currents. Surface currents are caused by wind. Scientists name currents to help identify their locations in the ocean. California, Peru, and East Australia are current names, for example.

Greenland

Gulf Stream

California

North Equatorial

South Equatorial

Peru

Brazil

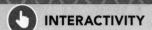
Suppose a sailboat was spotted drifting along the Gulf
Stream current. Several months later, the same sailboat was
spotted drifting along the East Australia current. Trace a
possible path of ocean currents that the sailboat followed.
Describe why you think the boat traveled that path.

Norwegian

North Equatorial

South Equatorial

West
Australia

East
Australia

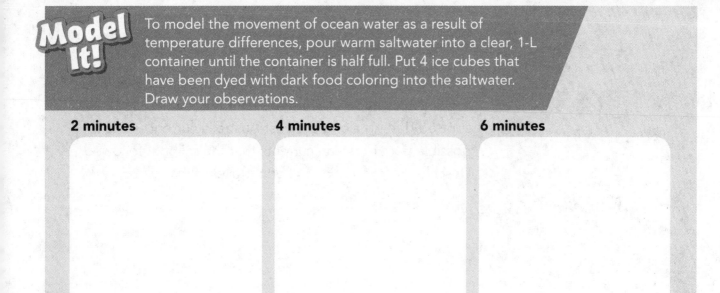

Model It!

To model the movement of ocean water as a result of temperature differences, pour warm saltwater into a clear, 1-L container until the container is half full. Put 4 ice cubes that have been dyed with dark food coloring into the saltwater. Draw your observations.

2 minutes	4 minutes	6 minutes

Salinity

Ocean water is salty, but salinity varies in different ocean areas. **Salinity** is the amount of salt dissolved in water. It is measured in parts per thousand. The surface waters of the Atlantic Ocean have higher salinity than the surface waters of the Pacific Ocean. In places where rivers empty into the ocean, freshwater mixes with saltwater. Those areas have lower salinity.

Salinity	
Body of water	**Salinity (parts per thousand)**
Indian Ocean	32–37 ppt
Caribbean Sea	35 ppt
Arctic Ocean	30 ppt
Antarctic Ocean	34 ppt

Identify Circle the body of water with the lowest salinity. Underline the body of water that most likely has the highest salinity.

Threats to the Shoreline

People throughout the globe have challenges in saving ocean shorelines. Building along a coast can cause pollution. Erosion and rising sea levels cause beaches to shrink. Accidents from ocean oil drilling spill oil into the water. Birds, fish, marine mammals, and sea plants suffer when oil coats the water. Polluted water from rivers or garbage dumped into the ocean can spoil shorelines. Tides and currents leave garbage and waste on the sand.

✅ **READING CHECK** **Draw Conclusions** Can oil spilled on land pollute the ocean? Explain your answer.

u Be a Scientist

Oil Spill in a Bottle
Fill a plastic water bottle 3/4 full of water. Add 6 drops blue or green food coloring. Swirl the water to mix the color. Add 1 cm of vegetable oil. Put the lid on tightly. Turn the bottle on its side and see how an oil slick spreads. Shake the bottle vigorously. Place the bottle on its side and wait a few minutes. What happens to the oil? Why can't the ocean get rid of an oil slick?

✅ Lesson 3 Check

1. **Explain** Through which processes in the water cycle is the ocean connected to all of Earth's water?

_____

_____

2. **Explain** On Tuesday, the water temperature at Emerald Beach is 27°C (81°F). On Thursday, the water temperature at the same beach is 30°C (86°F). What factors might have caused the temperature change?

_____

_____

Water Resources

Fill in the table based on what you have learned about water. Consider each source and its possibility of providing water for drinking. You need to consider the tasks you will complete as you get the water. You should also consider which tasks will cost money.

Glacier	Type of water: _____ Location: _____ Tasks involved: _____ _____ Factors affecting cost: _____
Groundwater	Type of water: _____ Location: _____ Tasks involved: _____ _____ Factors affecting costs: _____
Ocean	Type of water: _____ Location: _____ Tasks involved: _____ _____ Factors affecting costs: _____

Evaluate Which of these sources contains the greatest amount of water? What is one difficulty in making that water drinkable for humans?

_____

_____

_____

_____

_____

Can people live on Mars?

Phenomenon People may someday live on Mars. For humans to live on Mars, they will need a freshwater source. Recent studies by NASA show that Mars has plenty of water, but much of it is frozen. Water ice lies in an underground layer covering a large area of Mars. The water ice in this layer has about as much water as Lake Superior. Using radar, NASA looked at an area called Utopia Planitia. The water ice there covers more land than New Mexico. The water contains dust and rock. The chart shows a few other differences.

	Earth	Mars
Atmosphere	nitrogen, oxygen, argon, others	carbon dioxide, water vapor
Water content	97.5% saltwater, 2.5% freshwater	frozen, dirty freshwater, snowflakes of carbon dioxide
Climate	tropical, temperate, and polar regions	extreme cold to moderate, massive dust storms

Let's use what you know about finding and using water. Complete this claim: If people were to live on Mars, they would need food, water, and shelter. The water would come from

_____

_____

The process of obtaining water on Mars would be most like getting water from which sources on Earth?

_____

_____

The water could be made usable for humans by

_____

_____

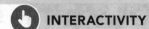
Water, Water Everywhere!

How can you make undrinkable water drinkable?

Phenomenon Apply what you learned to decide how to provide drinkable water to the two thirsty towns in the table.

Town	Nearest water source	Quality of water
Katherine, Australia	Katherine River	Little rain for many months of each year. Water contains soil particles from runoff.
Agadir, Morocco	Atlantic Ocean	Water source has salt content.

For each town, write a recommendation for how to solve its water problem. Do research to find additional information to support your recommendation. What challenges to success do you think might exist for each of the towns?

Katherine _____

_____

_____

_____

_____

Agadir _____

_____

_____

_____

Water Quality Specialist

Water quality specialists understand how water conditions affect people. These scientists study ways people get water and ways human activity pollutes water. They have two water sources to check. The first is raw water, or water as it exists in nature. They check how this type of water changes because of runoff from land and roads. The other is treated water, the water you get when you turn on a faucet at home.

Water quality specialists need degrees in chemistry, earth science, or biology. They travel to water sources to take samples and investigate possible problems. Some work is done in labs and some in offices, but at least 40 percent of this job is done outdoors.

Reflect In your science notebook, describe two or three things about being a water quality specialist that interest you.

1. **Vocabulary** A city dams a river and makes a lake that stores its freshwater supply. This is an example of an artificial _____.

Use the diagram for questions 2 and 3.

2. **Interpret Diagrams** Number 1 on the diagram represents which part of the water cycle?

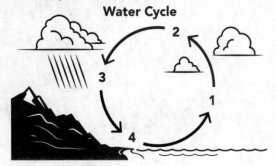

Water Cycle

A. evaporation

B. precipitation

C. condensation

D. collection

3. **Describe** Which of these best describes how the water cycle moves from 3 to 4 in the diagram?

A. Water falls on land as precipitation and collects in lakes, ponds, or the ocean.

B. Water collects in reservoirs, where surface water evaporates.

C. Water vapor in the air condenses when it cools and forms clouds that provide precipitation.

D. Rain falls on land and immediately begins the process of evaporation.

4. **Explain** A sealed plastic bottle falls into the ocean off Australia. Three years later, the bottle is found on a beach in France. Explain how that might happen.

_____

_____

_____

_____

_____

_____

_____

5. **Evaluate a Plan** Water can be a solid, liquid, or gas in Earth's water cycle. Identify two processes in the water cycle where water changes from one state to another state and then back to the original state.

_____

_____

_____

_____

_____

_____

_____

_____

6. Describe What does the ocean's connection to Earth's water reservoirs through evaporation and precipitation tell you about the ocean's role in the water cycle?

_____

_____

_____

7. Interpret Which of these would be an accurate title for the graph?

A. Distribution of Earth's Water

B. Earth's Saltwater Sources

C. The Water Cycle

D. Distribution of Freshwater

Surface/Other

freshwater **1.2%**

**Groundwater
30.1%**

**Glaciers
and
ice caps
68.7%**

8. Describe Which of these describes a drought?

A. In the last five years, an area in Australia has received less than half its normal rainfall.

B. A ski area in the French Alps has seen no rain for a month but has had 975 mm of snow.

C. A coastal town in Maine has no rainfall at all for the month of August.

D. A region in South Africa has almost no rainfall during the winter but a wet spring and summer.

The Essential Question

How much water can be found in different places on Earth?

Show What You Learned

You viewed several maps and graphs as you learned about Earth's water. Think about this evidence. What conclusions have you drawn about where saltwater and freshwater are found?

_____

_____

_____

_____

_____

_____

Use the table to answer questions 1–6.

Water source	Water volume on Earth (cubic km)	Percent of total water*
Ocean (saltwater)	1,338,000,000	96.53
Ice caps, glaciers, permanent snow	24,064,000	1.73
Fresh groundwater	10,530,000	0.76
Salty groundwater	12,870,000	0.93
Ground Ice and permafrost	300,000	0.02
Freshwater lakes	91,000	0.01
Saltwater lakes	85,400	0.01
Other freshwater reservoirs	34,305	0.01

*Percentages have been rounded.

1. **Draw** Choose 3 water sources and graph their amounts to help show how water is distributed on Earth.

2. **Identify** Where on Earth is most freshwater found?

   A. oceans

   B. lakes

   C. groundwater

   D. ice caps, glaciers, permanent snow

3. **Draw Conclusions** Which conclusion can be drawn from the data in the table?

   A. Almost no water is stored on Earth as ice.

   B. Freshwater on Earth is evenly distributed.

   C. Most of Earth's water is saltwater.

   D. Saltwater on Earth is evenly distributed.

4. **Explain** Is more of Earth's freshwater in lakes or in groundwater? Use evidence to support your answer.

   _____

   _____

5. **Evaluate** How would the information in the table change if half of Earth's ocean water permanently froze?

   _____

   _____

   _____

   _____

6. **Infer** Humans cannot drink saltwater, and the ice caps and glaciers are usually in places that people cannot live. Based on this information, why is it important to maintain our freshwater resources?

   _____

   _____

   _____

How can water move upward?

Phenomenon Engineers need to pump water from underground to test it. How can you build a device to pump water upward?

Design and Build

☐ **1.** Use the materials to design a device that will pump the greatest volume of water as quickly as possible.

☐ **2.** Draw a design for your device. Label the materials your device will use.

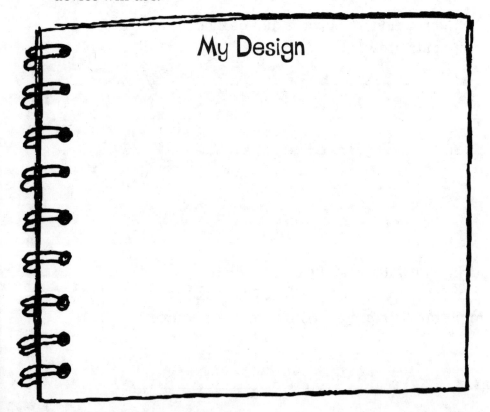

My Design

☐ **3.** How will you test your device? Remember to control variables.

_____

_____

Materials
- safety goggles
- squeezable plastic water bottle with a lid
- tape
- bucket
- water
- graduated beaker
- stopwatch

 Wear safety goggles.

Engineering Practice

Engineers **describe quantities,** to provide evidence.

4. Show your design and testing idea to your teacher before you begin. Record your observations.

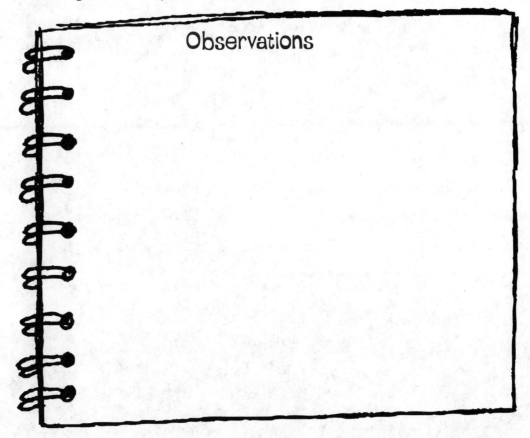

Observations

Analyze and Interpret Data

5. Compare and Contrast Compare your device with those of other students to identify the design that can pump the greatest volume of water in a specific time. What features do the most powerful devices share?

_____

_____

6. Infer How could you improve your model to make it more powerful?

_____

_____

_____

Human Impacts on Earth's Systems

Next Generation Science Standards

5-ESS3-1 Obtain and combine information about ways individual communities use science ideas to protect the Earth's resources and environment.

Go online to access
your digital course.

VIDEO

eTEXT

INTERACTIVITY

VIRTUAL LAB

GAME

ASSESSMENT

The Essential Question

How can we protect Earth's resources and environments?

Show What You Know

Each of these flags represents a native species that people planted near this lake. How might planting native species help organisms that live in the lake?

_____

_____

_____

_____

Take Care of Earth — It's Our Home!

How can we preserve and protect the resources we need?

Phenomenon Hi, I am Emma Elliot, an environmental scientist! My job is to find ways to protect our environment while we use the resources that it provides. In this problem-based learning activity, you will help make your school and classroom more environmentally friendly.

Similar to an environmental scientist, you will identify efficient and wasteful uses of resources in your school. You will also identify how your school can become more energy efficient.

Follow the path to learn how you will complete the Quest. The Quest activities in the lessons will help you complete the Quest! Check off your progress on the path when you complete an activity with a **QUEST CHECK ✓ OFF**. Go online for more Quest activities.

Quest Check-In 1

Lesson 1

Identify actions that use resources efficiently and wastefully.

Next Generation Science Standards
5-ESS3-1 Obtain and combine information about ways individual communities use science ideas to protect the Earth's resources and environment.

VIDEO

Watch a video about an environmental scientist.

Quest Check-In Lab 3

Lesson 3
Model the ways that people can build homes to reduce energy use.

Quest Check-In 4

Lesson 4
Evaluate a school expansion plan based on your school's conservation goals.

Quest Check-In 2

Lesson 2
Make a checklist to evaluate the efficiency of your school's energy use.

Quest Findings

Use evidence to suggest an action plan to reduce the impact your school has on its environment.

RECYCLE

SCHOOL

RECYCLE

How can we reuse materials to design new products?

Engineers design products that meet specific criteria. How can you design fun pet toys out of reused materials?

Suggested Materials

- used tennis balls
- used towels, rope, or other soft materials
- old toys or stuffed animals
- used clothing

Design and Build

☐ **1.** Choose a pet. Research and compare the design of at least two toys for this pet. Use approved sources from your teacher.

☐ **2.** Use your research to design a pet toy made out of reusable materials. Describe how you will build the toy. Have your teacher check your plan before you start.

_____

_____

Engineering Practice

Engineers **obtain information** to explain solutions to a design problem.

☐ **3.** Build your toy and then trade toys and criteria with a classmate. Give each other suggestions for ways that the toys could be improved. Write one of the suggestions you receive.

_____

_____

_____

Evaluate Your Design

4. Communicate Why is evaluating and communicating improvements for a design important? Could it help conserve materials?

_____

_____

_____

_____

_____

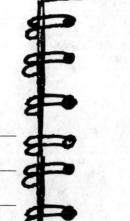

Design

Compare and Contrast

 GAME

Practice what you learn with the Mini Games.

When you compare and contrast objects or actions, you look for ways they are alike or different.

- Words such as *similar, both,* and *all* show how things are alike.
- Words such as *greater, smaller, more, less,* and *most* often show how things are different.

Read the following passage to learn about limited and unlimited resources.

Using Energy Resources

Most of our energy now comes from fuels, such as coal, oil, and natural gas. Many scientists predict that these will last as energy resources for about 100 more years. Other resources, such as sunlight and wind, are unlimited. These resources will not run out. A new supply is naturally made all the time. A tiny fraction of sunlight on Earth could provide for all of our energy needs.

In the past, collecting energy from limited resources has been less expensive than getting energy from unlimited resources. Now collecting energy from unlimited resources is getting less expensive. Both kinds of resources have environmental impacts, but the impacts are different. Most limited resources are fuels that are burned, so they produce pollution and affect the atmosphere. Some structures that collect unlimited resources, such as solar energy, take up a lot of land to produce energy.

☑ **READING CHECK** **Compare and Contrast** How are limited energy resources similar to unlimited resources? How are they different?

_____

_____

_____

_____

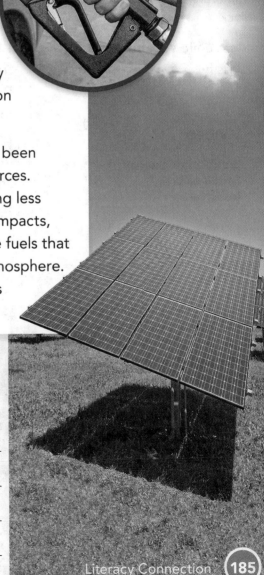

Earth's Natural Resources

I can...

Describe Earth's
natural resources.

5-ESS3-1

Literacy Skill
Compare and Contrast

Vocabulary
natural resource
nonrenewable
  resource
renewable resource
mineral
rock

Academic Vocabulary
classify
efficient

▶ **VIDEO**

Watch a video about
Earth's natural
resources.

LOCAL-TO-GLOBAL ❯ Connection

The people in the picture are gathering seabird
droppings. In places where millions of seabirds live,
the droppings, called guano, can build up quickly. On
islands near the coast of Peru, guano droppings can
be up to 6 meters (20 feet) deep! People have gathered
guano and used it to make fertilizers for at least 1,500
years. As in the past, Peru is the top producer of guano
today. The climate in Peru is ideal for high-quality
guano.

Guano contains many nutrients that plants need to
grow. People all over the world use guano to fertilize
their crops and home gardens. You probably can find it
in many stores that sell gardening supplies in your city.
But not all places on Earth have seabird populations
large enough to produce much guano—or the climate to
produce quality guano similar to that found in Peru. As
a result, most of the guano used in the United States is
shipped from Peru or other countries.

Infer Why is guano a good fertilizer?

_____

_____

_____

Where are the metals?

Scientists study how resources are obtained and used. How can you find out where some metals come from?

Procedure

☐ 1. Select five metal resources from this list:
aluminum, copper, gold, iron, nickel, silver, tin, zinc.

☐ 2. Use reference sources to find information about where your metal resources are naturally found. Record the metals and the information in the table.

Metal	Where it is found

☐ 3. Use the World Map to show the major places where each metal is found. Use symbols to represent each metal. Make a legend for your map that identifies the symbols you use.

Analyze and Interpret Data

4. **SEP Interpret** Examine the information on your map and the maps of classmates. Do all areas of the world have the same amount of metal resources? Explain your answer.

_____

_____

_____

_____

Materials
- reference materials about metals
- World Map
- colored pencils

Suggested Materials
- computer with Internet access

Science Practice

Scientists evaluate published information to explain natural phenomena.

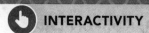
Natural Resources

Books, phones, shoes, bikes—all of the materials that make up these objects originally came from nature. A **natural resource** is something found in nature that humans use. The vegetables you eat come from growing plants. Metals are mined from underground. Glass starts out as sand, and plastics are made from oil.

One way we can **classify**, or put into groups, natural resources is based on how available they are. Some natural resources have a limited supply. A **nonrenewable resource** is one that is not made fast enough to replace what is used. Energy resources such as coal, petroleum, and natural gas are nonrenewable resources. They form naturally, but the process takes millions of years. That means the supply that exists right now is all that will be available to people.

A **renewable resource** is a material that is made by nature at least as quickly as people use it. Plants that we use as food are renewable resources. The sun supplies new solar energy every day. Wind used for energy is a renewable resource. Even the air that we breathe is a renewable resource because plants constantly produce oxygen. Resources, though, are renewable only if we do not use more of them than nature produces.

✓ **READING CHECK** **Compare and Contrast** What is the main difference between a renewable resource and nonrenewable resource?

_____

_____

Literacy ▸ Toolbox 🔧

Compare and Contrast
As you read, look for sentences that describe how one thing is similar to or different from something else. As you read this lesson, list words that could describe both renewable and nonrenewable resources.

Quest Connection

What is one way you can reuse something that you no longer need?

_____

_____

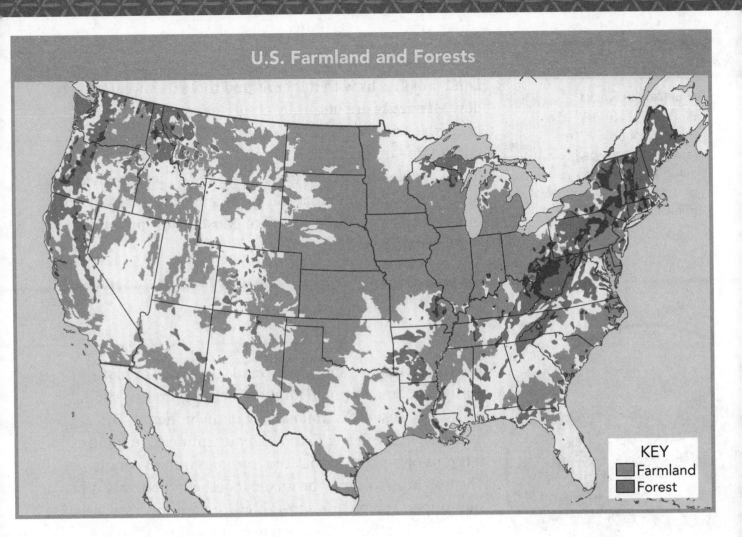

U.S. Farmland and Forests

KEY
Farmland
Forest

Land and Forest Resources

You may not think of land as a resource. But we use land to provide many things we need and want. We build houses and other structures on land. We use soil to grow crops and graze animals. Without soil, we would have very few kinds of food to eat. Soil can take hundreds of years to form, so using it wisely is important.

Without land, we would not have forests, which provide habitats for many organisms. Forests also provide materials for paper, medicines, and foods, such as nuts and fruits. In addition, forests play an important role in controlling the amount of carbon dioxide in the air. Too much carbon dioxide in the atmosphere can cause Earth's atmosphere to warm.

Relate The map shows the locations in the United States of farmland and forest. Why are these natural resources important?

_____

_____

Minerals and Rocks

Land provides us with minerals and rocks that we use every day. **Minerals** are naturally occurring, nonliving solids in Earth's crust. The particles that make up each kind of mineral are arranged in a specific pattern. Some minerals are available on Earth in large amounts. Others are available in much smaller amounts. Many minerals must be dug from mines deep below Earth's surface. Most metals are mined from minerals.

Identify Which material shown in the map is most plentiful in the United States?

Rocks are natural substances made up of one or more minerals. Some common kinds of rock are granite, chalk, and slate. Most rocks are made of many minerals. For example, iron is never found as a pure mineral in nature. It is part of iron ore, a rock that includes iron materials. The iron minerals may be mixed together with many other substances. The picture shows how iron ore can vary. Because iron ore and other rocks are found only at certain places on Earth, they are often carried by rail or ship to places far from where they were mined. Rocks and minerals take many thousands of years to form, so they are nonrenewable resources.

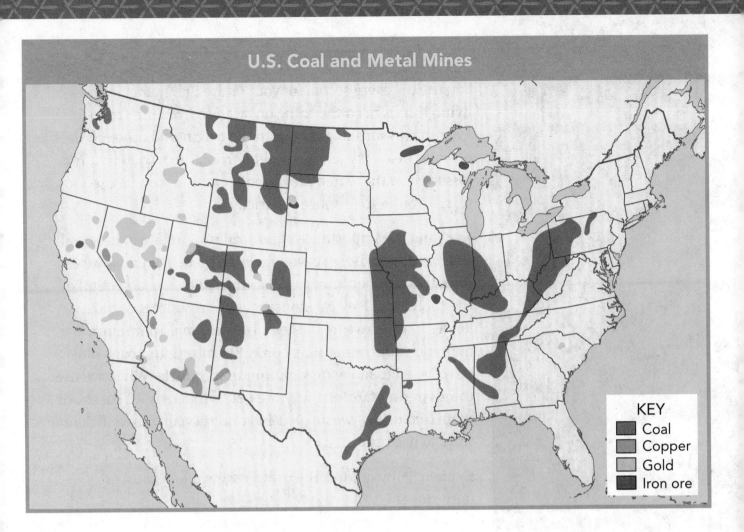

U.S. Coal and Metal Mines

KEY
- Coal
- Copper
- Gold
- Iron ore

Water Resources

The next time you take a drink of water, think of the water as a natural resource. Humans and all other living things need water to survive. We use water in other ways too—bathing, swimming, cleaning, washing clothing, cooking, growing crops, and raising animals. Industries also depend on water for processes such as cleaning, transporting, and mining. Water also powers turbines that help produce electricity.

Although water is a renewable resource, it is not evenly distributed around Earth. Some places do not have enough water. People living there treat ocean water to remove the salt, or they get water from places where it is plentiful.

Make Meaning In your science notebook, tell whether people who live where water is plentiful should take care of water resources. Tell why you think so.

Air Resources

You use air every second of your entire life. In fact, almost all living things need the same gas we use from air—oxygen. Even the organisms that live in the ocean and other bodies of water need oxygen. They get it from the oxygen that has dissolved in the water. Moving air, or wind, can be used to turn turbines to produce electricity.

Knowing the importance of natural resources will help you use resources wisely. As you have learned, even renewable resources can become scarce or unusable if we do not take care of them. Likewise, nonrenewable resources can last longer if we take care of them. For example, aluminum is a nonrenewable mineral resource. But aluminum cans may be recycled to make new aluminum products. When we use things in an **efficient** way, we get as much as we can from them and do not waste. Reusing and recycling are efficient ways to use resources.

Explain Why is carefully using renewable resources important?

_____

_____

_____

☑ Lesson 1 Check

1. Explain Why is steel from old cars not considered a renewable resource even though it is used to make new steel products?

_____

_____

2. Contrast What is the difference between a mineral and a rock?

_____

_____

Efficient or Wasteful

Some of the ways we use resources are efficient. Other activities can waste resources. For example, filling a bowl of water for your pet is an efficient use of a natural resource. Letting the water run over the top when the dish is full uses more water than is needed. Some people would say it is wasteful. People often have different opinions about whether an activity is wasteful enough to change the way they do it. One person might think buying a new phone is wasteful if the old phone still works. Someone else might think it is efficient because the new phone does things the old phone could not do.

1. List four ways resources at your school are used efficiently. List four ways resources at your school are used wastefully.

Efficient	Wasteful

2. Compare your list with those of other students. Discuss students' reasons for opinions that are different from yours. Did their reasons change your opinion? Explain.

_____

_____

_____

_____

uEngineer It! Design STEM

▶ **VIDEO**

Watch a video about how engineers update and improve electric cars.

Make Energy the Solar Way

Phenomenon You may have seen objects similar to the ones in the picture. They are solar cells. A solar cell is a device that changes the energy of sunlight to electrical energy. Solar cells produce electricity without adding harmful materials to the atmosphere or hydrosphere. As long as there is sunlight, solar cells can produce electricity without any more cost.

Because solar cells use the sun as their energy source, large rooftop panels of cells must be outside. As a result, solar cells tend to collect dirt, leaves, and bird droppings. These materials block sunlight. With less sunlight, the panels capture less energy and produce less electricity. To capture the most solar energy, the panels must be kept clean. While it is easy to clean a solar cell on a calculator, it is more difficult on a high, sloped roof.

Design It

Suppose you are an engineer working for a company that makes solar cell panels for rooftops. The company wants you to design a system that makes it easier to keep the panels clean. The engineering problem is to design a way to clean the solar panels without using a ladder.

☐ Brainstorm three ideas that solve the problem.

_____

_____

_____

☐ Choose one design solution. Explain how it will solve the problem.

_____

_____

_____

☐ Sketch your solution to the problem. Label parts and write a short description of how the device works.

_____

_____

_____

Earth's Energy Resources

VIDEO

Watch a video about energy resources.

ENGINEERING › Connection

Deep underground, Earth is very hot. The heat is contained in the rocks, steam, water, and other matter below Earth's surface. The underground steam and hot water are a source of energy called geothermal energy.

Different systems bring geothermal energy to the surface in places where it can be used. Some systems pump hot underground water directly to buildings to heat them or to roads and sidewalks to melt snow. Other systems use the hot water and steam to turn turbines connected to generators that produce electricity. The cooled water left over can be returned below ground where it will heat up and can be used again.

Geothermal energy is a renewable resource. It does not pollute, it is inexpensive to use, and it is available all the time in places where it can be used, such as places near volcanoes, where the ground is very hot. It does have some disadvantages, though. Drilling through miles of rock can be difficult and expensive.

Conclude Since geothermal energy is always available, why do you think we do not get all of our energy from this source?

_____

_____

_____

uInvestigate Lab

Which color is best at capturing solar energy?

Scientists investigate how variables affect an outcome. How does color affect how much solar energy an object absorbs?

Materials
- 3 identical plastic bottles
- red, black, and white paper
- water
- graduated cylinder
- thermometer

Procedure

☐ 1. Predict how you think the color of a container will affect how much solar energy the container captures.

_____

_____

Science Practice

Scientists analyze data to provide evidence.

☐ 2. **SEP Plan an Investigation** Write a plan to test your prediction. Show your plan to your teacher before you begin. Record your observations.

Observations

Analyze and Interpret Data

3. **Evaluate** Which container is best at capturing solar energy? How do you know?

_____

_____

Human Uses of Energy

People have always needed energy. Ancient civilizations used the energy of strong animals to travel, to move building materials, and to plow fields to grow food. They burned wood and other plant materials to stay warm and to cook. In the modern world, other sources of energy, such as the gas that produces this flame, have replaced animals and firewood.

Identify What kinds of energy do you use that ancient people also used?

_____

_____

Energy from Fuels

When fuel burns, the chemical energy of the fuel **transforms**, or changes, into heat and light. People have used this energy for many thousands of years by burning dried wood or other plant materials. Today, most of our energy comes from burning fossil fuels—coal, oil, or natural gas. These materials formed from plants and animals that died long ago and were compacted underground. Coal is a solid, rock-like substance made mostly of carbon. When it burns, it produces a lot of heat. Oil is a liquid that is used to make liquid fuels, such as gasoline. Oil is the main source of energy for transportation such as cars, boats, trains, and planes. **Natural gas** is a flammable gas. It is used to generate electricity in homes for heating and cooking.

☑ **READING CHECK** **Compare and Contrast** How do the energy resources available to people now compare to those available in the past?

_____

_____

_____

Energy from Nonfuel Sources

The water behind the dam may look as if it does not have much energy, but it is an important source of energy when it flows over the dam. As water falls through a dam, it turns blades that are inside a turbine. The blades are connected to a generator, which transforms the energy of the moving turbine into electrical energy. The energy that comes from the movement of water is called **hydroelectric energy**.

Wind can also be used to produce electricity. Similar to moving water, wind can turn the blades of a turbine. The turning blades are hooked to a generator that produces electricity.

Another energy source is the sun. The sun has always been the original source of energy stored in our food. People also use solar energy to provide heat and light. It can also be transformed into electrical energy using solar panels.

Infer Why are wind and water energy usually changed into electrical energy before they are used?

_____

_____

Science Practice
►Toolbox

Obtain Information Some places are more suitable than others for using wind energy. Use reliable websites, such as .gov and .edu sites, to research places where the greatest production of wind energy occurs in the United States. Show the locations on a map.

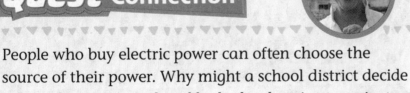

Quest Connection

People who buy electric power can often choose the source of their power. Why might a school district decide to buy electricity produced by hydroelectric power instead of electricity produced by burning fossil fuels?

_____

_____

_____

Where is electrical energy generated?

Much of the energy we use comes in the form of electrical energy. This electrical energy does not occur naturally. Generators change other forms of energy to electrical energy. A network of wires delivers the energy to the places where people use it.

! On the line near each source of energy, write the natural resource that is transformed into electrical energy.

LIBRARY

Find Your Impact

With an adult, figure out how you use energy in your home. Then figure out how that energy is produced. How big do you think your impact is from the energy you use?

Impacts of Energy Production

The picture shows how land can be changed to get energy sources such as coal. Mining and drilling operations make changes to Earth above and below the surface. Many of these changes cause changes to wildlife habitats. The changes may harm the organisms that live in the habitats.

Even sources of energy that do not need to be removed from within Earth can affect the environment. Dams change the flow of water in natural systems. Wind turbines can harm birds and bats. Large systems to collect solar energy cover land that could be used for other purposes. More efficient ways can be used to install solar technologies. One example is placing solar panels directly on rooftops. This provides power to homes and businesses without using additional land or connections to a power plant. People can also reduce impacts of energy production by reducing their energy use.

📓 **Write About It** In your science notebook, tell whether the need for energy sources should be more important than protecting land. Explain why you think so.

☑ Lesson 2 Check

1. Identify What is the original source of most energy that people use?

_____

_____

2. Explain What is another source of energy that people can use?

_____

_____

Save Energy!

What happens if you leave a door to your home open on a cool day? You probably notice cool air replacing some of the warm air inside the house. The home's heating system turns on to warm the cool air. It uses energy to do this. The heating system shuts off when the room is warm. This saves energy.

There are ways to save energy in your school. For example, turn off lights when you leave a room. That way energy is not wasted making light that is not needed.

1. Discuss ways that you could evaluate whether your school uses energy efficiently. Record your ideas.

_____

_____

_____

_____

_____

2. Use your ideas to make a checklist. The checklist should help you evaluate energy use at your school. Show your checklist to your teacher before you begin. Then do your evaluation of the school.

3. Review your evaluation. Look for ways the school uses energy efficiently. Also look for items that indicate that the school could improve its energy efficiency. List the places where you think energy efficiency could be improved.

_____

_____

_____

_____

Human Activity and Earth's Systems

I can...

Explain how human activities affect Earth's resources and environments.

5-ESS3-1

Literacy Skill
Compare and Contrast

Vocabulary
pollution

Academic Vocabulary
effect

 VIDEO

Watch a video about human activity and Earth's systems.

STEM Connection

The foggy layer that covers this city is caused by harmful gases and particles in the air. Many large cities around the world have the same problem. Exhaust gases from power plants, factories, and vehicles build up in the air. Even plant pollen can add to the problem. These materials can harm people, other living things, buildings, statues, and more.

Many cities have instruments that measure harmful materials in the air, such as ozone, sulfur dioxide, nitrogen, carbon monoxide, and pollen particles. The measurements taken by these instruments are often included in daily news and weather reports. If people note these reports, they can take actions to reduce their health risks.

Infer What actions could people take if a report showed that air quality was hazardous?

_____

_____

uInvestigate Lab

HANDS-ON LAB

5-ESS3-1, SEP.3

What happens to substances over time?

Soil is an important natural resource. How can you investigate what happens to materials that are buried in soil?

Procedure

☐ 1. Choose 3 different materials. Write a hypothesis about what will happen to the materials if they are buried in soil and kept in a warm place for two weeks.

_____

_____

☐ 2. **SEP Plan an Investigation** Write a procedure to test your hypothesis. Show your procedure to your teacher before you begin. Record your observations.

Observations

Analyze and Interpret Data

3. **Evaluate** Does your data support your hypothesis? Explain.

_____

_____

_____

4. **CCC Cause and Effect** What happens to a natural environment if trash is not disposed of properly?

_____

_____

Materials
- plastic gloves
- lab apron
- safety goggles
- potting soil
- water

Suggested Materials
- plastic cups
- tissue paper
- newspaper
- foam packing peanuts
- cardboard
- plastic wrap
- fruit peels
- aluminum foil
- leaves
- grass clippings

 Wear safety goggles.

 Wear plastic gloves.

 Do not taste materials in the lab.

Science Practice

Scientists carry out investigations to compare results.

How can human activities change Earth's Systems?

Earth has many systems that change as people use them. Some changes affect how the system works. These changes can make the system more useful or less useful to people.

Atmosphere

The atmosphere provides the air that we breathe. When substances are added to the air, the atmosphere changes.

Geosphere

The geosphere is the rock and soil beneath and around us. When people build places to live, they often change the geosphere.

Hydrosphere

The water on Earth and in its atmosphere makes up the hydrosphere. To use energy from the hydrosphere, people build large dams, which change the hydrosphere, geosphere, and biosphere.

Biosphere

The living things on Earth make up its biosphere. These living things include plants, animals, microorganisms, and even humans. When people cut down trees or grow plants, they change the biosphere.

! For each sphere, circle an example of how human activity has caused it to change.

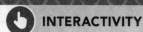
uBe a Scientist

Changes in Habitat

Take a walk in your neighborhood. Make a list of some of the things you think are different from the way they were before people lived there.

Human Resource Use and Pollution

Earth's systems are the source of the natural resources that all living things need to survive. Humans, though, use more resources than any other kind of organism. For example, beavers and humans build homes. They both remove many trees and alter water habitats by building dams. However, humans also use metals for pipes and wires, minerals for paints and plasters, and textiles for carpets and curtains. They use energy to run lights, ovens, and heaters.

Human activities have a huge effect on Earth's systems. An **effect** is a change that happens because of some kind of action. An effect can be the aim of an action, or it can be an unplanned result of an action. An unplanned result is called a side effect. The aim of farming is to produce food for people, but a side effect is that it replaces the type of organisms that normally live in an area. Factories use resources mined from the ground to produce goods that meet human needs. But they can produce gases that pollute the air. **Pollution** is the presence of substances in the environment that are harmful to humans or other organisms.

☑ READING CHECK **Compare and Contrast** Underline one positive effect of farming. Circle one negative effect of farming.

Quest Connection

How does the amount of resources that you use in school affect Earth's systems?

_____

_____

_____

Reduce Human Impacts

People can reduce unwanted impacts on Earth's systems. Activities that reduce our environmental impact are called ecofriendly. If we use fewer resources, then our impact is smaller. Using energy from sunlight is ecofriendly because it reduces the need for mining coal. Reusing materials means that fewer new resources are needed. Every act of conservation helps, no matter how small its effect might appear.

Reflect How can improving energy efficiency affect Earth's systems? Write your ideas in your science notebook.

Engineering Practice ▸ Toolbox

Design Solutions When engineers design solutions, they have criteria to measure whether their designs will be successful. What are some criteria that ecofriendly solutions have to meet?

☑ Lesson 3 Check

1. Describe How do humans affect Earth's natural resources?

_____

_____

2. Draw Conclusions How does human activity affect Earth's environments?

_____

_____

How do building materials affect energy efficiency?

Engineers choose from many different materials when they decide how to construct a building. How does the choice of building material affect energy efficiency?

Suggested Materials

- masking tape
- glue
- scissors
- ruler
- thermometer
- heavy paper or card stock
- parchment paper
- cardboard
- aluminum foil
- foam plastic sheets
- thin boards
- sheets of heavy plastic
- heavy canvas cloth
- plastic sheeting for windows
- strips of wood

Design and Build

☐ 1. **SEP Define the Problem** You will build a model room. What criteria does your room need to meet?

_____

_____

☐ 2. **SEP Design Solutions** Sketch the design of your room. Identify what materials you will use to make the walls and ceiling of the room.

 Be careful using scissors.

Engineering Practice

Engineers *compare multiple solutions* to evaluate how well they meet the criteria and constraints for a design problem.

3. As a class, plan a way to test the energy efficiency of each room. Remember to control variables and to consider where failures might happen. Make a class table that can be used to compare the test results for the rooms. Be sure to include a place on the table to list the materials that were used for each room.

4. Test your room. Record your data on the class table.

Evaluate Your Design

5. **SEP Analyze** Compare the designs to determine their success. Use the table to determine which materials were most energy efficient and which were least efficient. Provide evidence to support your answers.

_____

_____

_____

_____

_____

_____

_____

6. **Draw Conclusions** What properties of a material might make it more energy efficient?

_____

_____

_____

_____

_____

Protection of Earth's Resources and Environments

CURRICULUM ▷ Connection

In the first part of the 20th century, hunting eliminated all the wolves from Yellowstone National Park. The loss of the wolves led to some surprising results. The loss led to an increase in the number of wolf prey—deer and elk. Elk eat young willow and aspen trees. Beavers need these trees to build the lodges where they live. Because the elk ate more trees, the beaver population declined. With fewer beaver dams, there were fewer marshes.

Starting in 1995, scientists moved gray wolves from Canada into Yellowstone Park. Since then, the number of marsh habitats in the park has increased. This increase happened because wolves now help control the population of elk. Reintroducing wolves led to more animals thriving, not fewer.

Draw Conclusions What would likely happen if all of the elk in Yellowstone Park were removed?

_____

_____

How can you collect rainwater?

Engineers build their initial designs to evaluate solutions. They often make changes to initial designs to see whether they can be improved. How can you build a system to capture rainwater?

Design and Build

☐ 1. **SEP Design Solutions** Choose materials to plan and build a system to collect rainwater. Draw your design. Show your design to your teacher before you build it.

☐ 2. Pour water over your system to model rainwater. Vary the way you pour the water to model different types of rain. Record your observations.

Observations

Communicate Your Solution

3. **Compare and Contrast** Present your rainwater collection system to the class. Compare your system with those of other groups. What is one way that you could improve your system?

Materials
- water
- watering can

Suggested Materials
- sheets of hard plastic in several sizes
- aluminum foil
- funnel
- containers in various sizes
- plastic tubing
- duct tape

Engineering Practice

Engineers apply scientific principles to design a solution.

Resource Protection

Most of the natural resources that we need have a limited supply. That is why **conservation**, the practice of protecting the environment and using resources carefully, is important. Governments and organizations can help lead conservation efforts. National and state parks often preserve natural areas with rare features. Two examples are the colorful geysers at Yellowstone National Park and the canyons of Grand Canyon National Park. Other parks protect important ecosystems, such as wetlands or large areas of forest.

Individuals can also practice conservation. Reducing the amount of waste materials that you make helps reduce the amount of resources you use. Riding your bike instead of having someone drive you is fun and saves fuel. Filling a reusable water bottle instead of buying bottles of water saves resources.

Infer How do school buses that carry several students to school at the same time help conserve natural resources?

_____

_____

_____

Environmental Conservation

Humans now use more than half of the world's lands. Human activities have major effects on the environment, so conservation is important. Environmental conservation includes all the ways that people work to reduce the harmful environmental effects of human activity. Scientists play an important role. They gather data about how human activity changes Earth's systems. They encourage conservation by sharing their findings with citizens, farmers, government officials, and industry leaders.

Individuals and organizations also play important roles. They can use what they learn about conservation to take steps to protect Earth's systems. Individuals help by changing their daily behavior. Every act of conservation helps, no matter how small its effect might appear. For example, people can recycle paper and plastics or purchase products from companies that also practice conservation. Engineers help by designing devices that use renewable energy or at least use less energy. For example, companies may install green roofs, solar panels, or wind turbines to reduce the amount of nonrenewable energy they use. Creative solutions can reduce the negative impacts of human activities even as they help people meet their needs and wants. For example, some crops, such as coffee, can be grown in the shade of existing trees. This protects habitat for native birds and other organisms. These crops also require less chemical fertilizer, which reduces pollution.

Summarize How do communities use science ideas to protect Earth's resources and environment?

_____

_____

_____

_____

_____

_____

Crosscutting Concepts ▸ Toolbox

Scale One reason that many parks cover large areas is to include all the parts of an ecosystem. How do different parts of the natural world work together to make a system?

How do people recycle?

Many materials that we use every day are recycled. These include paper, metals, glass, and plastic. When a plastic bottle is recycled, the plastic does not end up in a landfill. Instead, it becomes a new item.

1 The first step to recycle is to sort materials.

4 People use old plastic when they use the new product.

3 The plastic is used to manufacture a new product.

! For each step, write one word to describe how plastic is recycled.

1 _____

2 _____

3 _____

4 _____

2 The old plastic goes to a factory where it is melted and processed.

_____

_____

Reduce and Reuse

One way that people can practice conservation is to reduce the amount of resources they use. Reducing the resources that you use decreases the amount that needs to be produced. At home, turning off lights when they are not needed saves energy. You could also turn off heaters or air conditioners when you are away from home.

Reusing and recycling things instead of throwing them away reduces the need to produce new material resources. For example, canvas grocery bags can be used over and over. This decreases the number of paper and plastic bags that people need. Rechargeable batteries can replace disposable batteries that end up becoming waste.

PLASTIC   PAPER   GLASS

Quest Connection

▼▼▼▼▼▼▼▼▼▼▼▼▼▼▼▼▼▼▼▼▼▼▼▼▼▼▼▼▼▼▼▼▼▼

Some waste materials, such as food waste, can be made into compost. Compost can be used to fertilize a garden. Compost is made when food waste is broken down and mixed with soil. How could you add composting to the practices of your school?

_____

_____

Resource Use

Earth's systems are the source of all the materials that people use. Some resources, such as plants, can be replaced as people use them. Others, such as fossil fuels, cannot. For all resources, using them wisely will help reduce the human impact on the environment.

Besides reducing, reusing, and recycling, people can also plan and make choices wisely. Green homes are living places that are designed to reduce impact. They are built using as many recycled or renewable materials as possible. They are designed to use as little energy as possible and to use renewable energy when it is needed. Electric vehicles are another way to use energy resources wisely. Electric cars still use energy, but they have a smaller impact on the environment. If the electricity comes from a renewable resource, these cars also reduce the demand for fossil fuels.

 **READING CHECK** **Compare and Contrast** How are green homes and electric cars alike?

_____

_____

_____

INTERACTIVITY

Complete an activity about going green.

uBe a Scientist

Recycling Plastic Investigation

Plastic containers that can be recycled have a symbol that shows a triangle of arrows with a number inside. Look at plastic containers in your home and record the numbers. Then use the Internet to find out what kinds of plastics the containers are made of.

✓ Lesson 4 Check

1. Analyze What are two ways that you can protect Earth's resources?

_____

_____

2. Explain Some green homes include devices to produce electricity from solar energy. Why is this an important part of green building?

_____

_____

_____

Increase Conservation

Your school needs to expand and make new classrooms. They can build the expansion over part of the parking lot, over a field, or over part of a forest. What are some factors the school must consider for each solution? Which solution would help the school best meet their conservation goals?

1. Identify criteria and constraints for the expansion.

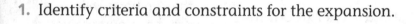

_____

_____

_____

2. Evaluate how each possible solution does or does not meet the criteria.

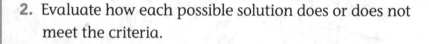

_____

_____

_____

_____

3. Make a recommendation. Which is the best solution for the school? Explain your reasoning.

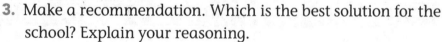

_____

_____

_____

_____

_____

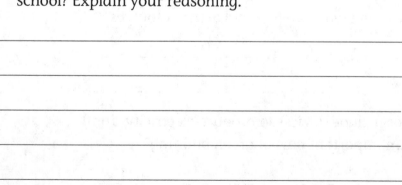

3, 2, 1, Touchdown!

Since the dawn of the space age in the 1950s, people have launched thousands of rockets into space. Most rockets are damaged when they re-enter Earth's atmosphere, and they cannot be used again.

The Falcon 9 rocket is different. It is built by a private company to carry materials into space for NASA and other organizations. Falcon 9, however, is designed to be reused within hours of a previous launch. The rockets carry their equipment high into the atmosphere. Then the main engine separates and returns to Earth's surface. It can be used again within hours. It can land on the ground or on the deck of a ship. By reusing the rockets, the company hopes to use fewer resources. Reusable rockets could help make space flight less expensive.

How do you think reuseable rockets could affect the space program of the United States?

_____

_____

_____

This Falcon 9 rocket returns to Earth after carrying a spacecraft to the International Space Station.

INTERACTIVITY

Organize data to support your Quest Findings.

Take Care of Earth — It's Our Home!

How can we preserve and protect the resources we need?

Research

Phenomenon Look back through the topic to collect ideas for changes your school can make in order to conserve resources.

Develop a Plan

Write a plan for one specific action that your school can take to conserve resources and protect the environment. Use data to explain how your action will decrease resource use. Then write a letter to your principal describing your plan.

_____

_____

_____

_____

_____

_____

_____

Environmental Scientist

Environmental scientists study Earth's environments. There are many different kinds of jobs that environmental scientists can do. They may work in forests or other natural environments. They can also work in cities or in schools. Other environmental scientists work in laboratories. These scientists analyze soil, water, and air samples to find out if they contain hazardous materials. Data from environmental scientists are useful in developing ways to protect plants and animals. Scientists also use data to plan recovery steps for damaged ecosystems. They help keep students and other people safe from hazardous materials where they live and work.

Another job of environmental scientists is working with governments, developers, and landowners to decide where buildings, roads, dams, and other projects should be built. The environmental scientist studies the natural and human systems and provides data that people can use to make decisions about building. If you want to help improve the environment and the health of others, you might make a great environmental scientist!

Reflect In your science notebook, describe how you were working as an environmental scientist when you developed a conservation plan for your school.

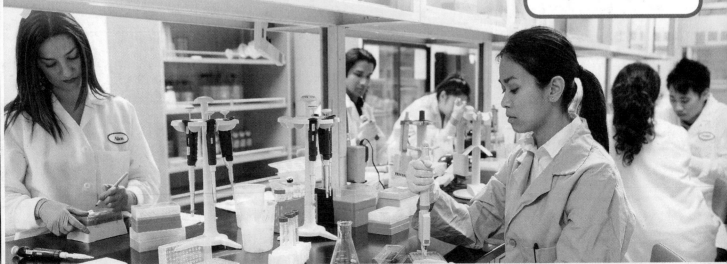

1. **Interpret** Which of these materials is a natural resource?

   A. air

   B. glass

   C. plastic

   D. steel

2. **Vocabulary** Which statement best describes a renewable resource?

   A. It is available to use all of the time.

   B. It is replaced by nature as quickly as it is used.

   C. It has energy that originally comes from sunlight.

   D. It is very inexpensive to produce and deliver to the point of use.

3. **Describe** How does pollution affect Earth's systems?

   _____

   _____

   _____

   _____

4. **Interpret** This symbol appears on a plastic bottle. What does the symbol mean?

   _____

   _____

   _____

   _____

5. Interpret Which picture shows a nonrenewable energy resource?

A.

B.

C.

D.

6. Explain Every human activity has some impact on the environment. How does using renewable hydroelectric energy from a dam have an impact?

_____

_____

_____

_____

The Essential Question

How can we protect Earth's resources and environments?

Show What You Learned

What are three different ways that you can practice conservation in your own life?

_____

_____

_____

_____

_____

_____

Read this scenario and answer questions 1–5.

The citizens in a small city studied the energy use in all the public buildings. They found that the heating systems in the city buildings needed to be replaced. The citizens decided to investigate different options for energy sources. The study showed five possible choices:

- Replace the oil-burning boilers with a new oil system
- Switch to a natural gas-burning boiler system
- Install electric heating systems that use power from a coal-burning plant
- Install solar panels on the roofs of the buildings to provide electric heat
- Build a dam on the river to provide electric power for heat

Possible Energy Sources			
Energy source	Is the source renewable?	Cost of energy system	Amount of pollution it causes
oil	no	medium	high
natural gas	no	low	medium
coal electricity	no	medium	high
solar electricity	yes	medium	none
hydroelectricity	yes	high	none

1. **Communicate** At a meeting to discuss the results of the survey, one citizen pointed out that hydroelectricity does not cause damage to the environment because it does not cause pollution. Explain why this argument is not completely correct.

_____

_____

_____

_____

2. **Synthesize** The citizens who answered the survey were in favor of using an energy source that has the least effect on the environment. Based on the survey, which action would they most likely prefer to provide energy for the new heating systems?

   A. replace the oil system with a new oil system

   B. build a dam in the river to provide electric power

   C. install solar panels on the roofs of the buildings

   D. buy electrical power from the power company

3. **Obtain Information** What evidence supports your answer to question 2?

   A. Solar energy production does not cause any pollution.

   B. The least expensive option is replacement of the boiler.

   C. Energy from natural gas causes less pollution than energy from oil.

   D. Hydroelectric power plants are more expensive than coal plants.

4. **Synthesize** The citizens decided that they needed to have a way to provide energy when their first source was not available. The backup system should be inexpensive because it would not be used very often. What backup system would you suggest for the city? Explain your answer.

   _____

   _____

   _____

   _____

5. **Evaluate** Which factor might make the citizens decide not to use solar power even though it does not cause pollution?

   A. There are times when solar power is not available.

   B. Solar power is more expensive than other renewable energy options.

   C. The citizens do not want to use a renewable energy source.

   D. Solar panels may produce too much energy.

How can you use the energy of **water?**

Phenomenon Engineers build solutions and then improve them based on input from other experts. How can you build a machine and improve it?

Design and Build

☐ **1.** Research and compare the design of at least two devices that use the energy of falling water to cause motion. Use approved sources from your teacher.

☐ **2. SEP Design Solutions** Design a device that uses the energy of falling water to cause motion. Choose materials. Sketch your design. Have your teacher review it.

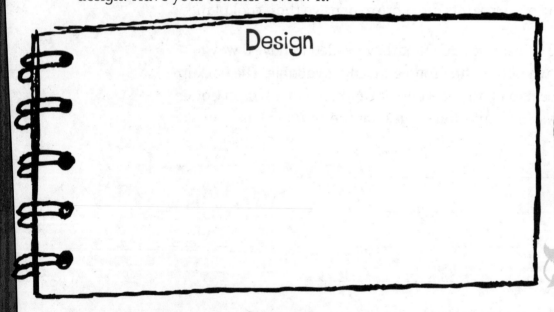

Design

☐ **3.** Build your device. Describe how it uses energy to produce motion. Where did the energy of the water come from?

_____

_____

_____

_____

Materials
- safety goggles
- water

Suggested Materials
- tape
- glue
- string
- plastic bottles
- plastic strips
- wheel and axle from old toy
- plastic tubing
- plastic tub
- strips of wood
- plastic container caps
- screws
- screwdriver

 Wear safety goggles.

 Be careful with the materials.

Engineering Practice

Engineers **obtain information** to explain solutions to a design problem.

Evaluate Your Design

4. **SEP Communicate Solutions** Trade devices with a classmate. What are some of the limitations of the system your classmate used to provide energy to the device? How could it be improved? Write your suggestions on a sheet of paper and give it to the designer.

_____

_____

_____

_____

_____

5. **SEP Evaluate Information** After you get feedback from a classmate, think of ways that you could improve how your device works. Write or draw your ideas.

6. **Evaluate** How can you improve your design to increase conservation of water and conserve Earth's resources?

_____

_____

_____

_____

_____

Topic 6
Solar System

Lesson 1 Brightness of the Sun and Other Stars

Lesson 2 Inner Solar System

Lesson 3 Outer Solar System

Next Generation Science Standards

5-ESS1-1 Support an argument that differences in the apparent brightness of the sun compared to other stars is due to their relative distances from Earth.

3-5-ETS1-1 Define a simple design problem, reflecting a need or a want that includes specified criteria for success and constraints on materials, time, or cost.

Go online to access
your digital course.

▶ VIDEO

📖 eTEXT

👆 INTERACTIVITY

📱 VIRTUAL LAB

🎮 GAME

☑ ASSESSMENT

The Essential Question

What is Earth's place in space?

Show What You Know

Earth is among many planets in our solar system. There are four planets in the inner solar system and four planets in the outer solar system. What makes Earth an inner solar system planet?

_____

_____

_____

STEM Keeping the Planets in Order

How can you model your own solar system?

Phenomenon Hello! I am Kelsey Patton, an astronomical technician. Your school could use a new model of our solar system. I am organizing a small group to help make the model. I think you would be a great addition to our group. Would you join our group?

In this problem-based learning activity, you and your classmates will be the chief advisors. You will guide the team in designing and building the model. One of your challenges will be making a model that fits in your lobby and that shows the correct size of each planet compared to the other planets!

Follow the path to discover how to complete the Quest. The Quest activities in the lessons will help you complete the Quest. Check off your progress on the path when you complete an activity with a QUEST CHECK ✓ OFF . Go online for more Quest activities.

Quest Check-In 1

Lesson 1
Apply what you learned in this lesson to make a large poster of the sun.

Next Generation Science Standards
5-ESS1-1 Support an argument that differences in the apparent brightness of the sun compared to other stars is due to their relative distances from Earth.

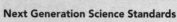

▶ VIDEO

Watch a video about an astronomical technician.

Quest Check-In Lab 3

Lesson 3

Use what you learned about Jupiter, Saturn, Uranus, and Neptune to build a model of the outer planets for your solar system model.

Quest Findings

Put your model solar system together, including any supporting visuals. Then write a supplemental information sheet that lists the important details of each planet.

Quest Check-In Lab 2

Lesson 2

Use your knowledge of Mercury, Venus, Earth, and Mars to build a model of the inner planets for your solar system model.

How **big** is the sun?

Astronomers investigate the scale and proportions of objects in space using models. How can you use a model to see how large the sun is compared to other objects in the solar system?

Materials
- modeling clay

Science Practice

Scientists **use models** to support an argument.

Procedure

☐ **1. SEP Model** The solar system contains the sun and the planets and their moons. Based on what you already know, make a model of our solar system with the modeling clay.

☐ **2. SEP Obtain Information** Research how much of the total mass of the solar system is taken up by the sun.

_____

_____

☐ **3.** Identify any changes you should make to your model based on data you collected in step 2. Rebuild your model.

Analyze and Interpret Data

4. SEP Use Evidence What changes did you make in your second model? What evidence do you have to support those changes?

_____

_____

_____

_____

_____

_____

_____

Use Text Features

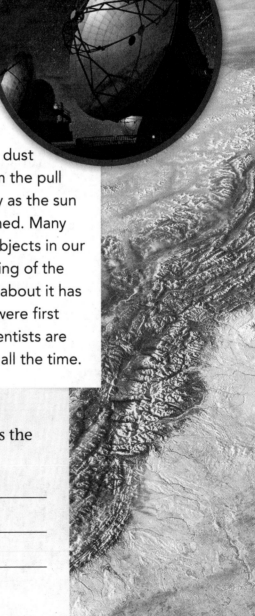

GAME

Practice what you learn with the Mini Games.

One important reading skill is to recognize and use text features. Here are some examples of how to use text features when reading.

- Look for headings and subheadings. These are the titles that start a new section.
- Note how the sections of text are divided.
- Get information from graphs, tables, illustrations, labels, photos, and captions.

Read the following text. Look for text features that will help you understand the information.

A Very Old System

Our solar system is estimated to be about 4.6 billion years old. It formed from a giant cloud of dust and gas. This cloud slowly collapsed in on itself from the pull of gravity. During this collapse, what we know today as the sun and the eight planets and their moons were all formed. Many other smaller objects were also formed. All of the objects in our solar system move around the sun. Our understanding of the solar system is not very old. Most of what we know about it has come from scientists using telescopes. Telescopes were first used to study the solar system in the year 1609. Scientists are still making new discoveries about our solar system all the time.

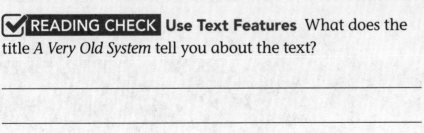

✓ READING CHECK Use Text Features What does the title *A Very Old System* tell you about the text?

_____

_____

_____

Lesson 1

Brightness of the Sun and Other Stars

I can...

Recognize that many stars are as big and bright as the sun. Explain how the apparent brightness of stars is related to their distances from Earth.

5-ESS1-1

Literacy Skill
Text Features

Vocabulary
star

Academic Vocabulary
apparent

 VIDEO

Watch a video about the sun and other stars.

LOCAL-TO-GLOBAL Connection

The sun, the only star in our solar system, provides energy for life on Earth. Scientists know a lot about the sun. Over time, they have discovered the existence of a vast number of stars throughout outer space. Our galaxy, the Milky Way, is one of more than 1 trillion galaxies in the observable universe. The Milky Way Galaxy has about 100 billion stars in it. Our sun is one of those stars. The sun is very large when compared to Earth. The sun has a volume that is about one million times the volume of Earth.

When was the last time you chewed a piece of gum from a gumball machine? Think of the sun as a gumball machine. It would take more than one million Earth gumballs to fill the sun gumball machine!

Compare and Contrast What are some differences between the sun and the stars you see in the night sky?

_____

_____

_____

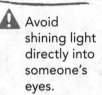
How are distance and *brightness related?*

Scientists compare the brightness of stars. How can you investigate how light and distance are related?

Materials
- flashlight
- construction paper
- metric ruler

⚠ Avoid shining light directly into someone's eyes.

Procedure

☐ **1.** How does the distance from a light source affect the brightness of the light? Make a prediction.

_____

☐ **2.** **SEP Plan an Investigation** Make a plan to use the materials to test your prediction. Show your plan to your teacher before you begin. Record your observations.

☐ **3.** Rank the brightness of the light from 1 to 4, with 1 being the brightest and 4 being the least bright.

Science Practice

Scientists *use evidence* to support a scientific argument.

Distance from source of light	Diameter of light (cm)	Brightness rank

Analyze and Interpret Data

4. **SEP Use Evidence** Explain how distance impacts the brightness of stars. Support your explanation with evidence from this lab.

_____

_____

_____

INTERACTIVITY

Complete an activity about star brightness.

Crosscutting Concepts ▸ Toolbox

Energy and Matter
Farming, or agriculture, is critical to maintaining life on Earth. Why does a farmer rely on our star, the sun, for growing crops and raising animals? Do farmers rely on any other star in outer space?

Earth's Sun

Earth's sun is a star that is in the center of our solar system. A **star** is a huge ball of very hot matter that gives off energy. Stars shine because processes in the stars produce huge amounts of energy. The temperature of the center of our sun is about 15,000,000°C (27,000,000°F).

Earth's sun is the largest object in our solar system, but it is not the largest star in the universe. It is a medium-sized star when compared to the billions of other stars in our galaxy. Earth's sun makes up more than 99 percent of the mass of our solar system.

Without the sun, Earth would be a drastically different place. Life on Earth could not exist without the sun's energy. And the planet would be very, very cold.

Identify List two characteristics of the sun.

_____

_____

Structure of the Sun

In addition to being much larger and hotter, the sun is different from a planet in another way. The main layers of the sun are the core, the radiative zone, and the convective zone. The core is where the sun's energy is generated. The radiative and convective zones carry the energy to the sun's surface.

The atmosphere of the sun has three layers: the photosphere, chromosphere, and corona. The photosphere is what we see when we look at the sun. The corona can be seen only during a total solar eclipse.

Make Meaning This photo shows a solar flare on the sun. Solar flares occur when energy heats the sun so much that it causes particles to explode into outer space. In your science notebook, write a short story about what happens when a solar flare explodes. Be sure to include the layers of the sun's atmosphere that the solar flare goes through.

Quest Connection

Why is it important to include the sun in your model of the solar system?

_____

_____

Light Sky, Dark Sky

Work with an adult. Stand in a brightly lit outdoor area at night. Look at the night sky. Then stand in a place that is dark. Look at the sky again. How did the amount of light affect how many stars you saw?

Distances of Stars

Have you ever been outdoors when the sun sets? At first, you do not see any stars. Then, as the sun disappears below the horizon, a few bright stars appear. The apparent size of stars is very small. **Apparent** means "the way something looks." Even though stars in the sky appear to be small, they are actually many, many times larger than Earth. They appear small because they are so far from Earth. The distances of stars from Earth are enormous. To measure the distances, scientists use the light year. A light year is the distance light travels in one year–9,460,800,000,000 kilometers. The closest star in our galaxy is 4.2 light years away. Stars can be millions of light years away!

Brightness of Stars

The sun is much closer to Earth than other stars are. That is why the sun appears so much larger than any other stars. You may have noticed that some stars appear brighter than other stars. The brighter stars are not necessarily bigger or brighter. The apparent brightness of a star depends on how bright the star actually is and how far away it is. A brighter star can appear less bright in the sky than a star that is actually dimmer—if the dimmer star is closer to Earth.

Star Temperature

If you go near a campfire that is burning very brightly, it will feel very hot. If you go near a campfire that is dim, it will not feel as hot. The same is true for stars. Stars that are hotter will be brighter than stars that are not as hot. However, the relative brightness you see will depend on how far away the stars are from Earth.

Identify What are two factors that affect how bright a star appears in the night sky?

_____

_____

You must demonstrate that the differences in apparent brightness of the sun compared to other stars is due to their relative distances from Earth. Describe a procedure you would use to support this concept.

_____

_____

_____

_____

Size of Stars

Stars that you see in the night sky are not in our solar system. They are many light years away from us. The closest stars to our solar system are part of the Alpha Centauri star system. Three stars are part of this system—Alpha Centauri A, Alpha Centauri B, and Proxima Centauri. This diagram shows the relative sizes of the Alpha Centauri star system and the sun. Proxima Centauri is the star closest to our sun. Since the sun and the Alpha Centauri system are the closest stars to Earth, they appear brighter than other stars in the sky.

✓ **READING CHECK** **Text Features** What does the photo on the page tell you about Proxima Centauri and the sun?

_____

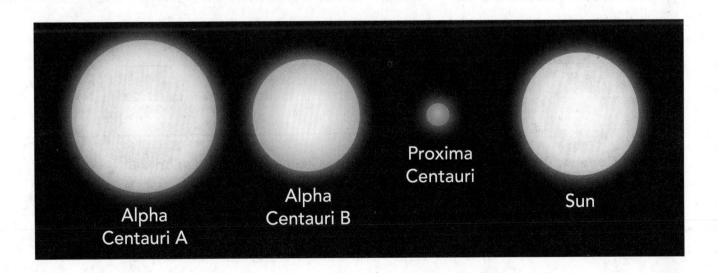

Alpha Centauri A

Alpha Centauri B

Proxima Centauri

Sun

Earth-Like Planets

In June, 2017, NASA, the United States space agency, announced that its Kepler telescope had discovered more than 200 new planets. These planets do not circle Earth's sun. Instead, they circle other stars in the universe.

Ten of these planets are about the size of Earth. They orbit their stars at a distance that is similar to Earth's distance from our sun. Scientists think these ten newly discovered planets might have temperatures that allow liquid water to exist on their surfaces. Scientists think that water is a key ingredient to support life.

Infer Why might scientists think these planets might have liquid water on their surfaces?

_____

_____

_____

_____

_____

The blue on this image of Earth is water. Scientists look for other planets that might also have water on their surface.

☑ Lesson 1 Check

1. List What are three characteristics of the sun?

_____

_____

_____

2. Connect Why are the sun and the Alpha Centauri star system brighter than other stars visible to us on Earth?

_____

_____

_____

Fun in the Sun!

The sun plays a significant role in the solar system. The first step in assembling your solar system model is to make a large poster of the sun.

1. **Recall** What are the three layers of the sun's atmosphere?

_____

_____

_____

2. Make a poster of the sun. On your poster, be sure to label and describe various characteristics of the sun.

3. **Evaluate** What is the significance of the sun?

_____

_____

VIDEO

Watch a video about observatory telescopes.

What's with the dust?

Phenomenon Dust is everywhere—even in outer space. The dust in outer space is known as cosmic dust. But cosmic dust is not like dust in your home. Cosmic dust consists of tiny particles of solid materials floating around in the space between stars. It is the material from which new stars and planets are formed.

Most cosmic dust absorbs and scatters visible light. The light is sent out again in a form of light we cannot see—mostly infrared radiation. Because the visible light is scattered, scientists had difficulty seeing into the far parts of the universe. Now they use instruments that detect the infrared light that we cannot see. Now scientists can look deep into space to learn more about many formerly unknown parts of the universe.

Model It

The technicians at a local laboratory have asked for your help. Astronomers have discovered a new object in space. They want to know whether the dust on Earth is similar to the cosmic dust in the object they have discovered. They would like you to develop a procedure for collecting dust on Earth to model how dust could be collected in space.

1. Brainstorm how many samples you will collect and where you will collect them. Record the information in the table.

2. What equipment will you use to collect the dust? Record the information in the table.

3. What procedure will you follow to collect the dust?

Samples I will collect	Materials I will need	Procedure I will follow

4. **Distinguish** What are the differences between the contents of dust on a classroom floor and cosmic dust?

_____

_____

_____

Lesson 2
Inner Solar System

I can...

Describe the inner planets of Mercury, Venus, Earth, and Mars.
Identify common characteristics of the inner planets.
Recognize the position of Earth within the solar system.

SEP.1

Literacy Skill
Use Text Features

Vocabulary
solar system
inner planets
orbit
moon

VIDEO

Watch a video about the inner planets of the solar system.

SPORTS > Connection

The game of tetherball is a common playground game. To play the game, you tie a string to one end of a pole. Tie a ball to the other end of the string. Hold the ball and throw it. The ball will eventually move around the pole in a circle.

Tetherball is similar to a planet traveling around the sun. But with our solar system, a string does not hold the planets in their path. Gravity is the force that pulls the planet toward the sun. A planet is moving with great speed, which prevents gravity from pulling it into the sun. What would happen if the string in tetherball broke? The ball would go flying away. If the sun suddenly lost its gravitational pull on Earth, we would similarly go flying away into space!

Compare and Contrast How is the pull of the string in tetherball similar to the effect of gravity?

_____

_____

_____

uInvestigate Lab

How does a *planet's* distance from the *sun* affect its *path?*

Like a tetherball that circles a pole, planets travel in a path around our sun. How does the distance from the sun affect the length of a planet's path?

Materials

• safety goggles

Suggested Materials

• string
• pencil
• scissors
• tape
• stopwatch
• colored paper

Procedure

☐ 1. **SEP Develop a Model** Plan a model to show how a planet's distance from the sun affects its path. Choose materials for your model.

☐ 2. Show your plan to your teacher before you begin. Record your observations.

 Be careful using scissors.

 Wear safety goggles.

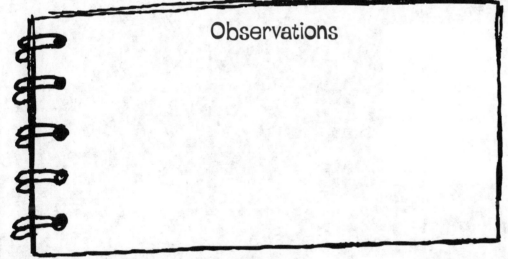

Observations

Science Practice

Scientists *use models* to support arguments.

Analyze and Interpret Data

3. **Draw Conclusions** How does distance from the sun affect the length of a planet's path around the sun?

_____

_____

4. **SEP Cite Evidence** What evidence do you have from your investigation to support your answer?

_____

_____

What is in our solar system?

Our **solar system** is a system of eight planets and the sun, along with moons, asteroids, and comets. Four of the eight planets are inner planets. Mercury, Venus, Earth, and Mars are called **inner planets** because they are closest to the sun.

Mars
- known as the red planet
- thin atmosphere
- iron-rich materials that form rust on the surface
- two moons

Venus
- hottest planet in the solar system
- thick, toxic atmosphere that traps heat
- surface covered with volcanoes and canyons
- no moon

A planet is a large body of matter that travels around the sun.

INTERACTIVITY

Complete an activity on the inner solar system.

> ! **Summarize what you have learned about the four inner planets.**
>
> _____
> _____
> _____
> _____
> _____

Earth
- largest of the inner planets
- atmosphere that allows for the existence of living things
- surface of landmasses: mountains, canyons, hills, and valleys
- one moon

Sun

Mercury
- smallest of the inner planets
- thinnest atmosphere of inner four planets
- made up of iron and nickel
- no moon

Question It! Astronomers recently discovered a planet called Proxima b. This planet is orbiting the small star, Proxima Centauri. Astronomers predict that this planet might have similar qualities to Earth that could one day make it livable. If you could ask an astronomer two questions about this planet, what would you ask?

_____

_____

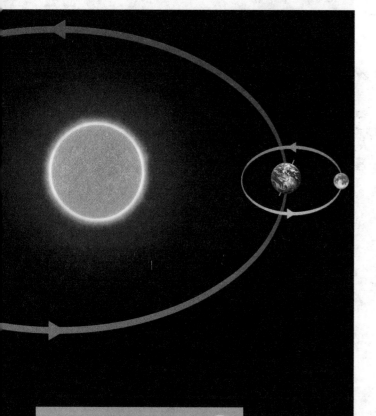

Planetary Orbit

The curved path of an object around a star, a planet, or a moon is called an **orbit**. Planets orbit the sun, and moons orbit planets. The amount of time each planet takes to orbit the sun is different because each planet is a different distance from the sun. The farther a planet is from the sun, the longer its orbit will be. Earth takes about 365 days to orbit the sun. The moon takes about 27 days to orbit Earth.

✓ **READING CHECK** **Use Text Features**
How does the picture help you understand what an orbit is?

_____

_____

Engineering Practice ▸ Toolbox

Evaluate Information Why do scientists need to know the orbits that rockets will take around Earth or other objects when the scientists are building them?

Quest Connection

How will the inner planets look compared to the sun in the model of the solar system?

_____

_____

Mercury

Venus

Earth

Mars

Moons

A **moon** is a satellite made of rock and ice that orbits a planet. Two inner planets, Earth and Mars, have moons. Earth's moon has a very important impact on Earth. The moon's gravitational pull helps to stabilize Earth's wobbling motion as it rotates around its axis. The entire solar system relies on gravity, a force of attraction, to keep planets, moons, and other objects in orbit.

📖 **Write About It** You are a new astronomer shadowing an experienced astronomer who is your mentor for the next week. You already know quite a lot about planet Earth, but you are interested in learning about the three other inner planets. In your science notebook, list five questions regarding the inner planets that you want to ask your mentor.

......⋃Be a Scientist..........

Satellites in the Sky
The moon is a natural satellite that you can observe. You can also observe human-made satellites. Research when you will be able to see the International Space Station above Earth. Then on a clear night, go outside with an adult to find the space station.

☑ **Lesson 2 Check**

1. Compare What are two differences between Earth and Mars?

_____

_____

_____

_____

2. Identify What is Earth's position in our solar system?

_____

What's inside the solar system?

You are on a Quest to rebuild a model of the solar system for your school's lobby. In this activity, you will make models of the four inner planets.

Materials
- ruler

Suggested Materials
- modeling clay
- clothespins
- string
- balls of various sizes

Procedure

☐ **1.** How will you determine how big to make each model planet?

_____

_____

_____

☐ **2. SEP Develop Models** Using your knowledge of the four inner planets, sketch what each planet in your model will look like.

Science Practice

Scientists develop and use models to support arguments.

☐ **3.** Use the materials to make a model of the four inner planets. Also include Earth's moon.

☐ **4.** Show your models to your teacher. Then arrange the models with the backdrop you have completed in the Quest so far.

Analyze and Interpret Data

5. CCC Systems and System Models How does your model compare to the actual order and sizes of the inner planets?

_____

_____

_____

_____

_____

_____

_____

6. SEP Use Models Explain how your model shows planetary orbit. If it does not, how could you improve your model to show orbits?

_____

_____

_____

_____

_____

Outer Solar System

I can...

Describe the outer planets of Jupiter, Saturn, Uranus, and Neptune.
Identify common characteristics of the outer planets.
Recognize that there are moons, asteroids, and comets in our solar system.

Literacy Skill
Use Text Features

Vocabulary
outer planet
asteroid
comet

Academic Vocabulary
characteristics

▶ **VIDEO**

Watch a video about the outer planets of the solar system.

CURRICULUM ⟩ Connection

All of the planets, except Earth, were named after Roman gods and goddesses. Jupiter and Saturn were given their names thousands of years ago. The ancient Romans could see them in the sky without a telescope. The other planets in our solar system were not discovered until telescopes were invented. Even then, the tradition of naming the planets after Roman gods and goddesses continued. Most of the moons are also named after the creatures, gods, and goddesses in Roman mythology.

Explain How did the planets get their names?

_____

_____

JUPITER

μInvestigate Lab

How **hard** do space objects **hit** Earth?

Scientists conduct research on space objects to determine the impact they have on Earth. What kind of impact do space objects have on Earth?

Materials
- blocks of various sizes and weights
- newspaper, various sizes, bunched up
- meterstick

Procedure

☐ 1. **SEP Develop Models** Make a plan to model the impact of differently sized space objects when they hit Earth's surface.

☐ 2. Show your plan to your teacher before you begin. Record your observations.

Science Practice

Scientists use models to support arguments.

Observations

Analyze and Interpret Data

3. **SEP Draw Conclusions** Use your data collected to explain the relationship between a space object and its impact on Earth's surface.

_____

_____

_____

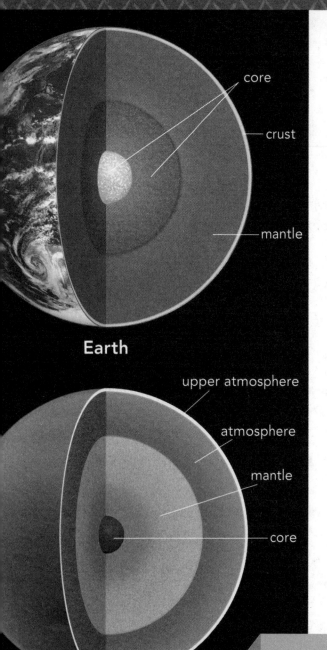

core

crust

mantle

Earth

upper atmosphere

atmosphere

mantle

core

Neptune

Gas Giants

Beyond Mars are four more planets in our solar system—Jupiter, Saturn, Uranus, and Neptune. These four planets are called **outer planets** because they are farther from the sun than the inner planets. They are also significantly larger than the inner planets. You may recall that the inner planets have rocky, Earth-like surfaces. Some inner layers of the inner planets are solid. The outer planets do not have clearly defined surfaces. We see only the atmospheres of the outer planets. These thick atmospheres are made of gas. This is why the outer planets are often referred to as the gas giants. However, they also have large, liquid inner layers and solid cores. Each outer planet has rings of particles and many moons orbiting it.

Use Text Features These diagrams reveal the interior of Neptune, an outer planet, and the interior of Earth, an inner planet. How is the outer layer of Earth different from the outer layer of Neptune?

_____

_____

Quest Connection

▼▼▼▼▼▼▼▼▼▼▼▼▼▼▼▼▼▼▼▼▼▼▼▼▼▼▼▼

Brainstorm what you might need to include in a model of the solar system. How would the outer planets compare to other objects in your model?

_____

_____

_____

Jupiter: Gas Giant with Many Moons

Jupiter, a gas giant, is the fifth planet from the sun and the largest planet in the solar system. Jupiter's atmosphere is made up of hydrogen and helium, and it shows many bands of color. Jupiter is a large planet, but it has a low density, which means that its mass is not packed tightly together. The planet rotates much faster than Earth. In the time that Earth takes to complete one rotation, Jupiter completes more than two rotations. Jupiter also has many moons. In 1610, a scientist named Galileo was the first person to see the four largest moons of Jupiter. He saw them through his telescope.

Classify How is Jupiter's rotation different from Earth's rotation?

jupiter rotates faster than earth.

Science Practice
▶ Toolbox

Engage in Argument from Evidence Each of the outer planets has many moons orbiting it. So far, scientists have found that Jupiter has 67 moons, Saturn has 62 moons, Uranus has 27 moons, and Neptune has 14 moons. Why do you think the outer planets have so many moons?

Saturn: A Planet with "Handles"

The sixth planet from the sun is Saturn. Jupiter and Saturn are very similar. Saturn is also a very large planet with a low density. Just like Jupiter, Saturn has an atmosphere that contains mostly hydrogen and helium. When Galileo looked at Saturn through his telescope, he saw what looked like a planet with handles. The "handles" are brilliant rings that orbit Saturn. The particles making up the rings are made up of ice, dust, and rock. They vary in size from tiny grains to boulders. The inner rings of Saturn revolve faster around the planet than the outer rings.

Relate What are two similarities and two differences between Saturn and Jupiter?

How are the outer planets aligned?

The planets in the outer solar system are much larger than planets in the inner solar system. The outer planets also have different characteristics, or qualities, from the inner planets.

Neptune
- most distant from the sun
- coldest planet in the solar system
- 14 moons

Uranus
- orbits the sun on its side
- first planet discovered with use of a telescope
- 27 moons

Saturn
- known for its many rings
- atmosphere made up of hydrogen and helium
- 62 moons

INTERACTIVITY

Complete an activity on the outer solar system.

Asteroid belt

- belt-shaped disc that separates inner planets from outer planets
- many asteroids within the disc

Summarize what you have learned about the four outer planets.

_____

_____

_____

_____

_____

sun

Jupiter

- largest planet in the solar system
- color bands due to particles in the atmosphere
- 67 moons

Uranus

Uranus is the seventh planet from the sun and the most distant planet visible without a telescope. Uranus's atmosphere contains hydrogen, helium, and methane. The planet is so cold that the methane in the atmosphere can freeze. Methane absorbs red light and reflects blue light, which gives Uranus its blue color. Uranus has rings and many moons, just like the other outer planets. Unlike the rings of Saturn, the rings of Uranus are dark and hard to see with Earth-based telescopes.

Neptune

Neptune is the farthest planet from the sun. It is too far away to see without a telescope. It takes more than one hundred Earth years for Neptune to orbit the sun. Neptune is the smallest of the outer planets. Even so, if Neptune were hollow, it could hold about 60 Earths. Neptune's atmosphere is like that of Uranus. Like Uranus, Neptune has a bluish color because of the methane in its atmosphere. Neptune also has bands of color like those of Jupiter. Of its 13 moons, the largest one is Triton.

Describe Why are the four outer planets also known as gas giants?

_____

_____

_____

📓 **Make Meaning** In your science notebook, tell which of the gas giants you would like to visit. Which characteristics of the planet make you interested in it?

Be a Scientist

Scale and Proportion
Find an object to represent Earth. If you were to model all the planets together, what objects would you use for the outer planets? Would your choice always be the same?

Comets and Asteroids

Asteroids and comets are fragments left over from the giant cloud of gas and dust that formed the solar system more than 4.5 billion years ago. **Asteroids** are chunks of rock that measure in size from a meter to several kilometers in diameter. They orbit the sun. Objects smaller than asteroids are called meteoroids. Scientists have found more than 1,000,000 asteroids that lie in the asteroid belt between Mars and Jupiter. **Comets** are chunks of ice and dust or rock that have stretched-out orbits around the sun. As comets heat up, gas and dust are released and trail behind them. The sun illuminates the trail of gas and dust, which is why some comets are visible in the night sky.

Infer Sometimes, comets have trails. Other times, they do not. What might cause a comet's trail to appear and disappear?

_____

_____

_____

comet

asteroid

☑ Lesson 3 Check

1. Draw a line from each object in the solar system to its correct description.

sun	satellite made of rock and ice that orbits a planet
planet	chunk of rock that orbits the sun in a belt between Mars and Jupiter
moon	chunk of ice and rock that has an elliptical orbit around the sun
asteroid	huge ball of very hot matter that gives off energy
comet	large body of matter that travels around the sun

What planets are **way** out there?

As you have discovered in this lesson, the outer solar system contains four gas giants. In this lab, you will make a model of the outer planets. As you build your model, ask yourself this: How will my new model work with my model of the inner planets?

Suggested Materials
- modeling clay
- clothespins
- poster board
- coloring supplies
- balls of various sizes
- string
- tape
- ruler

Procedure

☐ 1. **CCC Scale** How will you determine how big to make each of your model planets?

_____

_____

☐ 2. Using your knowledge of the four outer planets, sketch what each planet in your model will look like.

☐ 3. Use the materials to make a model that includes all four of the outer planets. Your model should also display the asteroid belt.

☐ 4. Show your model to your teacher and arrange the model with the backdrop you have completed in the Quest so far.

Analyze and Interpret Data

5. **Compare and Contrast** How does your model compare to the actual order and size of the outer planets?

_____

_____

6. **Reflect** What challenges did you encounter when planning and building your model?

_____

_____

Science Practice

Scientists use models to support their ideas.

Jupiter

Saturn

Uranus

Neptune

How many Earths can line up across the sun?

The size of the sun is much greater than that of the planets and Earth's moon. In this activity, you will calculate how many Earths you can line up straight across the diameter of the sun. Think about what tools will assist you in this activity.

Sun	diameter = 1,400,000 kilometers
Earth	diameter = 12,800 kilometers

Evaluate Your Model

1. **Predict** Make a prediction about how many Earths would be needed to line up straight across the diameter of the sun.

   _____

   _____

2. **Evaluate** Using the data in the table, divide the diameter of the sun by the diameter of Earth to calculate the number of Earths that can line up across the sun. Show your work in your science notebook.

3. Round your number to the nearest whole number.

   _____

4. **Evaluate** Earth is the largest of the four inner planets. Mars, another inner planet, has a diameter of 6,800 kilometers. Calculate how many Mars planets you could line up straight across Earth. Round to the nearest whole number.

   _____

   _____

5. **Reflect** Why is it not necessary for your numbers to be exact when doing your calculations?

   _____

   _____

Keeping the Planets in Order

How can you model your own solar system?

INTERACTIVITY

Organize data to support your Quest Findings.

Meeting the Challenge

Phenomenon It is time to get the model ready for your school's lobby! Put the finishing touches on your model and the supporting backdrop. Write an information sheet that lists important characteristics of each planet. Compare and contrast the properties of the inner and outer planets. Describe whether your model is to scale. If you were not able to model the planets to scale with the materials you used, explain why.

Construct Explanations

Synthesize Another school is making a model of the solar system, and they left out the sun! Write a short letter to the students in charge of the solar system model at the other school explaining why they must include the sun in their model.

_____

_____

_____

_____

_____

_____

QUEST CHECK ✓ OFF

Astronomical Technicians

Astronomical technicians play a vital role in helping scientists perform successful research projects. They give astronomers the technical support that they need, from setting up telescopes in observatories to recording readings on instruments used to study space. Many of the technicians work in research laboratories, planetariums, observatories, or colleges and universities.

For those technicians that work at a college or university, they spend their days showing engineering, astronomy, and physical science students how astronomy instruments are used in laboratories, planetariums, and observatories. Technicians are also responsible for staying up-to-date on any changes, additions, or modifications to equipment, such as telescopes and refractors. These technicians are a great help to astronomers!

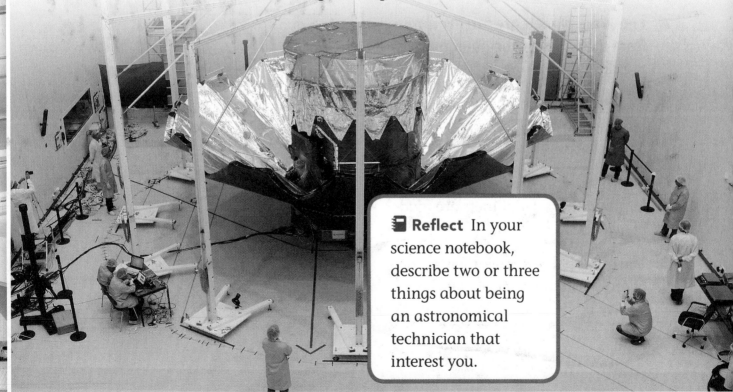

> **Reflect** In your science notebook, describe two or three things about being an astronomical technician that interest you.

1. **Vocabulary** A __star__ is a huge ball of very hot matter that gives off energy.

   A. comet

   B. asteroid

   C. star

   D. planet

2. **Identify** Which planet is farthest from the sun?

   A. Neptune

   B. Venus

   C. Jupiter

   D. Mars

3. **Contrast** Which of the following explains a difference between the inner planets and outer planets?

   A. The inner planets are farther away from the sun, and the outer planets are closer to the sun.

   B. The inner planets do not have any moons, and the outer planets each have a moon.

   C. The inner planets are made up of gas, and the outer planets are made up of rock.

   D. The inner planets are largely made of rock, and the outer planets are largely made of gas and liquid.

4. **Summarize** What is a moon? How does Earth's moon affect our planet?

   it affects our planets with water tides high and low. a moon is a natural satelite that orbits a planet.

5. **Compare and Contrast** Connect the game of tetherball to planetary orbit.

   the ball is the planet the pole is the sun when you spin it it is orbiting the sun.

6. Interpret Is this a picture of an asteroid or a comet? How do you know?

it is a comet because comets have trails like this one.

7. Explain How did comets and asteroids form?

from bigger things

8. Compare Describe common characteristics of all eight planets in our solar system.

Mercury closest to sun, venus the hottst earth has life capability mars is rusty red, jupiter, the biggest, saturn has the largest rings, uranus is sideways, neptune is the farthest.

The Essential Question *What is Earth's place in space?*

Show What You Know

Earth is one of eight planets in our solar system. There are four planets in the inner solar system and four planets in the outer solar system. What makes Earth an inner solar system planet?

because it is rocky and that is an inner planet thing.

☑ Evidence-Based Assessment

Use the data from the table to answer questions 1-5.

All of the stars in the chart, except for the sun, have similar actual brightnesses. The numbers 1–4 are a ranking of the four stars according to apparent brightness when viewed from Earth.

Apparent Brightness of Stars		
Name of star	Distance from Earth (light years)	Apparent brightness (rank; 1 = brightest, 4 = dimmest)
Sun	0	1
Hadar	320	2
Acrux	510	3
Adhara	570	4

1. **Infer** The sun is the smallest of all the stars listed in the table. It also releases the least amount of energy. Why does the sun appear to be the brightest star in the sky?

   that is becuase it is WAY closer to our planet than the other stars.

2. **Connect** When viewed from Earth, the sun appears larger than any other star in the sky. Which of these models explains why?

   A. A snowball tends to get larger as it rolls down a hill.

   B. Light bulbs that use more electricity give off more light.

   C. A train whistle gets louder as it approaches your location.

   D. Your thumb appears larger than the moon when the thumb is extended.

3. **Synthesize** All of the stars in the table except for the sun are roughly similar to each other in actual brightness. Which star appears dimmest from Earth?

   A. Sirius

   B. Adhara

   C. Acrux

   D. Hadar

4. **Explain** Justify your answer to Question 3.

   adhara is the dimmest it says
   in the graph and the farthest
   so of course its adhara

5. **Use Evidence** Which two stars in the table are the next closest to Earth after the sun?

   A. Acrux and Adhara

   B. Hadar and Adhara

   C. Hadar and Acrux

   D. Vega and Hadar

uDemonstrate Lab

How can you **compare** the **sizes** of objects in space?

Phenomenon Using a model to support your explanation, how can you describe the size of objects in space?

Materials
- classroom objects
- blocks
- balls

Science Practice

Scientists use models to support an argument.

Name of space object	Diameter
Earth	12,800 km
Mars	6,800 km
Uranus	57,000 km
Neptune	49,500 km
Earth's moon	3,500 km
Callisto (Jupiter's moon)	4800 km
Titan (Saturn's moon)	5200 km

Procedure

☐ **1.** Select a planet, a moon, and another object from the list. Circle your choices.

☐ **2.** Use the chart to help you make models of the objects you chose. How will this chart help you in your models?

_____

_____

☐ **3.** **SEP Develop Models** Develop your model. Write the steps you need to take to make your model accurate and useful.

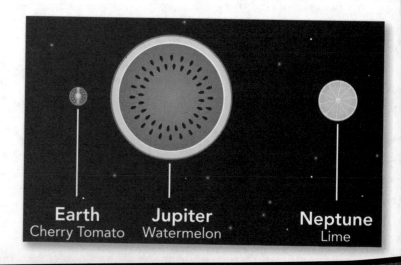

Earth
Cherry Tomato

Jupiter
Watermelon

Neptune
Lime

Step 1	Step 2	Step 3	Step 4	Step 5

☐ **4.** With your teacher's permission, use your procedure and the materials to make your model.

Analyze and Interpret Data

5. Explain How did you decide what objects to use for your model? How were you able to correctly model the space objects?

_____

_____

_____

_____

6. CCC Scale Why are some objects in space so much larger than others?

_____

_____

7. Reflect Suppose you are teaching your model to second graders. What would you tell them about the sizes of objects in space compared to the size of Earth?

_____

_____

_____

Patterns in Space

Next Generation Science Standards

PS2-1 Support an argument that the gravitational force exerted by Earth objects is directed down.

ESS1-1 Support an argument that differences in the apparent brightness the sun compared to other stars is due to their relative distances from th.

ESS1-2 Represent data in graphical displays to reveal patterns of daily anges in length and direction of shadows, day and night, and the asonal appearance of some stars in the night sky.

Go online to access
your digital course.

▶ VIDEO

📖 eTEXT

👆 INTERACTIVITY

🧪 VIRTUAL LAB

🎮 GAME

☑ ASSESSMENT

The Essential Question

How do patterns change from day to day and season to season?

Show What You Know

What is happening to the sun in this picture? Why do you think it is happening?

_____

_____

_____

Plan a Trip Around the World of Patterns

Where on Earth is it the middle of the night?

Phenomenon Hi, I'm Jackie Matters, a planetarium curator. I'm planning an exhibit about patterns in space. In this problem-solving learning activity, you will go on a trip around the world to observe patterns in the sky.

At the end of your journey, you will make a brochure that explains the patterns you observed at each stop. We'll use your brochure at the museum to teach others about space patterns.

Follow the path to learn how you will complete the Quest. The Quest activities in the lessons will help you complete the Quest! Check off your progress on the path when you complete an activity with a QUEST CHECK ✓ OFF. Go online for more Quest activities.

Quest Check-In Lab 1

Lesson 1

Learn about how gravity affects the positions of Earth, the sun, and the moon in space.

Next Generation Science Standards

5-ESS1-2 Represent data in graphical displays to reveal patterns of daily changes in length and direction of shadows, day and night, and the seasonal appearance of some stars in the night sky.

VIDEO

Watch a video about a planetarium curator.

Quest Check-In 2

Lesson 2

Use what you learn about Earth's movement to plan a trip to different countries to see day and night.

Quest Findings

Complete the Quest! Make a brochure to explain patterns in the sky. Include visuals in your brochure to illustrate the patterns.

Quest Check-In 3

Lesson 3

Research moon phases at each of your destinations.

How can spinning affect a planet's SHAPE?

Astronomers often build models to study objects in the universe. Earth spins around in space. How can you make a model to show how spinning affects Earth?

Materials
- construction paper
- scissors
- tape
- hole punch
- pencil
- ruler

Procedure

☐ 1. Make a sphere by crossing two strips of paper to form an X. Tape the spot where the paper crosses. Tape together the loose ends.

☐ 2. **SEP Use Models** Use the rest of the materials to show what happens when Earth spins. Show your plan to your teacher before you begin.

☐ 3. Draw a bar graph to compare the width of your model before and while you modeled Earth's rotation.

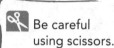 Be careful using scissors.

Science Practice

Scientists engage in argument using evidence from models.

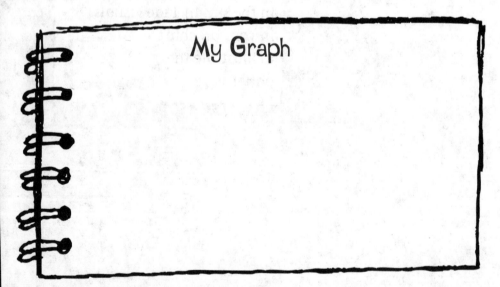

My Graph

Analyze and Interpret Data

4. **SEP Use Evidence** How did the shape of your model change when you modeled Earth's rotation?

_____

_____

Sequence

When you read, identify events that take place. Then sequence the events. When you sequence events, you put them in the order they happen

- Look for signal words: *after, before, then, first, next, last, finally,* and *later.*
- Ask yourself questions such as What happened first? Then ask what happened.

Read the following passage. Look for signal words to understand the sequence of events.

Shadow Play

Eli was studying how the movement of shadows in his yard is related to the position of the sun. Early in the morning, Eli placed a meterstick in the ground. Next, he measured the length of the shadow. Then, he noted the direction the shadow was pointing. He recorded these data. After four hours, Eli measured the shadow again. He recorded his observations. Later that afternoon, Eli repeated the process. Finally, Eli studied his data. He concluded that as the sun appears to move across the sky, the length and direction of shadows change.

☑ **READING CHECK** **Sequence** Underline the signal words in the paragraph. List three steps that Eli took to complete his study. Make sure to write the steps in the same order that Eli did them.

_____

_____

_____

Earth's Gravitational Forces

I can...

Demonstrate that Earth's gravity pulls objects toward the center of Earth.

5-PS2-1

Literacy Skill
Sequence

Vocabulary
gravity

Academic Vocabulary
exert

 VIDEO

Watch a video about Earth's gravity.

STEM Connection

A rocket stands on a launch pad at the Kennedy Space Center. Over at the mission control center, the countdown to blastoff begins. *"Three, two, one...we have liftoff!"* The engines below the rocket fire, thrusting the rocket upward into the sky. From Earth's surface, the rocket travels into the atmosphere and then into space.

Most rockets have two or three rocket boosters. The boosters contain fuel that is ignited at liftoff. The fuel burns and produces gases that push against Earth's surface. As the fuel burns, the boosters are released. Most rockets weigh hundreds of tons. So a huge amount of force is needed for the rocket to lift off. The escape velocity, or speed the rocket must achieve to leave Earth, is at least 40,234 kilometers (25,000 miles) per hour. That is more than 11 kilometers (7 miles) per second.

✓ **READING CHECK** **Predict** Write the order of events that occur when a rocket is launched.

_____

_____

_____

HANDS-ON LAB

5-PS2-1, SEP.2, SEP.7

How long do objects take to fall?

Scientists gather evidence to explain natural occurrences. How can you gather evidence to find out whether all objects fall at the same speed?

Suggested Materials
- ball
- pencil
- rock
- balance
- gram cubes
- meter stick

Procedure

☐ **1.** Make a plan for how you could use the materials to test whether different objects fall at the same speed. Write your plan.

_____

_____

_____

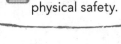 Be aware of physical safety.

☐ **2.** Show your plan to your teacher. Record your observations.

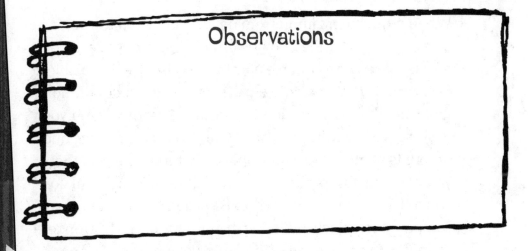

Observations

Science Practice

Scientists **construct arguments** that are supported by evidence.

Analyze and Interpret Data

3. SEP Construct an Argument Did the objects fall at the same speed? Use evidence from your experiment to support your answer.

_____

_____

_____

_____

Literacy ▸ Toolbox 🔧

Sequence
Sequence is the order in which events happen. Tell a partner the sequence of events that occur from the time a parachuter jumps from a plane until the parachuter comes to a stop on the ground.

Gravitational Force

When parachuters jump from a plane, they fall toward Earth. They are pulled downward by the force of Earth's gravity. **Gravity** is a force of attraction between two objects. Everything that has mass **exerts**, or applies, a gravitational force on other objects. Gravity exists between you and your desk, so why do you not feel it? Only objects that have huge amounts of mass exert, or apply, gravitational forces that you can feel. The pulling force of your desk is too weak for you to feel it. However, Earth has a huge amount of mass compared to objects on it. Earth's gravity is much stronger than the objects we see being pulled down.

A piece of tissue falls at a slower rate than a ball. This is because of the air. If there were no air, all objects would fall at the same rate. At first, a skydiver falls very fast. When the parachute opens, the person falls slowly. The jumper slows because air pushes against the parachute, slowing the fall.

Identify Draw arrows to show the direction of gravity and of the force of the air. Label the arrows *G* for gravity and *R* for air resistance.

Gravity on Earth

Gravity is a constant force. It cannot be "turned off," even when objects float or rise. Think about being on a moving swing. When you swing upward, Earth's gravity will always pull you back down. Earth's gravity always pulls objects toward Earth's center.

▢Be a Scientist

Explore Gravity Put a small hole in the bottom of a paper cup. With your finger over the hole, put some water in the cup. With the cup over a bucket, remove your finger. Observe how the water flows. Repeat but this time hold the cup so that the hole points sideways. Compare and explain your observations.

Use Evidence from Text Draw arrows to show the direction of the gravitational force on each object in the diagram. What evidence in the text explains why the arrows are facing that direction?

_____

_____

Engage in Argument from Evidence A friend says that Earth's gravity does not always pull objects downward. She says the proof is that gravity acts on people on the opposite sides of the planet. So Earth's gravity must pull objects both upward and downward. How would you respond? What evidence would you use to support your argument?

Gravity in Space

Gravity exists between all objects in space. Stars stay in their galaxies because of gravity. Our sun has much more mass than Earth or the planets and objects that revolve around it. So, its gravitational force is greater than the force of gravity of the objects that revolve around it. As a result, the gravity of the sun holds Earth and other objects in space in their orbits. Artificial satellites also stay in their orbits because of Earth's gravity. In the same way, the gravity of Earth holds the moon in its orbit.

📓 **Make Meaning** In your science notebook, tell about a time when gravity helped you complete a task.

Quest Connection

Will the strength of Earth's gravity on the moon change as you travel to different places on your Quest? Explain.

_____

_____

_____

☑ Lesson 1 Check

1. **Explain** How is a rocket being launched into space able to overcome the force of gravity?

_____

_____

2. **Predict** A soccer player kicks a ball high in the air. What will happen to the soccer ball? How do you know?

_____

_____

How does gravity affect matter?

Scientists use models to investigate gravity. How can you model the effects of gravity on objects?

Materials
- large foam cup
- string, 80 cm
- safety goggles
- pencil

 Wear safety goggles.

 Be aware of physical safety.

Procedure

☐ **1.** Use a pencil to carefully make two holes on opposite sides of the cup near the top. Tie the string through the holes, leaving at least 60 cm (2 ft) of string as a handle.

☐ **2. SEP Use Models** Make your plan to use the cups and string to model how the force of Earth's gravity affects objects. Include what happens if the strength of the gravitational force changes.

☐ **3.** Show your plan to your teacher before you begin. Record your observations.

Science Practice

Scientists use models to explain how systems work.

Analyze and Interpret Data

4. SEP Explain How did you represent gravity in your model? How did you test gravitational forces of different strengths?

_____

_____

_____

_____

5. CCC Systems Suppose that the sun did not exert a gravitational force. How do you think it would affect the solar system?

_____

_____

Observations

Earth's Movements in Space

I can...

Demonstrate that night and day are caused by the rotation of Earth around its axis once a day. Explain that Earth revolves around the sun about once a year. Describe why the amount of daylight is different depending on the time of the year.

5-ESS1-2

Literacy Skill
Sequence

Vocabulary
axis
rotation
revolution

Academic Vocabulary
pattern

▶ **VIDEO**

Watch a video about Earth's movements in space.

LOCAL-TO-GLOBAL ▶ Connection

Suppose the time is 3 p.m. in your town. Does that mean the time everywhere on Earth is 3 p.m.? No. When the time is 3 p.m. in New York, California time is 12 noon. The sun appears in the sky in New York about 3 hours before it does in California every day. That is because Earth spins around once every 24 hours. As a result, the sun only shines on one half of Earth at any specific time. So when the sun is rising where you live, it is setting in other parts of the world.

To adjust time to this difference, places all over the world are divided into time zones. For example, New York is in the Eastern time zone, and California is in the Pacific time zone. With different time zones, the sun rises in the morning at about the same local time, and it sets at about the same local time at night. When you travel east, time changes forward. When you travel west, time changes backward.

Calculate Draw the hands of the clock to show the time in New York when in California the time is 11 a.m.

CALIFORNIA   NEW YORK

uInvestigate Lab

How are we spinning?

Scientists use models to study Earth's movements. How can you use a model to observe some effects of Earth's spinning motion?

Materials

- rotating chair
- lamp
- index cards
- yarn

Suggested Materials

- camera
- glue
- yellow crayon

Procedure

☐ 1. **SEP Plan an Investigation** Make a plan to use the chair and the lamp to model Earth's spinning motion and some of its effects. Show your plan to your teacher before you begin.

☐ 2. **SEP Carry Out an Investigation** Carry out your plan. Pause to record your observations. You can draw your observations on index cards or take photos.

☐ 3. Make your model creative. Combine your drawings or photos into a flipbook and "play" it from beginning to end.

⚠ Be careful as you spin on the chair.

⚠ Do not look directly at the lamp.

Analyze and Interpret Data

4. **SEP Explain** Which way did you spin? Which way did things appear to move as you were spinning?

_____

_____

Science Practice

Scientists use models to explain phenomena.

5. **CCC Cause and Effect** Based on your model, infer some effects of Earth's spinning motion. Explain your inference.

_____

_____

_____

_____

_____

_____

_____

_____

Math ▸ Toolbox

Convert Measurements
Someone standing at the equator travels about 25,000 miles each day. Roughly how fast is that in miles per hour?

Earth's Rotation

You cannot feel Earth moving, but our planet is constantly moving in space. You can, though, observe the effects of this movement when you see the apparent movement of the sun across the sky. This effect is a result of Earth spinning on its axis. An **axis** is an imaginary line that goes through the center of an object. Earth's axis passes through the North Pole, the center of Earth, and the South Pole. The spinning of Earth and other bodies in space on an axis is called **rotation**. Earth makes one complete rotation about every 24 hours. One rotation is about equal to about one day on Earth.

As Earth rotates, different areas of Earth face the sun. The side of Earth that faces toward the sun experiences day. The side that faces away from the sun experiences night. During the day, the sun appears to rise in the east. Then it moves across the sky and finally sets in the west. The sun appears to move this way because Earth rotates from west to east. If you watch the stars and moon at night, you will observe the same pattern of movement. A **pattern** is a group of objects or events that repeat in the same order.

Identify The diagram below shows what you would see if you looked from space at Earth's North Pole. The curved arrows show Earth's rotation. It is noon at Place A. Write these labels on the diagram at the correct place: sunset, sunrise. Mark an X where Place A will be on the diagram after 12 hours.

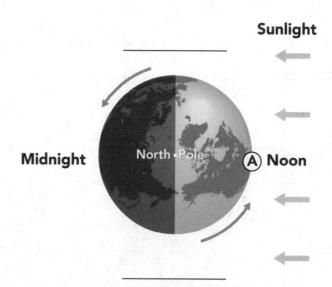

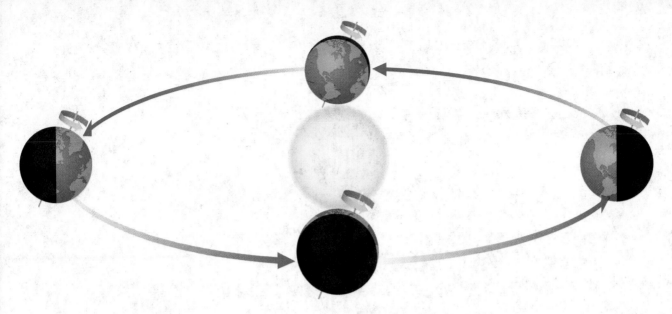

Earth's Revolution

When you celebrate your birthday each year, you are actually celebrating a complete trip around the sun! As Earth rotates, it also travels in a path around the sun. Earth's motion around the sun is called a revolution. A **revolution** is the movement of one object around another object. Earth takes about 365 days, or one year, to complete one revolution around the sun.

As Earth revolves around the sun, places on Earth receive different amounts of sunlight. Sunrise and sunset times change during the course of one year. So, the amount of daylight changes as well. A location gets more daylight in the summer than it does in winter.

Quest Connection

Where would you travel to experience a sunrise sooner? Why?

_____

_____

What is the movement of Earth's moon in space?

The moon revolves and rotates in space, similar to Earth's movement in space. The moon makes one complete rotation on its axis about every 29 days it takes the same amount of time for the moon to revolve around Earth.

1 On day 1, the sun seems to rise in the sky. The side of the moon we see from Earth faces the sun. Sunlight reaches this side of the moon for 14 days as the moon revolves around Earth.

sunlight

2 On day 14, the sun seems to set in the sky. The side of the moon we see from Earth faces away from the sun. Sunlight does not reach this side of the moon, so the moon appears dark in the sky.

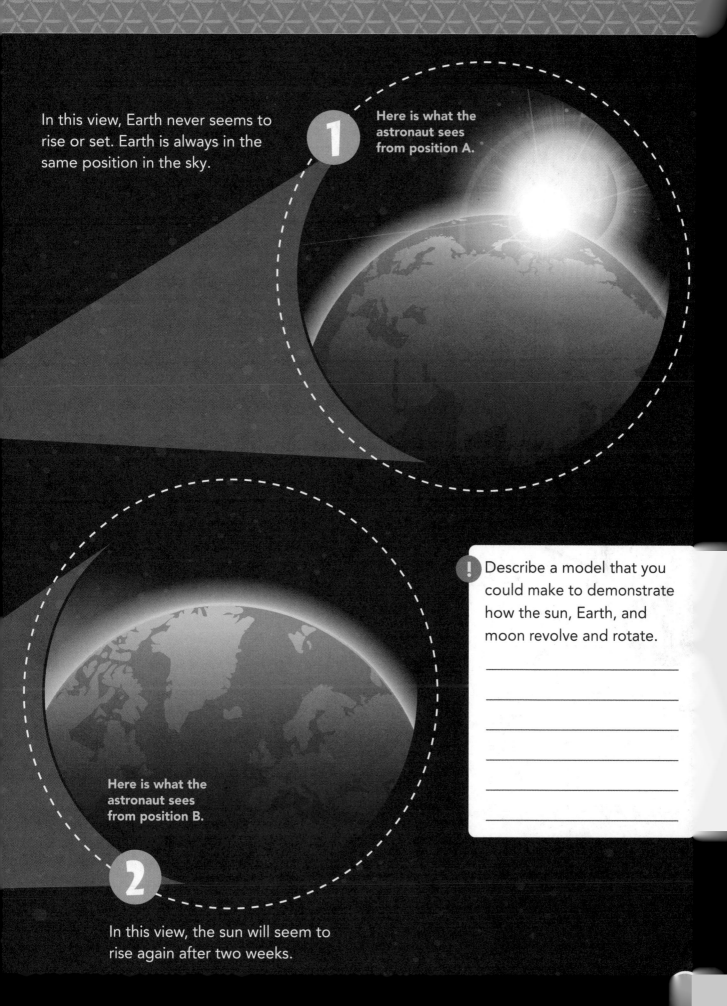

In this view, Earth never seems to rise or set. Earth is always in the same position in the sky.

1

Here is what the astronaut sees from position A.

Here is what the astronaut sees from position B.

2

In this view, the sun will seem to rise again after two weeks.

! Describe a model that you could make to demonstrate how the sun, Earth, and moon revolve and rotate.

_____
_____
_____
_____
_____
_____

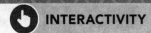

INTERACTIVITY

Complete an activity about Earth's movements in space.

Seasons

The tilt of Earth's axis and Earth's revolution around the sun cause Earth's seasons. The diagram shows that Earth's axis always tilts in the same direction at the same angle of 23.5 degrees. Earth's tilt and revolution affect how much direct sunlight different places on Earth receive at different times of the year.

In June, the Northern Hemisphere tilts toward the sun and causes summer. People there experience more hours of daylight and fewer hours of darkness. At the same time, it is winter in the Southern Hemisphere. There are more hours of darkness there than of daylight.

Interpret Diagrams Write the caption for June.

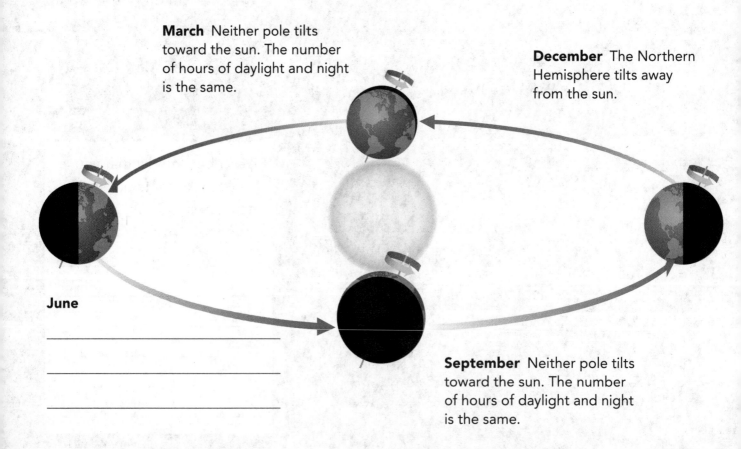

March Neither pole tilts toward the sun. The number of hours of daylight and night is the same.

December The Northern Hemisphere tilts away from the sun.

June

_____

_____

_____

September Neither pole tilts toward the sun. The number of hours of daylight and night is the same.

As Earth continues along its orbit from June until December, the Northern Hemisphere points farther away from the sun. In December it is winter in New York City and other places in the Northern Hemisphere. People there experience fewer hours of daylight than darkness. Places in the Southern Hemisphere, such as Buenos Aires, just the opposite is happening. It is summer there, so people experience more hours of daylight than of darkness.

Earth's tilt causes the angle of the sun's rays that Earth receives to change from season to season. In winter, the sun's rays are spread out, so the weather becomes colder. In summer, the sun's rays are more direct, so the weather becomes warmer. This pattern happens over and over and causes summer.

📓 **Make Meaning** In your science notebook, write about patterns you can observe as seasons change.

New York City

Buenos Aires

☑ Lesson 2 Check

1. Describe Why do the sun and moon appear to move across the sky?

_____

_____

2. ☑ READING CHECK **Sequence** What sequence of events does the revolution of Earth around the sun cause?

_____

_____

_____

Sun Up, Sun Down

What do you think the sky at the other side of Earth looks like outside right now? What might you see in the sky?

Look at the destinations shown in the table. These are the places you will visit on your trip around the world. You will fly to each of these cities and arrive on the day and time shown in the table. Your trip will begin in Seattle. For each city, describe what the sky is like when you arrive.

Quest Itinerary				
Location	Sunrise	Sunset	Time of arrival	Sky observations
Seattle	5:46 a.m	6:40 p.m	4:30 p.m. Monday	
Boston	5:38 a.m	6:22 p.m	8:00 p.m. Tuesday	
London	5:24 a.m	6:35 p.m	11:00 p.m. Wednesday	
New Delhi	7:08 a.m	6:49 p.m	6:45 p.m. Friday	
Tokyo	5:26 a.m	8:30 p.m	1:00 p.m. Saturday	

When you arrive in Tokyo, you will be on almost the opposite side of Earth from Boston. If it is the middle of the day in Tokyo, what will the sky look like in Boston?

_____

_____

_____

How long does it take to orbit?

You have learned that Earth orbits the sun. Other objects in the solar system orbit the sun too. Jupiter is a giant planet that moves around the sun. Halley's comet, an object with a glowing tail, also blazes a path around the sun.

The table shows the time each space object takes to make one orbit around the sun. Study the table, and then rank the objects according to their orbit time. Start with the shortest orbit time and end with the longest.

Object in space	Orbit time	Rank (shortest to longest)
Earth	365 days	
Pluto	248 years	
Jupiter	11.9 years	
Halley's comet	76.1 years	

Patterns Over Time

I can...

Demonstrate why the sun, moon, and stars appear at different times.
Describe why shadows change size and direction during the day.

5-ESS1-1, 5-ESS1-2

Literacy Skill
Sequence

Vocabulary
shadow
constellation

Academic Vocabulary
related

 VIDEO

Watch a video about patterns over time.

CURRICULUM Connection

During the spring and fall equinoxes, the hours of daylight and nighttime on Earth are about equal. Ancient civilizations marked these equinoxes with celebrations and rituals. About 700 c.e., the Mayans built a pyramid in the ancient city of Chichén Itzá, which is in present-day Mexico. The angles of the pyramid were built to celebrate the exact moment the equinox occurs. As the sun shines on the corner of the pyramid, it casts a shadow against the steps. The shadow appears as an image of a serpent moving down the staircase. Can you find the serpent in the photo. Hint: The carved head of the snake is at the bottom of the pyramid, representing the mythical god Kukulkan. Today visitors from all over the world come to this ancient city to view this spectacular event.

Infer Why were the Mayans able to predict the exact dates of the spring and fall equinox?

_____

_____

_____

What star patterns can you see?

The time is 7 p.m. What star patterns can you see? Are these same stars still visible at 11 p.m.? Make a star finder to explore the night sky.

Procedure

☐ **1.** Use the Star Finder Sheet to make a star finder.

☐ **2.** Choose a time and a date. Record the star groups you could see at that time.

_____

_____

Be careful using scissors.

☐ **3.** Describe how you can use the star finder to find out whether those same star groups are always in the same spot throughout the night.

_____

_____

_____

_____

_____

Science Practice

Scientists **use models** to support an argument.

☐ **4.** Carry out your plan and record your observations.

_____

_____

Analyze and Interpret Data

5. CCC Patterns Use what you know about how Earth moves to explain your results.

_____

_____

_____

Shadow Play

Place a meterstick vertically in the ground outside on a sunny day. Measure the length of its shadow at different times of day. When is the shadow the longest? When is it the shortest? Explain your results.

Shadow Patterns

Earth's rotation and revolution cause patterns in space. When light shines on an object and does not pass through it, the object casts a shadow. A **shadow** is a dark area or shape that is made when an object blocks a source of light. Have you ever noticed how shadows change throughout the day? As Earth rotates, the sun appears to move across the sky in an arc. So sunlight shines on objects at different angles throughout the day. As a result, shadows change their size and position during the day.

Earth's revolution causes seasonal patterns in shadows. During winter, the sun appears very low in the sky, and shadows are longest at the winter solstice. In summer, the sun appears much higher above the horizon, so shadows are shortest at the summer solstice.

Model It! Draw a model of how a shadow changes length and direction during one day in summer.

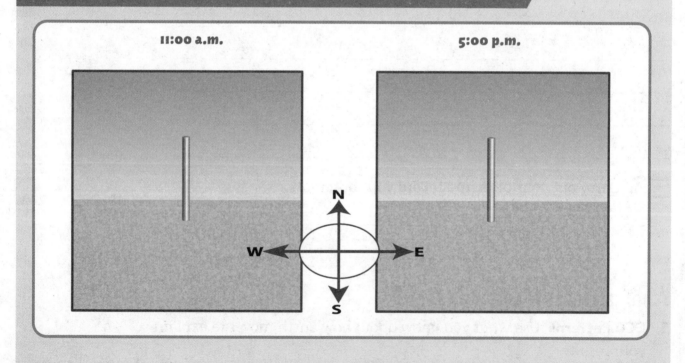

Stars and Constellations

Stars can also form shapes in space. A group of stars that, when seen, make a shape or picture is called a **constellation**. You may have seen a constellation at night called the Big Dipper. Stars in constellations may appear to be near each other, but they are actually different distances from Earth.

Some stars in a constellation may appear brighter than other stars in the constellation. How bright a star appears to people on Earth is **related**, or connected, to its distance.

For example, the sun is a star that is much closer to Earth than other stars, so the sun seems much brighter than other stars. However, many stars that are farther than the sun from Earth are much brighter.

Describe Why does the sun appear brighter than other stars? Cite evidence from the text to support your answer.

_____

_____

_____

INTERACTIVITY

Complete an activity about patterns over time.

How do we identify star patterns in the sky?

From our perspective on Earth, stars move in predictable ways during the year. To help identify star patterns during different seasons, scientists can use star maps. The star maps below show the positions of constellations as seen from the Northern Hemisphere at the same time of night during January and June.

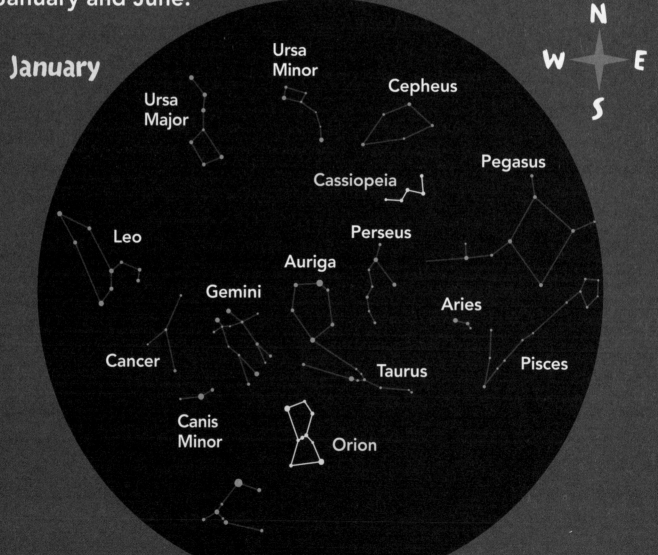

January

Ursa Minor
Cepheus
Ursa Major
Pegasus
Cassiopeia
Perseus
Leo
Auriga
Gemini
Aries
Cancer
Taurus
Pisces
Canis Minor
Orion

N
W   E
S

Orion is a bright winter constellation in the Northern Hemisphere. In the summer, Orion is too low in the sky for you to see.

! **Compare the position of Cassiopeia in the winter and summer sky. How does it change?**

_____

_____

_____

_____

June

Cassiopeia

Cepheus

Gemini

Ursa Minor

Cygnus

Ursa Major

Cancer

Lyra

Hercules

Aquila

Bootes

Leo

Corona Borealis

Sagittarius

Libra

Virgo

Scorpius

Moon Phases

Sometimes you can see a big, round moon at night. Sometimes you can even see it during the day. During both day and night, the moon looks as if it were shining with its own light. But the moon does not produce its own light. You can see the moon because sunlight reflects off the moon's surface.

If you look at the moon at different times of the month, its shape appears to change. However, the moon does not actually change shape. Half of the moon always faces the sun, and sunlight is reflected from half of it. The diagram shows how the lit portion of the moon that we see changes as the moon revolves around Earth. The changing pattern of the moon in the night sky is known as the moon's phases. One complete cycle of moon phases takes about 29.5 days.

✓ **READING CHECK** **Sequence** What is the sequence of moon phases between a full moon and a new moon?

_____

_____

_____

Quest Connection

Find out the phase of the moon for the current day. Predict when you will see the next full moon. Explain how you made your prediction.

_____

_____

First quarter

During a first-quarter moon, one half of the lighted half of the moon, or one quarter of the entire moon, is visible.

Waxing gibbous

In the waxing gibbous phase, more and more of the moon's lighted half is visible.

Waxing crescent

A waxing crescent moon follows a new moon. Waxing means the moon appears to be growing larger. You can see a sliver of the lighted moon.

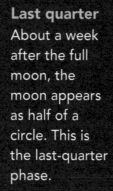

Earth

Sun

Full moon

During a full moon, the entire half of the moon that faces Earth is lighted. You see the moon as a full circle. A full moon appears about a week after the first-quarter moon.

Waning gibbous

Gradually, you see less and less of the moon. The moon is in the waning gibbous phase.

Last quarter

About a week after the full moon, the moon appears as half of a circle. This is the last-quarter phase.

Waning crescent

A waning crescent moon follows the last quarter. You can see a sliver of the lighted moon. Waning means the moon appears to be getting smaller.

New moon

During a new moon, the moon's dark, unlighted side faces Earth. You cannot see a new moon.

Keeping Track of Time

Since ancient times, people have used repeating events, such as the rising and setting sun, to keep track of time. Many cultures used a sundial, such as the one in the photo, to know what time it was. They knew that when the sun was directly above them, shadows were shortest. They called that time of day noon. As the sun moved across the sky, the shadow moved around the center of the sundial. The position of the shadow told them what time it was. This sundial tells that the time is 9:00.

People used the phases of the moon to predict when a year began and ended. Calendars were developed based on these predictable patterns. By observing the location of constellations in the sky, people could figure out when to plant their crops and when to harvest them.

Cause and Effect What causes the movement of the shadow on a sundial?

_____

_____

☑ Lesson 3 Check

1. Explain How are the motions of Earth and the apparent movement of stars connected?

_____

_____

_____

_____

2. Cause and Effect If a tree casts a shadow to the west at 11 a.m., how will the shadow appear at 5 p.m.?

_____

_____

Moon Sightings

On your trip, you will observe the moon phase at each of your destinations. Some of the phases are already identified for you in the table. Fill in the blank spaces to identify what the phase would be for each remaining city. Use what you observed in the Quest Check-In for Lesson 2 to help.

Quest Itinerary

Location	Day	Moon phase
Seattle	Monday	waxing crescent
Boston	Tuesday	
London	Wednesday	
New Delhi	Friday	first quarter
Tokyo	Sunday	

The moon orbits Earth about once a month. If you traveled around the world in a day or two, what would you notice about the moon phases?

_____

_____

_____

_____

Bonus question! Look at the moon phase for your first destination. Predict how many days until a full moon.

_____

_____

_____

uEngineer It! Design STEM

 INTERACTIVITY

Go online for help with completing your design project.

Coding **Moon** Phases

Phenomenon A code is a way of using numbers, symbols, or words to represent things. Computer scientists use codes to instruct a computer to carry out tasks. People can also use codes to order a sequence of events, such as moon phases. How can you use a code to show the pattern of moon phases?

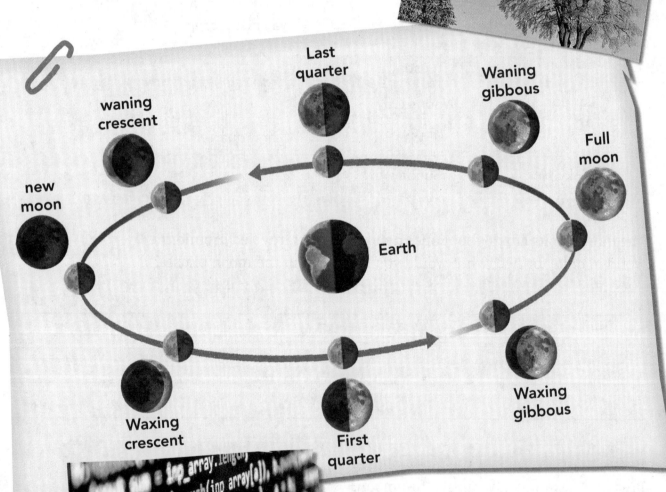

Design It

☐ Look at the diagram of the eight moon phases. Calculate how many days the moon remains in each phase. Remember that a complete cycle of moon phases takes about 29.5 days.

☐ Choose a phase to start coding. Decide how many days this phase will be visible.

☐ Next, figure out how many days each of the remaining phases will be visible.

☐ Design a code that tells what moon phase it will be on different days.

Write Your Code

Plan a Trip Around the World of **Patterns**

Where on Earth is it the middle of the night?

Make a Space Patterns Brochure

Phenomenon In this Quest, you traveled around the world to observe patterns in space. Now use your observations to make a brochure that summarizes what you experienced at each stop on your trip. Remember that the purpose of the brochure is to help others learn about patterns in space. Consider the following questions as you make your brochure.

• Is the location experiencing day or night?

• How long is it until sunrise or sunset?

• How will the moon look?

• How may the appearance of stars change over time?

Include drawings of Earth in space to illustrate Earth's patterns. Make pie charts that compare the length of day and the length of night at some locations. Research and include a visual that compares the seasonal appearance of some stars at one location.

Planetarium Curator

A curator is a person who is responsible for the items in a museum. A planetarium is a place where scientists study objects in the sky. The curator of a planetarium is in charge of the planetarium's collection. The collection includes space objects and historic items related to stars, the sun, the moon, and other objects in the universe. A planetarium curator gathers items for the planetarium's collection and makes sure the items are taken care of properly. He or she often decides how the items will be displayed for the public to see. The planetarium curator might also be involved with community activities for the museum.

Most planetarium curators must have at least four years of college education. Many planetariums look for curators with even more college training. Planetarium curators should have good critical thinking skills, be good at organizing things, and be able to talk with the public.

📔 **Reflect** In your science notebook, write why you think being able to think critically and organize information is important for a planetarium curator.

1. **Vocabulary** Which statements describe gravity? Circle all that apply.

   A. It exists only between heavy objects.

   B. It holds objects in space in their orbits.

   C. It pulls objects toward the center of Earth.

   D. It is a force of attraction between two objects.

2. **Cause and Effect** Which statement tells what causes the sun to appear to move across the sky?

   A. Earth rotates on its axis.

   B. Earth is tilted on its axis.

   C. Earth revolves around the sun.

   D. Earth has different time zones.

3. **Explain** Why do the positions of constellations change with the seasons on Earth?

   _____

   _____

   _____

   _____

4. **Use Evidence** What evidence supports the idea that gravity exists on Earth?

   A. All people on Earth observe that objects fall toward Earth's center.

   B. People are able to launch rockets into space.

   C. Earth rotates and revolves around the sun.

   D. The pull of gravity is stronger on planets that have less mass than Earth.

5. **Infer** Study the diagram. What season is it at the place marked X? Explain how you know.

   _____

   _____

   _____

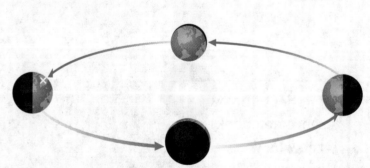

6. Sequence Which picture correctly shows the missing phase in the sequence of the moon phases?

A.

B.

C.

D.

7. Predict How might the length of a shadow change from 9:00 a.m to 12 noon on a sunny day? Explain.

_____

_____

_____

_____

How do patterns change from day to day and season to season?

Show What You Learned

Describe how daily patterns on Earth are different from seasonal patterns. Use the words *rotate* and *revolution* in your answer.

_____

_____

_____

_____

_____

_____

_____

_____

_____

_____

_____

_____

Read this scenario and answer questions 1–4.

Huxley was curious about whether he could use shadows to learn about patterns of Earth's movement. On a Sunday at 3:00 p.m., he placed a 1-meter-tall pole in an open field. Then he measured the length and direction of the pole's shadow. He returned every Sunday for a year to repeat his measurements. Some of his data are recorded in the table. Use the table to answer the questions.

Week	Shadow length (m)
1	3.9
4	2.9
8	2.1
10	1.7
15	1.1
21	0.9
28	0.8
32	1.0

1. Observe Patterns What season was it when Huxley began his experiment? Explain how you know.

_____

_____

_____

_____

2. **Analyze Data** During which week was the sun at its highest point during the observations?

   A. week 1

   B. week 10

   C. week 28

   D. week 32

3. **Use Graphs** Which choice describes how Huxley should use a graph to show the pattern of shadow lengths?

   A. Huxley should use a bar graph to show the length of the shadows each week.

   B. Huxley should use a line graph to show how the direction of the shadows changed.

   C. Huxley should use a pie chart to show how each week's shadow length compares to the total.

   D. Huxley should use a pictograph to show how many weeks it takes for the shadows to reach each length.

4. **Patterns** How long will the shadow of the pole be on week 52 of the experiment?

   A. 1.0 meters

   B. 2.0 meters

   C. 3.0 meters

   D. 4.0 meters

What can we tell from shadows?

Suggested Materials

- light sources
- pipe cleaner
- modeling clay
- ruler
- opaque objects
- protractor

Phenomenon Shadows change throughout the day, from day to day, and across seasons. How can you build a model to show how shadows change throughout these time periods?

Procedure

☐ **1.** Make a plan to model how shadows change. Which materials will you use for each part?

_____

_____

_____

_____

_____

Science Practice

Scientists **represent data** to describe phenomena.

☐ **2.** Show your plan to your teacher before you begin.

☐ **3.** Use data from your model to make a graph showing daily changes in shadows.

Analyze and Interpret Data

4. **Evaluate** What factors contribute to the daily changes in shadows? How does your model illustrate these changes?

_____

_____

_____

5. **Evaluate** What factors contribute to the seasonal changes in shadows? How does your model illustrate these changes?

_____

_____

_____

6. **Predict** Suppose Earth's axis was not tilted relative to the sun. How would this affect the daily and seasonal pattern of shadows?

_____

_____

_____

_____

_____

Topic 8

Energy and Food

Lesson 1 Energy in Food

Lesson 2 How Plants Make Food

Lesson 3 How Animals Use Food

Next Generation Science Standards

5-PS3-1 Use models to describe that energy in animals' food (used for body repair, growth, motion, and to maintain body warmth) was once energy from the sun.

5-LS1-1 Support an argument that plants get the materials they need for growth chiefly from air and water.

5-LS2-1 Develop a model to describe the movement of matter among plants, animals, decomposers, and the environment.

 Topic 8 Energy and Food

Go online to access
your digital course.

▶ VIDEO

📖 eTEXT

👆 INTERACTIVITY

📱 VIRTUAL LAB

🎮 GAME

☑ ASSESSMENT

The Essential Question

Where does food's energy come from and how is food used?

Show What You Know

How is energy from the sun transferred into the green plant the gorilla is eating?

_____

_____

_____

Plan Your Plate!

Why do plants and animals need food?

Phenomenon Hi, I am Shanay Marcus, and I am a nutritionist. I teach people which foods are best for their bodies. Many types of tasty foods can be found in the grocery store. Different categories of food like vegetables, fruits, and meats contribute to a balanced diet. Each type of food contains energy, which humans and other animals need to survive.

In this problem-solving learning activity, you will construct a dinner plate choosing foods that provide energy to complete basic tasks.

Follow the path down the grocery store aisles to learn how you will complete the Quest. The Quest activities in the lessons will help you complete the Quest! Check off your progress on the path when you complete an activity with a QUEST CHECK ✓ OFF .
Go online for more Quest activities.

Quest Check-In 1

Lesson 1
Group foods on a shopping list to show whether foods come from plants or animals.

5-PS3-1 Use models to describe that energy in animals' food (used for body repair, growth, motion, and to maintain body warmth) was once energy from the sun.

Quest Check-In 3

Lesson 3

Analyze how different animals use energy from food. Compare energy needs for each animal.

Quest Check-In Lab 2

Lesson 2

Use a nutrition table to investigate which plant food provides the most energy and nutrients.

Quest Findings

Complete the Quest! Construct a sample dinner plate choosing foods based on the amount of energy and nutrients they contain. Use what you have learned in each Check-In to guide your choices.

How much food do you need?

Scientists use models to explain how processes or actions work together. What is the relationship between food, activity, and energy?

Procedure

☐ 1. Predict if more or less food will give you enough energy to do three activities.

_____

_____

☐ 2. **SEP Develop a Model** Write a plan to model and test your prediction. Identify which materials represent you, food, energy, and activities.

☐ 3. Show your plan to your teacher before you begin. Record your observations and data.

Analyze and Interpret Data

4. **CCC Systems and System Models** How did your model help explain the relationship between food, energy, and activities?

_____

_____

_____

_____

_____

5. **Infer** Why does your body need food?

_____

_____

_____

_____

Materials

• beaker with 50 mL warm water
• crushed ice
• 3 small cups, 2 oz
• teaspoons

Science Practice

Scientists use models to explain natural processes.

Observations

Use Evidence from Text

 GAME

Practice what you learn with the Mini Games.

Scientists collect facts from reading reliable texts. They read closely, paying attention to important information. They underline or circle this information to keep track of where it is in the text. Then they use this information as evidence to support their analysis, reflections, and conclusions.

Read the text passage to find out how scientists designed a probe to investigate the sun.

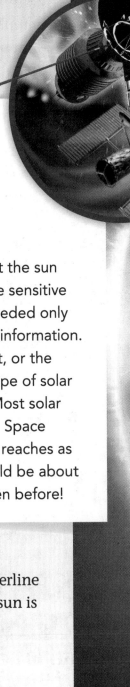

Taking the Heat

Each day, the sun shines its powerful light on Earth. It is the main energy source for life on Earth. Our sun is blazing hot. It can reach temperatures hotter than 5,600 °C (10,000 °F) at its surface. Human body temperature is only 37 °C (98.6 °F). Scientists sent a space probe called Helios 2 to orbit the sun in the early 1970s. They had to find ways to keep the sensitive instruments on Helios 2 from melting. The probe needed only 4 percent of the sun's light for power and to gather information. It needed to reflect the other 96 percent of the light, or the probe would get too hot. Scientists engineered a type of solar panel that could both absorb and reflect sunlight. Most solar panels are designed to only absorb sunlight energy. Space engineers are hoping to shoot a space satellite that reaches as close as 5 million kilometers from the sun. That would be about 39 million kilometers closer than we have ever gotten before!

✓READING CHECK **Use Evidence from Text** Underline evidence in the text that supports the claim that the sun is much hotter than the human body.

Energy in Food

I can...

Use a model to describe how the energy in an animal's food was once energy from the sun.

5-PS3-1

Literacy Skill
Use Evidence from Text

Vocabulary
herbivore
carnivore
omnivore

VIDEO

Watch a video about energy in food.

CURRICULUM Connection

Do you know how much energy your body needs? Children between 10 and 12 years of age need a minimum of 2,200 Calories each day, although the number varies depending on other factors. A Calorie is a unit of energy. All foods supply energy. The labels on packaged foods list the number of Calories in each serving. They also list ingredients and nutrients in the food.

The minimum energy needed by living things changes depending on body size and activity level. An elephant, for example, needs 70,000 Calories each day. A hummingbird may only need 7 Calories. This may seem like a small amount, but it is actually quite a lot of energy for such a small bird. If humans were as active as hummingbirds, we would need 155,000 Calories each day!

Calculate Why might an elephant need so many more Calories than a hummingbird?

_____

_____

_____

How is the sun involved in your meals?

Scientists make charts, diagrams, and drawings to represent data and information. How can you construct a model to describe how energy from the sun travels to the food on your plate?

Suggested Materials
- drawing paper
- colored pencils
- index cards
- yarn

Science Practice

Scientists use models to describe natural processes.

Procedure

☐ 1. Write what you eat in a typical meal. Include at least three different types of food.

_____

☐ 2. **SEP Develop Models** Look at your list and plan a model that shows where each food you ate got its energy. Choose materials to make your model.

☐ 3. If any of the foods you ate had eaten something else for energy, add that to your model to show where that energy came from.

Analyze and Interpret Data

4. **Compare and Contrast** Examine your classmates' models. How was your model similar to and different from other models in your class?

_____

_____

_____

_____

5. **CCC Energy and Matter** Where did the energy in your food start?

_____

_____

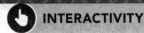
Literacy ▸ Toolbox

Use Evidence From Text
Scientists use evidence to support scientific claims. Underline information in the passage that supports the claim that plants change the energy of sunlight into chemical energy.

Plants and Energy

All living beings need energy from food. Plants get food by making it. They use matter from the environment and the energy of sunlight to build food molecules such as sugars or starch. These molecules store chemical energy. Starch is a long chain of sugar molecules. As plants perform life processes, they break down starch and sugars to release energy. Plants must continually replace the food molecules they use. This is why plants that do not get enough time in the sun each day do not stay healthy.

Not all the sugars a plant produces are used as food. Plants use some sugars along with other materials that the plant gets from the soil, to make plant parts. The amount of energy in the sugars a plant produces is less than the amount of energy the plant receives from the sun.

All plants use energy to grow, reproduce, and perform other activities. Some species of bamboo, for example, can grow almost 1 meter (3 feet) in one day! While plants may look very different, they all have structures to support the production and distribution of food molecules. Many have leaves or other broad, green surfaces to capture sunlight and exchange gases with the air.

Infer Seeds, which contain a young plant, usually begin to sprout below ground, where there is little sunlight. What else do you think is inside seeds? Why do you think this?

_____

_____

_____

Animals and Energy

Animals cannot make their own food, so they must eat to get energy. When animals eat plants, their body breaks down the molecules of the plant's body to obtain energy and nutrients. Like plants, animals use some food molecules for energy and others to make body parts. All living organisms use and store chemical energy.

Different kinds of animals eat different kinds of food. The grasshopper in the photo is a herbivore. A **herbivore** eats only plants. Deer, giraffes, and bees are herbivores. Plant material can be difficult to digest. Many herbivores have complex digestive systems to help them break down food.

A **carnivore** is an animal that feeds on animals or products animals make, such as eggs. Some examples of carnivores are tigers, wolves, snakes, and sharks. Carnivores have sharp teeth to catch and eat their prey.

An **omnivore** is an animal that eats both plants and animals. Some omnivores you might know are pigs and some birds. These animals have structures that allow them to eat both types of food.

✓ READING CHECK **Use Evidence from Text** Could a carnivore and a herbivore compete for the same food source? Use evidence from the text to support your answer.

_____

_____

Quest Connection

▼▼▼▼▼▼▼▼▼▼▼▼▼▼▼▼▼▼▼▼▼▼▼▼▼▼▼▼▼▼▼▼▼▼

How can you classify different foods that you eat?

_____

_____

_____

What is a trophic level?

Trophic levels sort animals and plants according to where they are in the food chain and how they obtain energy. This pyramid diagram shows four trophic levels in a prairie ecosystem. Energy flows through each level, from bottom to top. Some energy is used along the way. The levels get narrower toward the top to show that less and less energy is left.

Secondary consumers eat primary consumers. They convert and store about 10 percent of the energy from animals they eat. The other 90 percent is used or transformed and released as heat.

Tertiary consumers convert and store about 10 percent of the energy from the secondary consumer animals they eat. The other 90 percent is used or transformed.

Primary consumers eat plants. They convert and store about 10 percent of the energy they obtain from plants. The other 90 percent is used for life processes or released as heat.

Plants are **producers**, which means they make their own food through photosynthesis. Plants are able to use only about 11 percent of the solar energy they receive during food production.

The same principle of energy levels works underwater as well.

Draw each organism in the trophic level where it belongs.

Energy Paths to the Sun

All the energy in the food you, and other animals, eat can be traced back to the sun. Sometimes that path is not easy to see. An example is an egg. An egg comes from a chicken. When a chicken produces an egg, some of the energy and matter stored in the chicken passes to the egg. Chickens on many farms eat the food a farmer feeds them. The food comes in different shapes, such as pellets or grains. So how can the chemical energy in an egg be traced back to the sun?

The food that farmers feed their chickens contains ingredients such as alfalfa, corn, peas, wheat, or oats. All of these ingredients are plants or come from plants. The plants used energy from the sun to make the food that they stored in their body. That energy is then stored in the food that the farmer feeds the chickens.

Identify Draw a simple diagram that shows the flow of energy from the sun to the food chickens eat.

Foods Made with Plants
Look through the canned or packaged foods in your home. Predict which contain fruits or vegetables. Look at the ingredients labels to find out whether your predictions are correct.

☑ Lesson 1 Check

1. Review What are two ways that plants use energy from food?

_____

_____

2. Compare and Contrast How are a herbivore and a carnivore different? What is one way they are similar?

_____

_____

_____

Sorting Foods

Plants and animals use the energy and matter that are released when food molecules are broken down. They use the energy and matter to build molecules that their bodies need to carry out life processes. Look at the foods on the grocery shopping list. Decide whether each item on the list comes from plants or animals. Write the name of the food item in the correct column of the table.

Shopping list

turkey	tuna
lemon	berries
chicken breast	almonds
eggs	low-fat milk
salmon	veggies
herbs	garlic
shrimp	fruits

Plant products	Animal products

How Plants Make Food

I can...
Describe how plants make food using sunlight, air, water, and materials in soil.

5-LS1-1, 5.LS2-1

Literacy Skill
Use Evidence from Text

Vocabulary
photosynthesis
chlorophyll

Academic Vocabulary
obtain

▶ **VIDEO**

Watch a video about photosynthesis.

STEM ▷ Connection

Plants provide our world with many services. They prevent soil erosion, filter water, and release oxygen into the air. They also are a source of medicines and beauty products. Every plant plays an important role in its ecosystem. Some plants provide products or services that no other plant can. Protecting plants from extinction also protects the goods and services they provide.

Engineers created the Svalbard Global Seed Vault to protect all plant species. The vault can hold up to 2.5 billion seeds. Keeping seeds ensures that plants do not become extinct. The seeds come from many countries and habitats. About 50 seeds of each type are placed in a tube or bag and sorted in the vault. The vault is kept very cold to preserve the seeds and to keep them from sprouting. The Svalbard Global Seed Vault is located between Norway and the North Pole. This location is far from most human interaction and protected from natural disasters.

▤ **Reflect** In your science notebook, describe which seeds you would take to grow in a garden, if you could visit the seed vault.

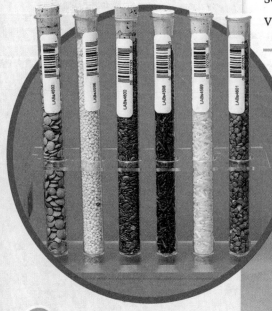

uInvestigate Lab

What matter do plants need to make food?

Scientists study how plants use matter to help them grow. How can you make a model of a sugar molecule to determine what kinds of matter is needed?

Procedure

Science Practice

Scientists use models to investigate natural processes.

☐ **1.** Sort the colored beads into three groups. Choose one color to represent carbon, one for oxygen, and one for hydrogen.

☐ **2.** Build 6 carbon dioxide molecules and 6 water molecules. Water is made up of 2 hydrogens and 1 oxygen. Carbon dioxide, a gas in the air, is made of 1 carbon and 2 oxygens.

☐ **3.** **SEP Develop Models** Use the picture to construct a model of a sugar molecule, using the water and carbon dioxide molecules. Record how many of each type of molecule you used to construct one sugar molecule.

Number of water molecules = _____

Number of carbon dioxide molecules = _____

Analyze and Interpret Data

4. **SEP Use Mathematics** When you put the glucose molecule together, did you use all parts of the carbon dioxide and water molecules? Explain.

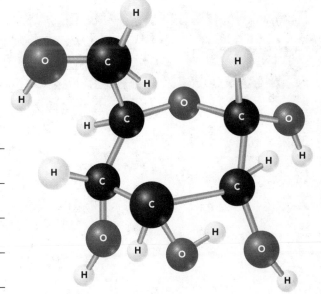

_____

_____

_____

_____

_____

_____

Photosynthesis

Plants use water and carbon dioxide from the air to make a sugar called glucose. In the process, they give off oxygen into the air. This process is called **photosynthesis**. Plants use glucose as food or store it in long, chain-like molecules called starch.

Several structures help plants **obtain**, or get, the matter and energy they need for photosynthesis. Water travels from the ground into plants through roots and then up to the leaves through tubes in the stem. Carbon dioxide in the air enters plants through stomata, small openings on the surface of the plant. Plants trap sunlight energy in structures called chloroplasts. Chloroplasts contain **chlorophyll**, a substance that absorbs sunlight energy. Chlorophyll gives plants their green color.

Infer Where does the matter that plants use for photosynthesis come from?

_____

Model It! Draw a diagram that shows how plants obtain the materials they need for photosynthesis.

How Plants Gain Mass

Have you observed how rapidly plants can grow? Little sprouts can grow into seedlings with leaves in just days. How is this rapid plant growth possible? Scientists have determined that the mass of a new plant is made mostly of carbon, oxygen, and hydrogen.

Water provides the hydrogen that the plant needs to build glucose. Air provides both carbon and oxygen.

Chlorophyll in the chloroplasts absorbs energy from the sun. The plant uses this energy to combine water and carbon dioxide into glucose.

water

+

O C O

carbon dioxide

+

sunlight

=

plant growth

As plants grow, they also need nutrients such as nitrogen, potassium, and phosphorus.

Plant Growth and Light Color

The bean sprouts at the grocery store are young plants. You can plant them in soil, and they will grow. Design an experiment to see how light color affects bean sprout growth. Make sure you use sunlight for one of the plants for comparison.

Photosynthesis and Temperatures

Plants cannot live where water is always frozen. Frozen water cannot travel into roots or up the tubes in stems. Also, photosynthesis includes many reactions. Some of these reactions take place only around certain temperatures.

Plants in very hot areas, such as deserts, must store water when it becomes available. They can store water in their roots, stems, or leaves.

When plants open their stomata to take in carbon dioxide or release oxygen, water can exit plants and travel into the air. This process is called transpiration. Transpiration happens more when it is hot. To reduce transpiration, many desert plants open their stomata only at night. They store carbon dioxide until daytime, when photosynthesis can occur.

☑ **READING CHECK Use Evidence from Text** What evidence in the text supports the claim that too much transpiration can be bad for a plant?

_____

_____

_____

Quest Connection

Why would a nutritionist encourage people to include fruits and vegetables in the food they eat each day?

_____

_____

Nutrients from Soil

As plants absorb water from the ground into their roots, they also take in minerals and nutrients. Nitrogen, phosphorus, iron, and potassium travel into groundwater from soil. Plants need nitrogen and phosphorus to build proteins. They need potassium and iron for a variety of processes. For example, plants use potassium as they open and close stomata. All animals depend on plants directly or indirectly, and plants make these important nutrients available to animals. Many of the nutrients are important to human nutrition. For example, humans need phosphorus to build bones and teeth.

Summarize What are three things animals can get from eating plants?

_____

_____

_____

_____

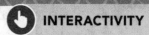 **INTERACTIVITY**

Go online to learn about photosynthesis.

Engineering ▸ Toolbox

Growing Plants in Space
What would astronauts need to grow plants in space? Explain how they could provide all that plants need in a small space with no windows.

☑ Lesson 2 Check

1. Explain How does a plant make glucose?

_____

_____

_____

2. Infer What materials can farmers add to a field in order to help their plants grow?

_____

_____

_____

What plant foods provide the most energy and nutrients?

Materials
- soil
- fast-growing seedlings
- artificial light source
- potting materials

Nutritionists use data to determine what plants are healthier. How can you use data to decide whether plants grown in sunlight are more or less healthy than plants grown in artificial light?

Science Practice

Scientists use evidence to support an argument.

Procedure

☐ 1. Which plants are healthier? Make a hypothesis.

_____

_____

☐ 2. **SEP Plan and Carry Out an Investigation** Plan a procedure to test your hypothesis. Show your plan to your teacher before you begin. Make a table to organize your data.

☐ **3.** Which plants were healthier? Use your data to explain your answer.

_____

_____

_____

Analyze and Interpret Data

4. CCC Energy and Matter How did all of the plants obtain energy and nutrients?

_____

_____

_____

5. SEP Use Evidence Construct an argument to support this claim: Food grown year-round indoors is just as healthy as food grown in season outdoors. Use evidence to support your argument. Give an example.

_____

_____

_____

_____

_____

_____

_____

_____

µEngineer It! Design STEM

VIDEO

Go online to watch a video about coding.

A Code for Plant Matter

Phenomenon Coding is a way to put information into a different format. When something is coded, there are numbers, letters, and symbols assigned to have specific meanings. Software engineers write codes for computers in a language that the computer knows. The computer knows what it is supposed to do for each command given in code. A program is a list of commands for performing a specific task. Programs can give a computer very complicated instructions. Using computer programs helps many jobs go quickly. Some scientists write code to analyze complicated data sets. Engineers may also use code to tell machines how to do complex tasks.

Design It

You are developing a software program that mimics photosynthesis.
Follow the steps to determine how you can develop your code.

☐ A sugar is made from carbon, oxygen, and hydrogen. Choose a letter or other symbol to represent each ingredient.

_____

☐ The materials the plant can use will be carbon dioxide and water. Write out how you can use code to represent those materials.

_____

☐ A sugar molecule includes six carbon atoms, twelve hydrogen atoms, and six oxygen atoms. How many units of each material will the plant need to get enough materials to make a sugar molecule? Write your answer using your code.

_____

☐ Computer codes have inputs and outputs. Your input is what you wrote on the previous line. What will the output of your code be?

_____

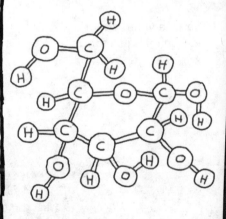

☐ Did the process you coded produce anything besides sugar? How is your process similar to what a real plant does in this way?

_____

_____

_____

How Animals Use Food

I can...

Explain how animals use the energy they get from food.

5-PS3-1

Literacy Skill
Use Evidence from Text

Vocabulary
endotherm
ectotherm
metabolism

Academic Vocabulary
maintain

▶ **VIDEO**

Watch a video about how animals use food.

SPORTS ⟩ Connection

If you eat a lot of food at one time, someone might say you eat like a horse! Horses do need to eat a lot of food to keep their bodies working. Racehorses are some of the hardest working horses. They use kinetic energy to reach speeds from 64 to 69 kilometers (40 to 43 miles) per hour while racing. The average thoroughbred racehorse weighs about 454 kilograms (1,000 pounds). It may eat between 7 and 9 kilograms (15 and 20 pounds) of food a day. Many large animals are carnivores, but horses are herbivores. A racehorse eats a mixture of alfalfa, grass, oats, cracked corn, wheat bran, and linseed meal.

Explain What are two reasons that a racehorse eats so much more than you?

_____

_____

uInvestigate Lab

HANDS-ON LAB

5-PS3-1, SEP.2

How do animals get energy from the sun?

Scientists develop models of interactions in ecosystems. How can you develop a model to show how animals get the energy they need?

Materials
- reference materials

Suggested Materials
- construction paper
- yarn
- markers
- scissors
- Internet

Procedure

☐ 1. **SEP Obtain Information** Select an animal you would like to research. Find out whether the animal is a herbivore, a carnivore, or an omnivore. Record two to three foods the animal eats.

_____

_____

☐ 2. Are the prey animals herbivores, carnivores, or omnivores? Record two to three foods each prey animal eats.

_____

_____

_____

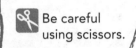 Be careful using scissors.

Science Practice

Scientists use models to describe natural processes.

☐ 3. Determine how many steps are involved when the energy of sunlight travels through other living beings to reach your animal. Construct a model that shows these steps.

Analyze and Interpret Data

4. **CCC Energy and Matter** How does your animal use the energy it gets? How can you show this step on your model?

_____

_____

_____

_____

Lesson 3 How Animals Use Food ⠀ **339**

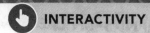

INTERACTIVITY

Complete an activity about how animls use energy to maintain body temperature.

Crosscutting Concepts ▸ Toolbox

Energy and Matter Energy can be transferred between objects. This means that one object gives energy to another. Draw a model of a prey animal giving energy to a predator animal. Use arrows to indicate the direction of energy transfer and labels to specify what forms of energy are involved.

Energy and Body Heat

Animals use energy for everything they do. But not all uses are easy to identify, such as the energy some animals use to maintain body heat. When you **maintain** something, you keep it stable and consistent. If you have ever taken your temperature, the thermometer should have shown your temperature to be near 37 °C (98.6 °F). That is the normal body temperature for a human. The normal body temperature for other animals can be different.

At a normal temperature, the processes that keep your body alive and healthy can take place. Even if your environment is very cold or very hot, your internal body temperature stays close to that temperature. This is because humans are endotherms. An **endotherm** is an animal that uses energy stored in its body to keep its body within a normal range. Endotherms are often called warm-blooded. All mammals and birds are endotherms.

Snakes are ectotherms. An **ectotherm** is an animal that depends on its environment to warm its body. Most fish, all reptiles, and all insects are ectotherms. Ectotherms often get energy by lying in the sun. If the environment cannot warm the animal's body to a correct temperature, the animal will reduce its need for warmth by remaining inactive.

✓ **READING CHECK** **Use Evidence from Text** Underline the text that tells why all animals need their bodies to be in the normal temperature range.

Energy and Metabolism

When an animal eats food, it is taking in chemical energy stored in the plant or animal it eats. Animal cells use some of this energy during the process of cellular respiration. In the process, the chemical energy stored in food is released to provide cells with energy they need to perform life processes. For example, animals use some energy to build complex molecules from simple ones. These complex molecules help animals grow, perform daily tasks, heal, and reproduce. Animals may eat more food than their bodies need. The unused food may be used to build fat tissue that is stored in the body. Or the unused food may be expelled from the body as waste.

The collection of chemical processes that break down and build molecules in a living organism is called **metabolism**. Animal metabolism can be fast or slow. For example, the speed of an ectotherm's metabolism depends on temperature. When the body of an ectotherm is warm, its metabolism speeds up. When the body is cold, its metabolism slows.

Very active and small endotherms often have a faster metabolism than slower or larger organisms. Small animals also become cold faster than large animals. To stay warm, small animals break down more food to release heat. This causes a faster metabolism. A pocket mouse has a fast metabolism. A sloth has a very slow metabolism. Animals with a fast metabolism need foods that provide energy quickly. Many plant foods provide an immediate source of sugars or starches that can provide energy quickly.

Infer Would an animal with a slow metabolism or a fast metabolism need to eat more often? Why?

_____

_____

_____

_____

Energy Tracker

Write a list of all the ways you use energy during one hour of the day. Start at the beginning of the hour and list ways your body moved. Why do you think eating food is necessary to complete all of these actions?

Energy and Movement

Movement, such as the jump of this rabbit, is often the most obvious way that an animal uses energy. An animal's body needs energy for body parts to move. The chemical energy in an animal's food can be transformed into the kinetic energy of movement.

Body movements can be categorized into locomotor movements and nonlocomotor movements. Locomotor movements involve moving the body from one place to another place. When animals walk, run, jump, chase, fly, sprint, and swim, they are doing locomotor activities. Non-locomotor movements do not transport the animal but involve movement of body parts at a fixed point. Twisting, shaking, bending, and stretching are all nonlocomotor movements.

Quest Connection

Why should a person's dinner plate include some foods that are high in Calories?

_____

_____

_____

_____

_____

Internal Uses of Energy

You could easily see this elephant and her young walk. But you cannot see other activities happening inside their bodies. The heart, kidneys, liver, lungs, and all of the organs in an animal's body need energy to function. Thinking, breathing, and sweating all require energy. Growth is also the result of internal processes. The young elephant will increase in size and mass from the time it is born until it is a full-sized adult. Animals must also use energy to grow new tissues when they heal.

When animals use energy, they must replace the energy by eating more food. Even though digestion of food in the stomach helps replace energy, the digestion process also requires energy!

Animals have bodies that are more complex than the bodies of plants. As a result, they need a variety of foods to provide the matter, nutrients, and energy needed for more complex structures.

📓 **Make Meaning** In your science notebook, explain why you need to use energy even when you are asleep.

☑ Lesson 3 Check

1. **Infer** An animal has a body temperature of 39 °C (102°F) one morning and 45 °C (113°F) the next morning. Is this animal an endotherm or an ectotherm? Explain.

   _____

   _____

   _____

2. **Identify** What are two ways you use energy that cannot be seen and two ways you use energy that can be seen?

   _____

   _____

   _____

Animals Using Energy

Choose one of the animals in the pictures. List 10 words to describe how the animal uses energy.

_____

_____

Research to find out what foods your animal eats to get the energy it needs. Find out how many Calories it needs each day.

dog

_____

_____

Use your information to fill out the card. Compare your card with the cards of classmates who chose a different animal.

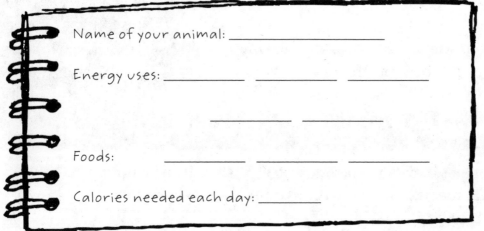

Name of your animal: _____

Energy uses: _____ _____ _____

_____ _____ _____

Foods: _____ _____ _____

Calories needed each day: _____

kingfisher

What patterns do you observe in the animal activities, diets, and Caloric needs?

_____

_____

_____

_____

elephant

EXTREME science

The Hungriest Animals!

Most animals eat according to their size, but some small animals have huge appetites. The hummingbird eats twice its weight in food each day. A typical hummingbird weighs about as much as a few pennies. They eat a lot of nectar because their wings flap many times per second. That movement takes a lot of energy.

The American pygmy shrew is the smallest mammal on Earth. It has a mass of only 2 grams. You would think it would eat less than 1 gram of food each day, but it can eat three times that much! It eats about 6 grams of food each day. The pygmy shrew does not sleep more than a few minutes at a time. That way it can be continuously hunting and eating. The American pygmy shrew has a very fast metabolism!

How much would someone your age, who had a mass of 32 kilograms, have to eat in order to be one of the hungriest animals?

Start with the person's mass in kilograms (kg).

_____

How many kilograms of food would the person have to eat to be as hungry as an American pygmy shrew?

_____

7,700 Calories are needed to build 1 kilogram of body mass. Calculate how many Calories the person would need to eat in one day to triple the person's body mass.

_____

INTERACTIVITY

Complete an activity to help with your Quest Findings.

Plan Your Plate!

Why do plants and animals need food?

Phenomenon It is now time to construct a food plate for each meal a person eats in a day. The food on the plates should give the person the energy and nutrients that he or she needs for an active day.

List the criteria your meals must meet. Remember that a human needs a variety of plant and animal foods. Also consider whether humans have a fast metabolism.

_____

_____

_____

_____

Decide what foods the person should eat in a day. Then organize those foods into three meals.

Breakfast	Lunch	Dinner
_____	_____	_____
_____	_____	_____
_____	_____	_____
_____	_____	_____
_____	_____	_____

Use your list to draw each meal on a separate paper plate.

Nutritionist

Nutritionists help people make healthy food choices. They evaluate the quality of a person's diet and make suggestions about what foods to add or remove. Nutritionists know the type of vitamins a person needs and what foods provide them. They can help people lose or gain weight. Sometimes nutritionists make a meal plan for their clients. This tells clients exactly what to eat at each meal.

People working as a nutritionist usually need a four-year college degree. They often must work in a training program and pass a test to be certified to work in the job.

To be a nutritionist, you should be good at working with people. Nutritionists are skilled at dealing with numbers and charts. Some tools they use are scales, nutrition tables, and calculators.

Nutritionists can work in private practices, physician offices, hospitals, long-term care facilities, and other institutions. They also work in food services in schools, prisons, hospitals, and cafeterias.

▌ Write About It
In your science notebook, tell whether you would like to be a nutritionist. Why or why not?

1. Interpret Diagrams How would you fill in the missing part of this model to show how a lion's food contains energy that was once energy from the sun?

A. draw a lion eating a plant

B. draw a zebra sitting in the sun

C. draw the plant sitting in the sun

D. draw a lion sitting in the sun

2. Identify Which food comes from a source that gets energy directly from the sun?

A. a pork chop

B. a glass of milk

C. an ear of corn

D. a slice of cheese

3. Summarize How does a plant make food? Include the three important resources necessary for plant growth.

_____

_____

_____

_____

_____

_____

_____

_____

_____

4. Vocabulary A snake relies on the sun to keep its body temperature at a safe range. This snake is a(n) _____.

A. ectotherm

B. endotherm

C. omnivore

D. herbivore

5. Describe What are three different ways an animal uses energy from its food?

_____

_____

_____

_____

_____

_____

_____

_____

6. Infer Which animal is not using energy from its food to do its activity?

A. A polar bear sleeps when it hibernates.

B. A tiger rests as it digests its food.

C. A lizard sits in the sun to get warmer.

D. A crocodile lays eggs in a nest.

7. Identify Which choice is a kind of matter that plants use to make food?

A. nitrogen

B. sunlight

C. oxygen

D. sugar

The Essential Question

Where does food's energy come from and how is food used?

Show What You Learned

Write a short story telling how energy enters a herbivore and travels through an omnivore to reach a carnivore.

_____

_____

_____

_____

_____

_____

_____

_____

_____

_____

_____

_____

_____

_____

_____

_____

Read this scenario and answer questions 1–4.

A scientist was taking observations in a forest. She wanted to understand the flow of matter and energy through the ecosystem. She recorded her observations in the table.

Organism	What it eats	What it is food for
mouse	oak tree (seeds)	owl
owl	mouse	
deer	fern	vulture
fern		deer
oak tree		mouse
vulture	deer	

1. The scientist did not fill in the box for what the fern eats. What is the best explanation for this?

   A. The scientist did not observe the fern eating another organism.

   B. Ferns need energy to survive, but they do not need matter.

   C. Ferns feed underground, so the scientist could not observe the food source.

   D. Ferns can survive for long periods without any food.

2. The scientist argues that matter from the oak tree can be found inside of the owl. Explain why you either do or do not think the scientist is correct.

   _____

   _____

   _____

3. What should the scientist include in the middle box to complete this model?

    A. a fern

    B. a deer

    C. a mouse

    D. a vulture

4. The scientist finds out that humans will be hunting deer in the forest she is studying. She argues that hunters who eat the deer will eat food that gets energy from the sun. Explain why you either do or do not agree with the scientist.

_____

_____

_____

_____

_____

_____

_____

_____

_____

How does matter move through an ecosystem?

Suggested Materials
- colored clay
- drawing paper
- markers

Phenomenon Scientists build models to explain interactions. How can you build a model to explain the interactions between matter, energy, and living things?

Science Practice

Scientists use models to explain natural processes.

Procedure

☐ **1.** How does matter move through an ecosystem?

_____

_____

_____

☐ **2. SEP Develop a Model** Design a model to demonstrate the movement of matter in an ecosystem. Use any of the materials. Write or draw your idea.

☐ **3.** Show your plan to your teacher before you make your model.

Analyze and Interpret Data

4. **Evaluate** Why was it important that your model showed matter from animals returning to the environment?

_____

_____

_____

5. **Analyze** Do all of the organisms in the photo get matter from the same source? Explain why or why not.

_____

_____

_____

Matter and Energy in Ecosystems

Next Generation Science Standards
5-LS2-1 Develop a model to describe the movement of matter among plants, animals, decomposers, and the environment.

Go online to access
your digital course.

▶ VIDEO

📖 eTEXT

👆 INTERACTIVITY

🧪 VIRTUAL LAB

🎮 GAME

☑ ASSESSMENT

The Essential Question

How can you model the interaction of living things in an ecosystem?

Show What You Know

This surprised cricket feeds on field grasses. What might happen to the chameleon population if a drought greatly reduces the grass population?

_____

_____

_____

STEM Public Relations Gone Wild!

How can we improve public opinion of important, but disliked, animals?

Phenomenon Hi, I'm Daphne Suh, a zoologist that works to protect important animals. Many animals that need help seem dangerous or creepy to people. Bats may seem scary, for example, but they can help control insect populations. While insects are an important food source for many organisms, some can be harmful.

I need your help to improve the public image of some disliked animals. On this Quest, you will create a video to improve an animal's public reputation.

Follow the path to learn how you will complete the Quest. The Quest activities in the lessons will help you complete the Quest! Check off your progress on the path when you complete an activity with a QUEST CHECK ✓ OFF . Go online for more Quest activities.

Quest Check-In 1

Lesson 1
Choose an animal and research its ecosystem.

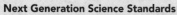

Next Generation Science Standards
5-LS2-1 Develop a model to describe the movement of matter among plants, animals, decomposers, and the environment.

VIDEO

Watch a video about a zoologist.

Quest Check-In 4

Lesson 4

Find out how your animal helps transfer energy and matter through its ecosystem. Explain what might happen if your animal disappeared from its community.

Quest Check-In Lab 3

Lesson 3

Investigate how your animal responds to changes in its environment.

Quest Findings

Create a video that helps people understand the important role your animal plays in its ecosystem. Give your animal a public relations boost!

Quest Check-In 2

Lesson 2

Identify the unique role your animal has in its ecosystem.

STEM uConnect Lab

How do the parts in a *fish* *tank* make up a **system**?

Scientists make models of systems to understand how they function. How can you model an aquatic ecosystem?

Develop a Model

☐ **1.** Write a sentence that explains why a fish tank is a system.

_____

_____

☐ **2.** Make a list of all the living and nonliving things fish may need to survive and thrive in a fish tank.

_____

_____

_____

☐ **3. SEP Develop Models** Using your list and the materials, plan how you can build a model fish tank. Show your plan to your teacher, and then build your model.

Analyze Models

4. Use the table to identify how each part of your model fish tank interacts with the other parts.

Fish tank part	Interactions

Suggested Materials

- plastic aquatic animals
- plastic plants or plant cuttings
- construction paper
- modeling clay
- scissors

 Be careful using scissors.

Science Practice

Scientists use models to explain natural processes.

Compare and Contrast

When you are learning about a new idea, you often can compare and contrast the information with what you already know.

- When you compare things, you look for how they are alike.
- When you contrast things, you look for how they are different.

Read the following paragraph about bicycles.

Bicycle Basics

The bicycle is a system with many parts that work together to make the bicycle move. Each part of the bicycle has an important role in making the bicycle work. The rider provides the force to make the bike move. The metal frame supports the rider's weight. The pedals turn the wheels. The wheels help the bicycle move smoothly across a surface.

☑ **READING CHECK** **Compare and Contrast** How are a fish tank and a bicycle alike and different?

_____

_____

_____

_____

Ecosystems

I can...

Describe the components of an ecosystem.

5-LS2-1

Literacy Skill
Compare and Contrast

Vocabulary
ecosystem
abiotic
biotic
community

Academic Vocabulary
interact

▶ **VIDEO**

Watch a video about ecosystems.

SPORTS Connection

At a volleyball match, the server tosses a ball high in the air. She leaps and smacks the ball over the net. The defender on the far side dives, but he is a moment too late. The ball hits the court just inside the boundary line—it is in! The players, net, ball, and referees are all part of a system that makes a volleyball match work.

What would a volleyball match look like if some parts, such as the ball, did not work the way they should? No action would take place. Each part of a system has a specific role that helps the whole system function. Without certain parts, the system functions poorly or not at all.

Draw Conclusions What would happen to a volleyball match if there were no rules or referees?

_____

_____

_____

_____

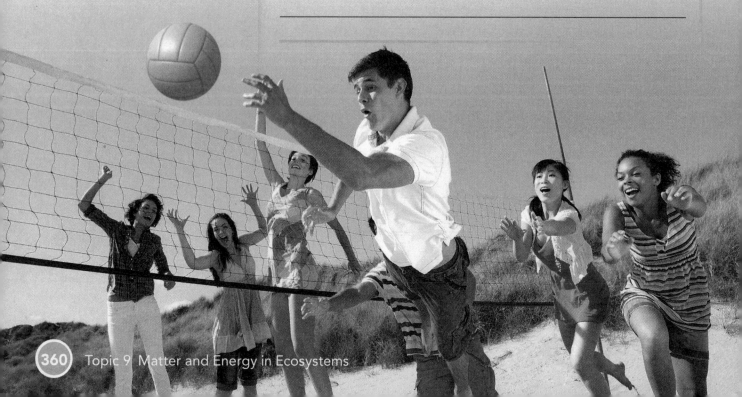

How do the parts of an ecosystem work together?

Scientists plan investigations to collect specific data to answer a scientific question. How can you investigate what parts form a natural system?

Procedure

☐ 1. **CCC Systems** Identify a system that you can observe. The system should have both living things and nonliving things. Record the system you will observe.

_____

☐ 2. Write a plan to observe how the living and nonliving parts of the system work together. Use any of the materials.

☐ 3. Show your plan to your teacher before you begin. Record your observations.

Nonliving things	Living things	Interactions

Suggested Materials
- binoculars
- hand trowel
- magnifying lens
- thermometer
- bowls
- spoons

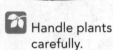 Handle plants carefully.

Handle animals carefully.

Science Practice

Scientists plan and carry out investigations to answer a scientific question.

Analyze and Interpret Data

4. **CCC Systems and System Models** How do the living and nonliving parts of the system you observed work together?

_____

_____

Ecosystems

A poison dart frog begins its climb up a tall tree in this tropical forest. Eventually, the frog reaches a bromeliad plant with stiff leaves. Frequent rains cause small puddles in the bromeliad's leaves. The frog places its tadpoles in one of these puddles. The tadpoles are far from the ground and away from snakes. They will feed on algae and mosquito eggs in the puddled water until they develop into full-grown frogs.

The frog, bromeliad, algae, mosquitos, air, and water are parts of an ecosystem. An **ecosystem** is all the living and nonliving components in a particular area. The components of the ecosystem interact. When two things **interact**, they affect one another. There are ecosystems anywhere that living things are found, including the highest mountain, the deepest ocean, the hottest desert, or the coldest Arctic place.

Describe Write about the interaction of two organisms that you have seen.

_____

_____

_____

Quest Connection

What is one reason an animal can be important to its ecosystem?

_____

_____

_____

Parts of an Ecosystem

Scientists refer to the nonliving parts of an ecosystem as **abiotic** factors. Abiotic factors include air, water, rocks, soil, sunlight, and temperature. The living parts of an ecosystem are **biotic** factors. The biotic parts of an ecosystem can be as small as a bacterium or as large as the tallest tree on Earth. All the organisms living together in an ecosystem make up a **community**. The community's members depend on one another to fill needs, such as mates or protection.

Water, temperature, and sunlight determine the number and types of organisms that can live in an ecosystem. The rain forest of Colombia has many types of organisms. The desert of Libya has only a few types of organisms. The graph shows the difference in the amount of rainfall each place gets. The warm, wet conditions of rain forests can support many organisms. The dry conditions of a desert cannot support a large number of organisms.

☑ **READING CHECK** **Compare and Contrast** Choose two ecosystems from the graph. How are their biotic and abiotic factors similar? How are they different?

_____

_____

_____

_____

_____

_____

_____

_____

_____

Compare and Contrast
Does an interaction have to be between two living things? How does the meaning of the word change in different situations?

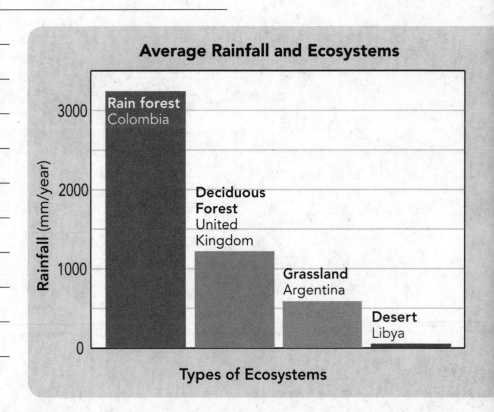

Average Rainfall and Ecosystems

Rainfall (mm/year)

3000

Rain forest
Colombia

2000

Deciduous
Forest
United
Kingdom

1000

Grassland
Argentina

Desert
Libya

0

Types of Ecosystems

How do factors interact in a forest ecosystem?

Identify Circle the biotic factors you observe in the forest ecosystem. Draw a square around the abiotic factors you observe.

Describe What are two ways that abiotic factors and biotic factors interact in this ecosystem?

👆 **INTERACTIVITY**

Complete an activity about interactions in an ecosystem.

Ecosystem Size

If you have an aquarium at home, you have your own ecosystem! An aquarium is a small ecosystem. The aquarium walls are its boundary. The continent of Australia is a large ecosystem surrounded by oceans. Ecosystems can be any size. They can be as small as a drop of water or larger than an entire forest. In fact, the entire Earth is an ecosystem. Regardless of their size, all ecosystems consist of abiotic and biotic components that interact.

Explain What are two ways that the biotic and abiotic factors in an aquarium interact?

_____

_____

_____

☑ Lesson 1 Check

1. Explain How is a neighborhood park a system?

_____

_____

_____

2. Identify What are two biotic factors and two abiotic factors in your classroom?

_____

_____

_____

Unwelcome Inhabitants

Choose an important, but disliked, animal to research. Before you start your Quest, confirm with your teacher that the animal is a good candidate for a public relations boost.

Animal I have chosen: _____

☐ Why do some people dislike this animal? Does the reason have to do with its interaction with humans or a pattern of behavior?

_____

_____

_____

_____

_____

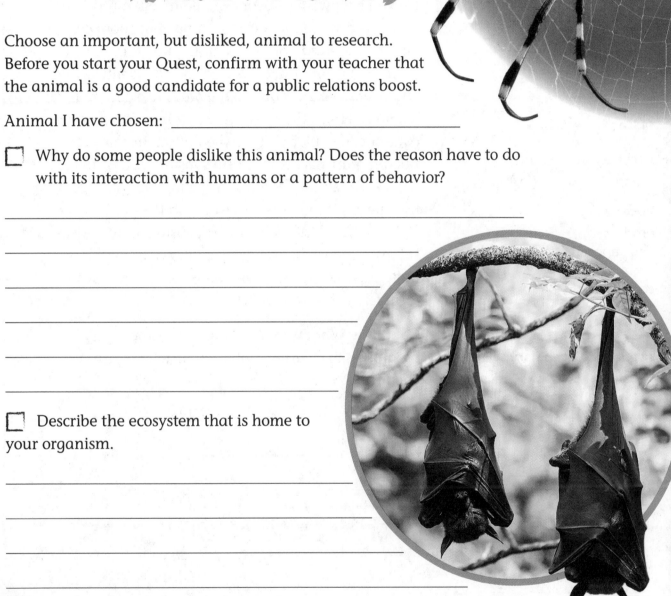

☐ Describe the ecosystem that is home to your organism.

_____

_____

_____

_____

_____

_____

_____

Organisms Within Ecosystems

I can...

Describe how organisms use matter. Describe the relationships between organisms in an ecosystem.

5-LS2-1

Literacy Skill
Compare and Contrast

Vocabulary
producer
decomposer
microbe
consumer
food chain
food web

Academic Vocabulary
transfer

▶ **VIDEO**

Watch a video about organisms and ecosystems.

STEM ⟩ Connection

Do you ever wish someone would invent a robot to clean your room for you? Cleaning your room can be difficult—and boring! Cleaning up oil in seawater after an oil spill is a lot more difficult. Scientists and engineers seek new and better ways to clean up toxic chemicals from the environment. One method they continue to explore is bioremediation. In this process, microorganisms use harmful substances as a food source. For example, some oil-eating bacteria use the oil that is in the ocean water. In the process, they change the oil into a harmless substance. Scientists have successfully used bioremediation to clean up harmful materials, such as sewage, industrial wastes, pesticides, farm fertilizers, and gasoline.

Compare What is an advantage of using living organisms to clean up pollution instead of using chemicals?

_____

_____

_____

How can matter change in an ecosystem?

Scientists study how matter from organisms becomes part of the soil in an ecosystem. How do bananas break down in soil?

Materials
- sealable plastic bags
- banana slices
- yeast
- soil
- spoon
- apron
- plastic gloves

 Wear plastic gloves.

 Wear safety apron.

 Do not taste materials.

Procedure

☐ 1. What do you think will happen to banana slices when they are buried in soil? How do you think adding yeast to the bananas will affect what happens? Write a prediction.

_____

_____

_____

☐ 2. **SEP Plan an Investigation** Write a procedure to test your prediction. Show your procedure to your teacher before you begin. Record your observations.

Observations

Analyze and Interpret Data

3. **CCC Cause and Effect** Do your results support your prediction? What do you think caused the results?

_____

_____

_____

Science Practice

Scientists interpret data to explain relationships.

Producers

Every kind of organism must get energy and matter from its environment. Organisms need energy to carry on life processes, such as moving and reproducing. They need matter to grow, to reproduce, and to repair damaged body parts. All organisms get matter and energy from food, but different kinds of organisms get their food in different ways.

An organism that makes its own food using nonfood matter and energy from the sun is called a **producer**. Plants are producers. They use sugars as food, but they make these sugars from water and carbon dioxide, which are not food. Plants use the energy of sunlight to combine these ingredients and make the sugars they need.

Producers need food, but they do not take food from the environment. Instead, a producer takes in energy and nonliving matter. It uses this energy and matter to build all of its parts. When other organisms eat a producer, they take in this matter and energy. Without producers, matter and energy would not be available to other organisms in an ecosystem.

Summarize What does the tree need from its environment?

_____

_____

_____

Growing crops on the same land year after year uses up soil nutrients that plants need. Fertilizers are applied to add nutrients back into the soil. But fertilizer use is linked to pollution in groundwater. Identify a problem to be solved in this situation. Write a question you could ask to help solve this problem.

Decomposers

Plants take nutrients from the soil and make them available to animals. So why do the essential nutrients in the soil not run out?

The rotting vegetables in the photo do not look like anything you would eat. They have started to decay, or rot. When organisms die, their bodies decay. This process releases nutrients from the dead organisms that can be returned to the soil. Decomposers are necessary for decay to happen. **Decomposers** are organisms that break down, or decompose, other organisms' bodies after they die. They also break down the wastes that animals produce. If you see mushrooms growing on a dead log, then the matter in the dead log is being broken down by decomposers. Even if you do not see decomposers on something that is rotting, they are at work. Many decomposers are microbes. **Microbes** are organisms that are too small to see. These include bacteria and very small fungi. Larger decomposers include earthworms and flies.

✓ **READING CHECK** **Use Evidence** Why are decomposers an important part of an ecosystem?

Visual Literacy Connection

Who eats whom?

Organisms that cannot produce their own food must eat other organisms. They are called consumers. Some consumers eat only producers, some eat only other consumers, and some eat both. The arrows in this diagram show how matter and energy flow from food source to consumer.

Blue Whale

The largest animal in the ocean feeds on the smallest. Zooplankton gets caught in the comb-like sheets, called baleen, that blue whales have instead of teeth. Energy and matter flow from the zooplankton to the whale.

Phytoplankton

Zooplankton

Zooplankton are tiny animals that eat even smaller producers called phytoplankton. They are weak swimmers, so they drift along with currents.

! **What would happen if zooplankton were removed from this ecosystem?**

_____

_____

_____

_____

Clams

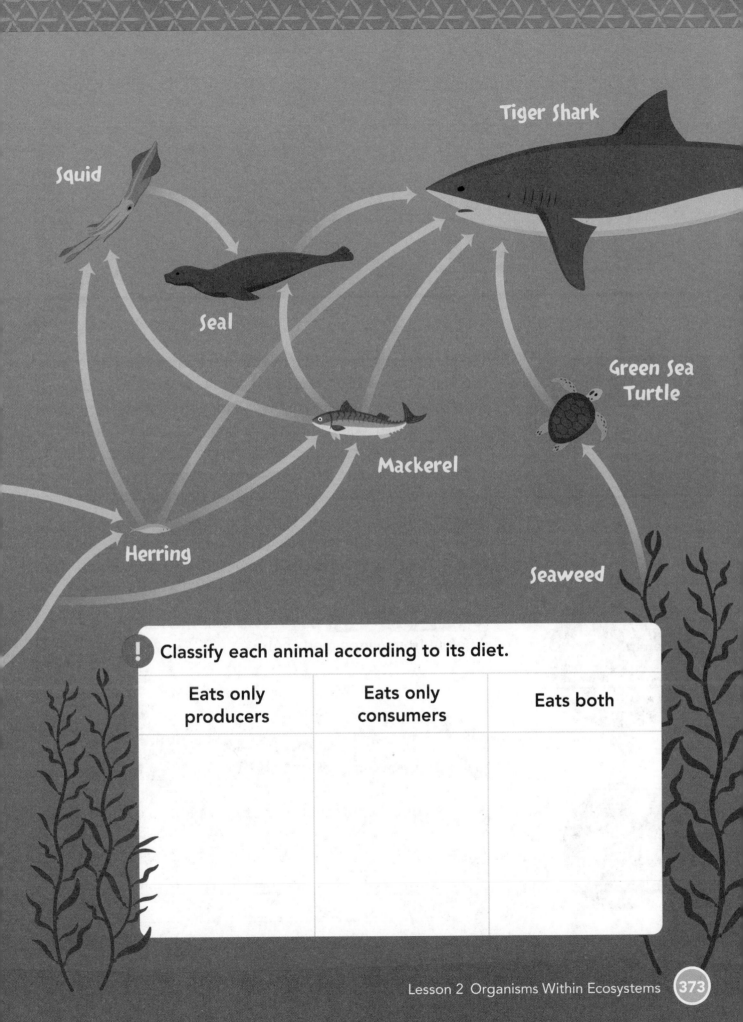

Squid

Tiger Shark

Seal

Green Sea Turtle

Mackerel

Herring

Seaweed

! Classify each animal according to its diet.

Eats only producers	Eats only consumers	Eats both

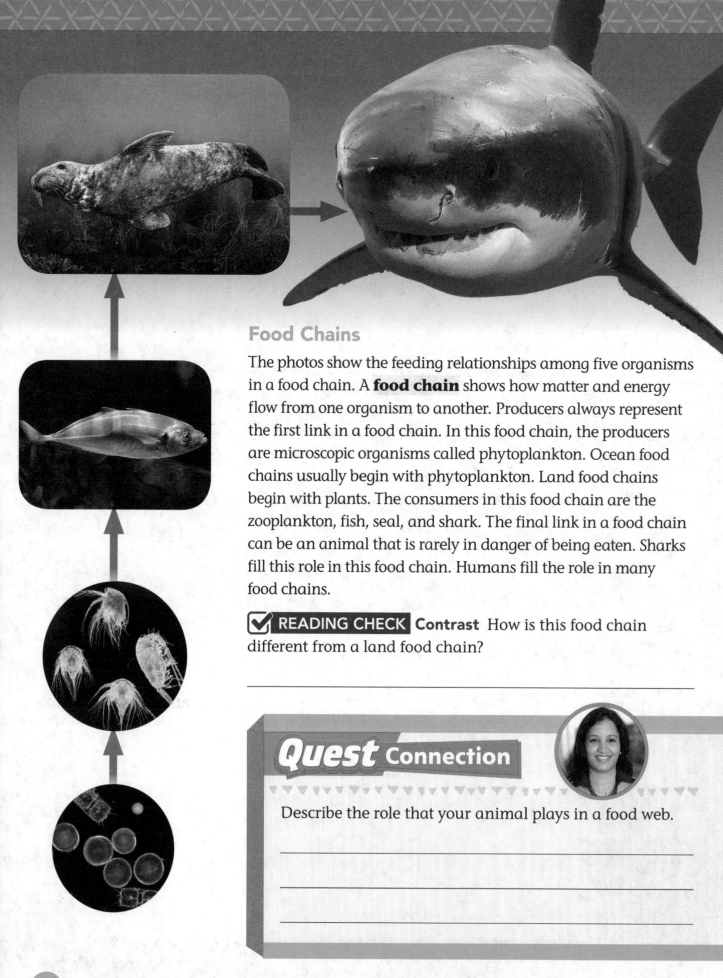

Food Chains

The photos show the feeding relationships among five organisms in a food chain. A **food chain** shows how matter and energy flow from one organism to another. Producers always represent the first link in a food chain. In this food chain, the producers are microscopic organisms called phytoplankton. Ocean food chains usually begin with phytoplankton. Land food chains begin with plants. The consumers in this food chain are the zooplankton, fish, seal, and shark. The final link in a food chain can be an animal that is rarely in danger of being eaten. Sharks fill this role in this food chain. Humans fill the role in many food chains.

✓ **READING CHECK** **Contrast** How is this food chain different from a land food chain?

_____

Quest Connection

Describe the role that your animal plays in a food web.

_____

_____

_____

Food Webs

Food chains can be longer than the one shown. And they can be made up of more organisms. For this reason, a food chain is not a good tool for describing the **transfer**, or movement, of matter and energy in an ecosystem. For example, the shark will eat more kinds of animals than just the seal. To get a better picture of the feeding relationships in an ecosystem, use a food web. A **food web** is a set of interconnected food chains. The feeding relationships that you read about on the Visual Literacy Connection make up a food web.

📖 **Make Meaning** In your science notebook, draw a food web that shows how you are connected to other organisms by feeding relationships.

INTERACTIVITY

Complete an activity about producers, consumers, and decomposers.

Polar bears are part of an Arctic food web.

✅ Lesson 2 Check

1. Identify How do organisms use matter?

_____

_____

2. Explain How are producers and consumers related?

_____

_____

_____

Connections to Others

To explain to others why an animal is important, you should provide information about how the animal interacts with other organisms.

☐ **1.** Research to find out what your animal's role is in its ecosystem. Find out what it does and how that action affects the ecosystem. Include information about where your animal fits in the ecosystem's food web.

☐ **2.** Decide whether each action has a helpful effect on the ecosystem or a harmful effect. Use the table to organize your information.

Helpful	Harmful

☐ **3.** Summarize the information you collected.

_____

_____

_____

_____

_____

QUEST CHECK ✓ OFF

STEM ⟩ Math Connection

Solve Word Problems

Plants and other producers use most of the energy they get from the sun to power the life processes that keep them alive. Only a small amount of the energy is stored in the cells of the producers. The same is true for consumers. They use most of the energy they get from food to stay alive. They store only a small amount of energy in their bodies. For this reason, consumers that eat tiny organisms must eat many, many individual organisms to get enough matter and energy. Giant anteaters, for example, must eat more than 30,000 ants each day to obtain the energy and matter they need.

How many ants would 6 giant anteaters need to eat in one year to get the matter and energy they need? Write a simple formula to help you solve the problem. Then find the answer.

Change Within Ecosystems

I can...

Identify the characteristics of a healthy ecosystem. Describe how change affects an ecosystem.

5-LS2-1

Literacy Skill
Compare and Contrast

Vocabulary
succession
competition

Academic Vocabulary
stable

▶ **VIDEO**

Watch a video about changes within ecosystems.

LOCAL-TO-GLOBAL ▶ Connection

In 2013, people living in Virginia greeted a rarely seen member of their ecosystem. Once every seventeen years this type of cicada emerges from the ground to feed and mate. Some people living in these areas find the cicadas pesky, especially their loud "singing." However, the cicadas do little damage to the area.

In other parts of the world, however, locusts cause heavy damage to crops. Like cicadas, locusts can gather in large numbers. A single swarm can include billions of locusts. The locusts shown swarming live in the dry areas of Africa and the Middle East. The swarming behavior of locusts is a response to overcrowding. When rare rainfall allows vegetation to grow in a normally dry region, the locusts feast on the vegetation until little or none remains.

☑ **READING CHECK Compare and Contrast** How are locusts different from cicadas?

_____

_____

cicada

locusts

How does change affect organisms in an ecosystem?

Scientists and engineers use models to study how changes affect organisms in ecosystems. How might the migration of more consumers into an ecosystem affect the ecosystem's producers and consumers?

Materials
• green, red, and blue colored chips

Science Practice

Scientists use models to understand how change affects complex systems.

Procedure

☐ 1. Use the colored chips to represent producers and consumers in a food chain: green chips = plants, red chips = rabbits, blue chips = wolves. Count out 40 plants, 10 rabbits, and 2 wolves to place in a community.

☐ 2. **SEP Develop Models** Find a way to use the information in the table to model the normal patterns of predation and reproduction during a single season.

☐ 3. Complete the table with the information you find.

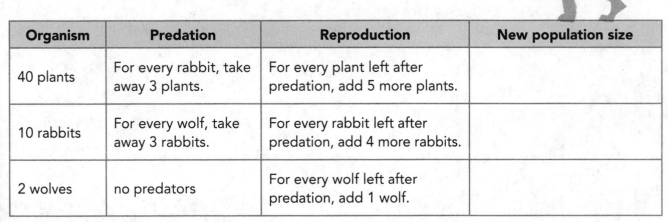

Organism	Predation	Reproduction	New population size
40 plants	For every rabbit, take away 3 plants.	For every plant left after predation, add 5 more plants.	
10 rabbits	For every wolf, take away 3 rabbits.	For every rabbit left after predation, add 4 more rabbits.	
2 wolves	no predators	For every wolf left after predation, add 1 wolf.	

Analyze and Interpret Data

4. **SEP Analyze Data** What will happen to the wolf and plant population sizes if a pack of 5 more wolves arrived? Why?

_____

_____

_____

What happens to a forest ecosystem after a fire?

Changes to ecosystems differ in how they affect ecosystems. For example, heavy spring rains might cause an increase in plant populations for a season. A large forest fire, however, has severe, long-term effects on an ecosystem. Succession refers to a series of changes in a community. Over time, ecosystems develop on land that has been damaged by fire. They also form on new land where no animals or plants lived before, such as land formed by volcanoes. When plants and animals start living on new land, the process is called primary succession. When plants and animals return to disturbed or damaged land, the process is called secondary succession.

Fire

Weeds, grasses, and flowering plants

0 years

after 1–4 years

Infer How does the community food web change over time during secondary succession? Why?

_____

_____

_____

_____

_____

_____

_____

_____

Apply Concepts Why do producers return to the ecosystem before consumers and decomposers?

_____

_____

_____

_____

Shrubs, pines, young oak and hickory

Mature oak and hickory forest

after 5–150 years

after 150 years

Stable Ecosystems

Organisms can survive only in ecosystems that meet their needs. A stable ecosystem can meet the needs of multiple species, or kinds of organisms. **Stable** means steady, or unchanging. For example, a stable lake ecosystem, such as the one in the photo, will have similar conditions from year to year.

The number of individuals of each species in a stable ecosystem may change a bit over time as conditions change slightly. But during the changes, the ecosystem remains stable. For example, during a particular season, some species may have more individuals than during another. In summer, the number of water plants in a lake may be much larger than the number of individuals of a fish species that eats them. In winter, however, the number of water plants may decrease, but the number of fish species may remain about the same. Each year, the cycle continues. The ecosystem is stable.

Describe If an ecosystem changes, is it unhealthy?

_____

_____

_____

Quest Connection

Describe ecosystem changes that your animal experiences on a regular basis. Tell how your animal reacts to the changes.

_____

_____

_____

_____

Threats to Ecosystems

In any ecosystem, organisms compete. **Competition** occurs when organisms in an ecosystem need the same resources. Competition is not a problem unless something causes it to become unbalanced. For example, if a new plant species is introduced into a stable ecosystem, the new plant will compete with other plants for sunlight and water. It may outcompete the other species and spread throughout the ecosystem. Eventually, it may cover the other plants, and they may die.

INTERACTIVITY

Complete an activity about changes in ecosystems.

Characteristics of healthy ecosystems	Threats to healthy ecosystems
• adequate shelter and nesting sites	• habitat loss due to human action and natural events such as forest fires
• balance of decomposers, producers, and consumers	• introduced species that crowd out other species
• a variety of species	• rapidly growing human population
• adequate supply of clean air, water, and nutrients	• overfishing or overharvesting
	• pollution
	• drought

☑ Lesson 3 Check

1. Summarize What are two characteristics of a healthy ecosystem?

_____

_____

_____

_____

2. Explain How can introducing a new species into an ecosystem negatively affect the ecosystem?

_____

_____

_____

How does change affect organisms in an ecosystem?

To understand your animal, you will need to know how it would react to environmental changes. How can you model how a freshwater fish might respond when it is exposed to saltwater?

Materials
- potato sliced into 1 cm disks
- tap water
- saltwater
- paper cups
- weight scale
- paper towels

⚠️ Do not taste.

Procedure

Science Practice

Scientists use models to investigate natural processes.

☐ **1.** Predict what will happen to a freshwater fish in saltwater.

_____

_____

☐ **2.** Look at the materials. Identify the material you can use to model body cells of a fish.

_____

☐ **3. SEP Develop and Use a Model** Write a plan to use your model to test your prediction. Make sure to control your variables and conduct multiple trials. Show your plan to your teacher before you begin.

☐ **4.** Draw a data table to record your measurements and observations.

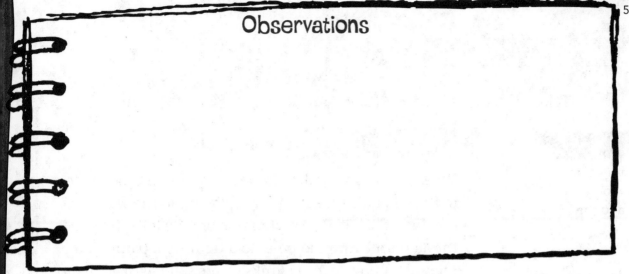

Observations

Analyze and Interpret Data

5. CCC Systems and System Models How did your model help you learn about freshwater fish in saltwater? What is different about your model and a freshwater fish?

_____

_____

_____

_____

6. SEP Explain Do your observations support your prediction? What evidence did you collect?

_____

_____

_____

_____

6. CCC Energy and Matter What can you infer from this investigation about how changes in ecosystems could affect your animal?

_____

_____

_____

_____

Lesson 4

Matter and Energy Transfer Within Ecosystems

I can...

Model the movement of matter among organisms and the environment.

5-LS2-1

Literacy Skill
Use Text Features

Academic Vocabulary
cycle

▶ **VIDEO**

Watch a video about matter and energy transfer in ecosystems.

ENGINEERING ⟩ Connection

When you flush a toilet, the water swirls and the waste in the toilet disappears. What happens to the waste after you flush it? The materials from the toilet flow through underground pipes to a treatment plant. There the wastes flow to large tanks where solid wastes sink to the bottom. In this way, the liquids separate from solids.

The wastewater is pumped into a tank full of tiny decomposers. The decomposers break down any solid waste particles in the remaining water. Then the water is filtered through sand. The resulting clean water is returned to nearby rivers, lakes, or the ocean.

The solid waste that has been collected is scraped into containers and taken to fertilizer plants. Some nutrients are still in the waste. These nutrients can be used to help plants grow better.

📘 **Write About It** All organisms produce waste. In your science notebook, write about how collected wastes contribute to ecosystems.

uInvestigate Lab

How does matter **move** through an **ecosystem**?

Materials
- 40 toy building bricks

Scientists use models to help develop explanations of natural processes. How can you model the movement of matter in an ecosystem?

Science Practice

Scientists use models to help explain natural processes.

Procedure

☐ 1. **SEP Develop Models** How can you model the movement of matter through an ecosystem? Use the building blocks to represent plants, animals, decomposers, and nutrients in the soil.

☐ 2. Brainstorm a plan. Choose one idea to develop as a presentation to other classmates. Draw your plan and then make your model.

☐ 3. **SEP Communicate Information** Present your model to other classmates.

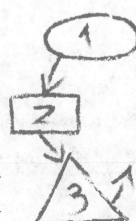

Analyze and Interpret Data

4. **SEP Use Models** How did your model show the movement of matter through an ecosystem?

_____

_____

_____

Research Cycles

Humans depend on cycles, just like plants and animals. Where do your recyclables go? How do they become other products? Investigate how your community recycles materials.

Flow of Matter in Ecosystems

Matter must enter and exit living organisms so that they can get the nutrients they need. The flow of matter in ecosystems cycles. To **cycle** means "to move through a series of steps that repeat." Matter cycles between the air, water, and soil and among plants, animals, and microbes as these organisms live and die. Organisms get matter from the environment, and they release waste matter back into the environment.

The first step in the cycle of matter happens when producers take in matter from the air, soil, and water. Matter travels to consumers when they eat plants or animals. Decomposers break down dead bodies and the wastes organisms make. The broken-down matter can be returned to the soil. New plants will use these nutrients as they grow.

Explain Why is the cycling of matter important?

_____

_____

_____

2 Mushrooms decompose the tree. They return matter to the soil, including nutrients.

3 New plants sprout in the nutrient rich soil.

1 The dead tree stores matter.

Plan It! Suppose you wanted to make a live model to observe the process of decomposition in an ecosystem. Make a drawing of the setup you would use. Label your drawing.

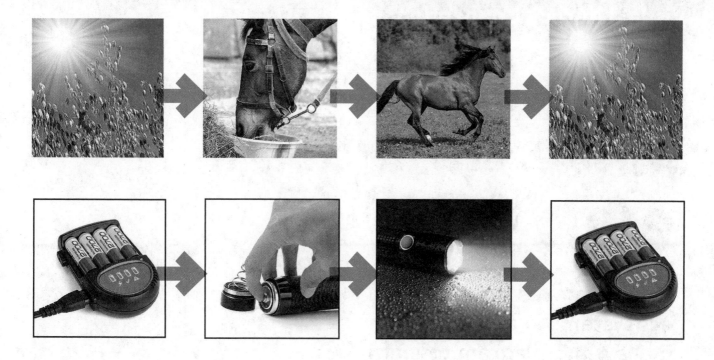

Energy Flow in Ecosystems

When you turn on a flashlight, the batteries in the flashlight provide the energy to cause the light bulb to glow. If you keep the flashlight turned on, eventually the batteries will no longer have enough energy to light the bulbs. The batteries will need to be recharged to gain energy. A similar process happens in ecosystems.

Very little energy that is in the food organisms eat gets stored in their bodies. Energy gets used up as organisms do different activities—moving, digesting food, thinking, breathing, talking, and others. Unless the energy of an organism is recharged, the organism will not be able to carry on life processes. It may die. That is why all organisms must have food—to recharge their supply of energy.

☑ **READING CHECK** **Compare and Contrast** How is energy in an organism similar to energy in a battery?

_____

_____

_____

_____

How does carbon move through ecosystems?

Carbon moves through ecosystems in a cycle. Review the diagram to learn about how carbon cycles.

When the cow breathes, it releases carbon dioxide gas. The carbon in this gas comes from the grass that the cow eats.

The grass takes in carbon dioxide from the air. It uses the carbon to make sugars and to build leaves and other plant parts. When the cow eats the grass, it takes in that carbon.

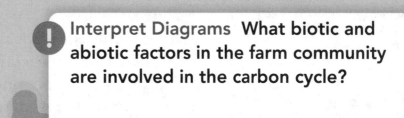

! Interpret Diagrams What biotic and abiotic factors in the farm community are involved in the carbon cycle?

_____

_____

_____

Trees take in carbon dioxide from the air and use it to make sugars, wood, and other kinds of organic matter. The carbon in the carbon dioxide becomes part of the matter that makes up the tree.

A fallen branch decays. Decomposers break down its organic matter. The carbon that was stored in this matter is released as carbon dioxide gas.

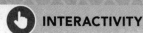
Literacy ▸ Toolbox

Use Text Features
Make an infographic using terms from this lesson to tell the public about one threat to the cycling of matter in ecosystems.

Cycles of Matter

Carbon is only one of the many kinds of matter that cycles again and again. The matter that makes up everything on Earth has been constantly cycling for most of Earth's history. The air you breathe is made up of matter that has been recycled many, many times. This cycling of matter is possible because of the interaction of living things with each other and with their environments. As matter cycles, it is combined and recombined in many different ways.

Infer Describe how the food you eat has been produced by cycled materials.

_____

_____

_____

_____

_____

_____

☑ Lesson 4 Check

1. Model Make a diagram to show how carbon cycles.

2. Cause and Effect What would happen over time to matter in an ecosystem if decomposers were removed?

_____

_____

Moving Matter and Energy

Understanding your animal's role in the cycling of matter and energy will help you explain its importance to the public.

☐ **1.** How does your animal obtain matter and energy?

_____

_____

_____

☐ **2.** What organisms depend on your animal for matter and energy?

_____

_____

_____

☐ **3.** What changes do you think would happen to the flow of matter and energy in the animal's ecosystem if the animal disappeared?

_____

_____

_____

_____

uEngineer It! Model STEM

INTERACTIVITY

Go online to plan an ecosystem.

Ecosystems in a Box

Phenomenon Biosphere 2 is an enclosed research facility in Arizona where scientists study large models of Earth's ecosystems. Biosphere 2 contains a small ocean, a wetland, and a rain forest. The rain forest at Biosphere 2 is warmer than most tropical forests. That is just what scientists want! They use the Biosphere 2 rain forest to model what rain forests might be like if Earth's temperature gets warmer in the future. Carbon dioxide in the air causes Earth temperatures to warm. In Biosphere 2, scientists can change how much carbon is in the rain forest's air. Then they observe how the change affects the ecosystem.

Plan It

Suppose your job at a research facility is to design a working biodome for a desert.

☐ **1.** List the biotic components you will include in your biodome.

_____

_____

_____

☐ **2.** List the abiotic components you will include in your biodome.

_____

_____

_____

☐ **3.** What information about a desert ecosystem would you like to study in the biodome?

_____

_____

_____

_____

☐ **4.** Make a drawing of your biodome.

INTERACTIVITY

Complete activities that will help you with your public relations task.

STEM Public Relations Gone Wild!

How can we improve public opinion of important, but disliked, animals?

Communicate

Phenomenon It is time to make a public relations video about your animal. In public relations, communication must be clear and convincing. Choose evidence, photos, and diagrams that will help people understand why your animal is important in its ecosystem. Be your animal's biggest fan!

Make a list of information, photos, and diagrams you want to include in your video.

Ideas / Photos & Diagrams

_____   _____

_____   _____

_____   _____

_____   _____

_____   _____

Explain

What key fact about your animal is most likely to change public opinion? Why?

_____

_____

_____

Communicate Make your video! Be sure to highlight the key fact you chose about your animal. Show the video to your classmates and ask them if it changed their opinion of your animal.

QUEST CHECK ✓ OFF

Zoologist

Zoologists are life scientists who study animals in the wild or in a laboratory. They investigate animal characteristics, behaviors, interactions, and diseases. Zoologists work at wildlife parks, universities, or conservation groups. To conduct research, they might travel to distant places or face harsh climates. Zoologists often use models to investigate how animals might respond to changes in their environment. They also spend time analyzing data and communicating what they learn to other scientists and the public.

Zoologists traveled 14.5 kilometers (9,000 miles) to study the birds of paradise in Papua New Guinea. To observe the birds, they hiked through thick forests and built platforms near the tops of trees. They used cameras to film the birds' beautiful feathers and elaborate mating rituals. Back at the university, the zoologists wrote scientific papers about the birds' ecosystem interactions. They also produced videos to educate students about the birds, and what it was like to conduct research in the rain forest.

Compare In your science notebook, write ways you are like a zoologist when creating your animal's public relations video.

1. Identify A tree makes its own food using matter from the air and soil. A tree is a

   A. decomposer

   B. producer

   C. consumer

   D. producer and consumer

2. Identify Use the photo of the otter to answer question 2. The abiotic factors in the otter's ecosystem include

   A. air and water

   B. air, water, and sunlight

   C. kelp and crabs

   D. water and kelp

3. Explain What is the connection between a healthy ecosystem and stability?

A healthy ecosystem is Stable, and if a ecosystem is stable it is healthy.

4. Sequence Mount St. Helens erupts. The volcano's mountainsides are blanketed by ash for many months. Number the photographs to show succession after the eruption.

③

②

①

5. Use Diagrams Why are cacti, such as the saguaro and prickly pear, important in a desert ecosystem?

It is because without it many animals wont have homes or food which they rely on affecting the whole ecosystem there.

6. In ecosystems, microbes and other decomposers

A. produce their own food

B. compete with plants

C. return matter to reservoirs

D. cause disease

How can you model the interaction of living things in an ecosystem?

Show What You Learned

Diagrams, analogies, and designed structures can all be used to model natural systems. What are two ways you can model the interaction of your animal with other organisms in its ecosystem?

(a fox gets a rat to eat 1 scenario)(the fox tries to get the rat but it escapes 2 scenario)(   )
    Extra scenarios: (the rat brings other rats to fight back)

Read this scenario and answer questions 1–5.

Many people fear sharks, yet sharks play a very important role in coastal areas. Sharks eat other large consumers, such as seals and rays, which eat fish, squid, and shellfish. Shark numbers are falling in many parts of the world. Humans hunt sharks for their fins and meat. Zoologists are worried about how the loss of sharks will affect coastal communities. They collected data about the numbers of sharks, rays, and scallops along the coast to investigate. Study the graphs of the data they collected, and then answer the questions below.

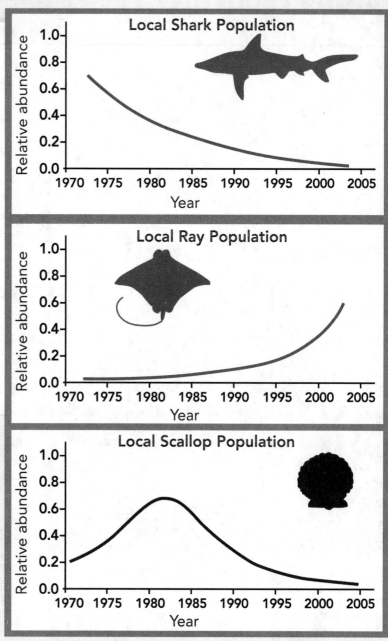

1. Infer What is one food chain in the coastal ecosystem?

A. sharks → scallops → rays

B. rays → scallops → sharks

C. scallops → rays → sharks

D. sharks → rays → scallops

2. Cause and Effect Which statement best explains what happens to scallops when shark numbers fall?

A. Scallop populations decrease because ray populations increase.

B. Scallop populations increase because ray populations decrease.

C. Scallop populations decrease because ray populations decrease.

D. Scallop populations do not change as shark and ray numbers change.

3. **Apply Concepts** Which animal pair shows two competitors?

A. sharks and scallops

B. rays and seals

C. scallops and seals

D. sharks and seals

4. **Use Evidence** What evidence suggests that sharks help stabilize other animal populations in the coastal ecosystem?

large consumer amounts are stable so are small ones. Without sharks large consumers would be out of control, while small consumers were almost none.

5. **Defend a Claim** Use evidence from the text and graphs to defend this claim:

Humans are the top consumer of the coastal food chain.

Humans eat all the coastal animals besides plants like kelp or just scallops. sharks eat large and small fish, large fish eat small fish, small fish eat small stuff so humans eat sharks, large fish, small fish.

How can you model matter cycles in the Earth system?

Phenomenon Earth is an ecosystem. Matter cycles through Earth's abiotic and biotic components. How can you use a model to explain the carbon cycle?

⚠️ Be careful while handling materials.

Design Your Model

Science Practice

Scientists use models to explain natural processes.

☐ 1. **CCC System Models** Use the materials to design a model of how carbon moves through the Earth system. Identify which materials will represent biotic and abiotic parts of the system.

☐ 2. **SEP Design Solutions** Draw a labeled diagram of your model design. Show the design to your teacher before you build your model.

☐ 3. Test your model by showing it to another student in your class, without explanations. Ask the student to identify the parts of your model.

Evaluate Your Model

4. Examine Use the checklist on the card to evaluate your model. Did you build an effective model and follow all constraints?

✓ The model uses all materials provided.
✓ Matter moves through the model.
✓ Another student could identify the parts of the model without needing labels or explanations.

_____

_____

_____

5. Analyze How did the starting amount of water affect your model?

_____

_____

_____

_____

_____

6. Improve Your Design If you were to build a second model, what would you change? How would the change better imitate the cycling of matter through Earth's system? Explain your choices.

_____

_____

_____

_____

_____

_____

7. Apply Identify the organisms in the photo. Then explain how each would be represented in your improved model.

_____

_____

_____

Science Practices

Ask Questions

Science is the study of the natural world using scientific tools and methods. The natural world includes things such as matter, energy, the planets, and living things. It does not include things such as opinions about art or music.

A scientist asks questions and then tries to answer them. For example, a scientist might wonder how a large whale finds its food deep in the ocean. The scientist could first study what others have already learned. Then the scientist could investigate questions that have not been answered. Questions could include "How can a whale hold its breath underwater when it makes a deep dive?" Or, "How does a whale find food in the darkness of the deep ocean?"

Ask Questions What question would you ask about the animal in the photograph?

_____

_____

_____

_____

_____

_____

_____

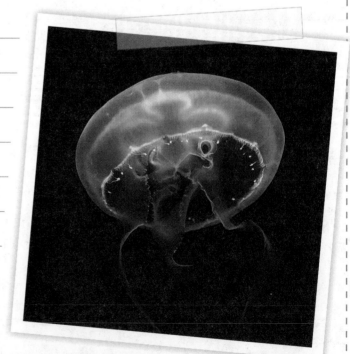

SEP.1 Asking questions and defining problems
SEP.3 Planning and carrying out investigations
SEP.4 Analyzing and interpreting data

Carry Out Investigations

Scientists use investigations and experiments to do their work. Part of an investigation is to observe the natural world to learn about how it works. When scientists make observations, they do not change anything. Scientists collect data from their observations. Quantitative data are expressed as numbers. Qualitative data describe something, such as how it smells or what color it is.

Scientists also investigate the world using experiments. In an experiment, scientists make a change to the object or process they are observing. For example, the amount of salt dissolved in ocean water is not the same everywhere. To find out how quickly salt dissolves in water at different temperatures, a scientist might put identical amounts of salt and water in several containers at different temperatures. The scientist changes the temperature of the containers and measures the time the salt takes to dissolve in each. The part of the experiment that the scientist changes is called the independent variable. The part that changes as a result is called the dependent variable. In this case, the independent variable is temperature, and the dependent variable is the time the salt takes to dissolve. All scientific investigations include collecting data.

Plan an Investigation A scientist is investigating how the amount of salt in water affects the growth of young fish. What are some quantitative data that the scientist can record?

_____

_____

_____

Science Practices

Science Tools

Scientists use tools to take measurements when they collect data. They also use tools to help make observations about the natural world. Scientific tools expand the type of observations that can be made.

Tools for measuring include rulers to measure length, certain glassware to measure volume, thermometers to measure temperature, and balances to measure mass. Different types of tools are needed for taking very small or very large measurements. It is important to use the right tool for the measurement that is to be taken.

Tools that expand what we can detect and measure include microscopes and telescopes. These tools allow people to observe things that are too small or too far away to see.

Cause and Effect Red tides occur when the population of tiny algae grows. The organisms can make toxic substances that harm wildlife and make the water unsafe for people. How would scientists use a microscope when they study a red tide?

_____

_____

_____

Digital Tools

Many modern tools operate using microprocessors or computers. These objects are digital tools. Digital tools include measuring tools such as digital balances and thermometers. They also include tools that scientists use to record and analyze data. Many scientific instruments have a computer that guides data collection and records results. Digital cameras are often a key part of telescopes, microscopes, and other tools used to make observations.

A solar panel provides power for the digital instruments and computer on this buoy. The instruments can measure changes in the ocean.

Computers and other digital devices make data collection faster. Processors can respond to changes and record data much faster than a human observer can. Computers are also important for keeping records and analyzing large numbers of data. Computers and other digital devices are an important part of communication networks that allow scientists to share data and results.

Communicate Scientists communicate in different ways. How could a scientist use a computer to communicate with another scientist?

_____

_____

Science Practices

Analyzing and Interpreting Data

Scientists use empirical evidence when they study nature. Empirical evidence is information that can be observed and measured. Scientific conclusions are always based on evidence that can be tested. These observations and measurements are data that can be used to explain the natural world.

Measurements and observations provide scientists with evidence of changes. For example, when a natural system changes, the change can affect organisms in the system. Scientists can observe and record the changes, such as how many organisms are living in an area at one time compared to another time. Then the scientists can analyze those data to make predictions about the effects of other changes.

Scientists analyze measurements and observations to answer scientific questions. Analyzing measurements of changes in an ecosystem can provide information about how different parts of the natural system work together.

Measure The temperature of water affects ocean currents and marine habitats. How could scientists get empirical evidence about the temperature of the water? Why is this empirical evidence?

_____

_____

_____

_____

Using Math

Careful measurements are necessary for collecting reliable data. Scientists make measurements several times to be sure that the results can be repeated. In general, scientists use digital instruments to collect quantitative data.

Scientists use mathematics to analyze quantitative data. They record measurements and compare them to find out what changes and what stays the same. A number of measurements can be compared to show if something changes over time. Mathematical analysis can also show how fast a change occurs.

When a scientist makes a claim based on evidence, other scientists can check the claim. When other scientists check the claim and find similar results, the claim or findings are supported by similar evidence.

Evaluate How do numerical data from measurements make it easier to compare results in an investigation?

_____

_____

Research ships carry many instruments that gather data.

Science Practices

Constructing Explanations

After scientists analyze data, they use their results to construct explanations of natural phenomena. A scientific explanation often uses the change in variables to relate one change to another. For example, as conditions in marine ecosystems change, organisms living in the water might change in response. Scientists observe changes in ecosystems and study populations of organisms to learn about effects of changes. Then they construct explanations about the organisms.

Developing and Using Models

Scientists often use models to help them understand something. Models are objects or ideas that represent other things. A model only shows part of the thing that it represents.

Scientists also use computers to make models. You can watch on a computer screen how ocean conditions change over time. The model can show you how plant and animal populations are affected. You can even make a model using words. When you describe something, you are making a verbal model of the object. Other people can learn about the object from your spoken model.

Evaluate How could you make a model to explain how a lobster survives on the ocean floor?

_____

_____

_____

SEP.2 Developing and using models
SEP.6 Constructing explanations and designing solutions
SEP.7 Engaging in argument from evidence

Engaging in Arguments from Evidence

Scientific observations are different from opinions. An opinion is a personal belief and is not always based on facts. An example of an opinion is that tuna tastes better than salmon. No facts support this opinion. An example of a fact is that salmon lay their eggs in fresh water. This statement can be supported by observation.

Scientists use evidence to support their conclusions. For example, the conclusion that whales migrate is based on evidence. Whales can be seen in some areas but not in others, depending on the season. Scientists can also track individual whales to see where they go.

When a scientist makes a claim or argument, other scientists can check the evidence that the claim is based on. Different people making the same observation will find the same evidence. Scientific explanations are always based on empirical evidence.

Explain No one has seen a giant squid with a length of 20 meters. How could scientists use evidence to decide whether these animals exist?

_____

_____

_____

_____

_____

Science Practices

Habits of Mind

Scientists must be creative when they design experiments. Science is focused on answering new questions. That often means that scientists must come up with new ways to answer questions. Designing a good experiment requires them to think of new ways to solve problems. They need to think about what could go wrong and how to fix it. For example, a scientist who studies tiny organisms in the ocean might try to count them using a medical machine that counts blood cells.

When scientists develop new methods, they evaluate them to be certain they are collecting the right data to answer the question. After they have analyzed data and reached a conclusion, scientists share the results. Other scientists then review and evaluate the methods and conclusions. This peer review process helps confirm that investigations were correctly designed. Other scientists may also repeat the investigation to confirm that they obtain the same results.

Plan an Investigation Sea urchins eat a lot of kelp, an underwater organism. A scientist concludes that increasing populations of sea otters would help restore kelp forests because otters eat sea urchins. How could other scientists confirm this conclusion?

_____

_____

_____

_____

Communicate Information

Scientists communicate with other scientists to share what they learned. The words that scientists use sometimes have meanings different from the same word used in everyday communication. *Current, heat,* and *record* are examples of words that have a specific meaning in science. In science, for example, *heat* refers to the flow of thermal energy. In everyday use, heat may refer to the temperature on a warm day.

Scientists around the world communicate and evaluate results.

Scientists do not perform a single observation or experiment and then come to a conclusion. They repeat experiments and gather the same kind of information. If the results cannot be repeated, then some of the observations may include errors. It is also important that scientific observations can be repeated by other researchers. Sometimes, other researchers cannot get the same result. Then the scientists compare their methods to find out what is different. An error could have happened in one of the methods.

Being able to repeat results makes a conclusion more reliable, so communication among scientists is important. Scientists communicate their methods and results, so other scientists can repeat them and then compare.

Evaluate A scientist repeats an experiment and gets a different result. What should the scientist do next?

_____

_____

_____

Engineering Practices

Defining Problems

Scientists study the natural world. Engineers apply scientific knowledge to solve problems. The first step of the engineering process is stating a well-defined problem. The engineering problem states exactly what the solution to the problem should accomplish. Engineers ask questions to define problems that need to be solved. For example, an engineer might want to build a probe to take samples very deep in the ocean. The engineer might start by asking "What kinds of tools can do that specific job?" Engineers use scientific knowledge and principles to solve the problem.

Before designing a solution, engineers identify criteria and constraints of the problem. The criteria are what the solution must accomplish. For example, one criterion when building a research submarine is that it must work well under the great pressure of the deep ocean. Constraints are limits on the solution. A constraint could be that a solution not go over a certain cost.

Evaluate A classmate says that the cost of an environmental project should not be considered a constraint. Do you agree? Why or why not?

_____

_____

_____

_____

SEP.1 Asking questions (for science) and defining problems (for engineering)
SEP.6 Constructing explanations (for science) and designing solutions (for engineering)
SEP.8 Obtaining, evaluating, and communicating information

Designing Solutions

Before designing a solution, engineers identify criteria and constraints of the problem. For example, one criterion of a solution to rebuild a harbor could be that it restores a habitat for certain animals. A constraint of the harbor restoration could be that it not cost too much money.

Engineers use the criteria and constraints to develop a solution to the problem. They may think of different ways to solve the engineering problem, then decide which way fits the criteria and constraints best.

After they decide on a solution, engineers build the solution and test it. They may use several different design ideas and evaluate each one. They often can combine the best features of each to come to a final design solution.

Design Solutions When ships release water from distant places, they can introduce invasive species. What kind of engineering solution would help prevent the spread of invasive species?

_____

_____

_____

_____

_____

Engineering Practices

Using Models and Prototypes

Similar to scientists, engineers frequently use models as they design solutions. Engineering models can be actual working devices of a proposed solution. Sometimes these devices represent the final solution, but perhaps on

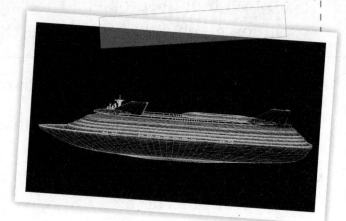

a smaller scale. They may only model one part of the solution. Other models are an actual device at full scale and perform all parts of the solution. This kind of model is called a prototype. Engineers use a prototype to collect data that can help them evaluate the design.

Engineers may use other kinds of models, such as drawings or computer models. A computer model can compare parts of a very complex solution. It allows engineers to make changes and observe what happens without investing a large amount of time or resources to actually build the solution. For example, an engineer investigating ways to restore a damaged ecosystem could use a computer to model changes to the system. The computer could model the effects of changes before the engineer decides which changes to make in a large area.

Infer Why would a computer model of a new ship design save time or money during the construction of the ship?

_____

_____

_____

Optimizing Solutions

Engineering is focused on solving problems. A successful solution must meet all of the criteria and constraints. Even if a solution is successful, a better solution may still be possible. When the design is tested, engineers may think of new ideas that might work. The criteria or constraints may also change during the process.

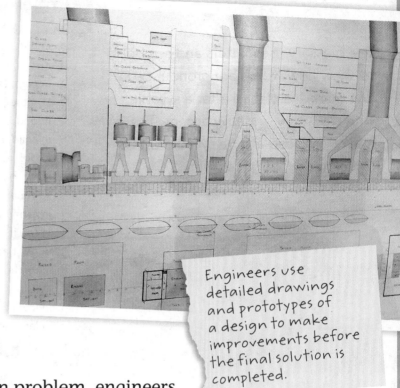

Engineers use detailed drawings and prototypes of a design to make improvements before the final solution is completed.

Even after solving the design problem, engineers continue to work on the solution to optimize it, or make it better. They evaluate the results and consider ways to improve on them. Then they may make a new prototype to determine whether it is a better solution. Like scientists, engineers make a change and then observe or measure the results of the change. After analyzing and evaluating their data, engineers may change the solution or develop a new engineering problem.

Optimize Solutions An engineer designs a project to restore a forest after a mining project. After the design is complete, more funding becomes available. How could the engineer optimize the design solution?

_____

_____

_____

_____

Glossary

The glossary uses letters and symbols to show how words are pronounced. The mark " is placed after a syllable with a primary or heavy accent. The mark ' is placed after a syllable with a secondary or light accent.

abiotic (ā' bī ot" ik) nonliving parts of an ecosystem

apparent (ə par" ənt) how something looks

aquifer (ak" wə fər) underground water supply

asteroid (as" tə roid') a chunk of rock in space that orbits the sun

atmosphere (at" mə sfir) the layer of gases surrounding Earth

atom (at" əm) the smallest part of an element that has the properties of the element

atomic theory (ə tom" ik thē" ər ē *or* ə tom" ik thir" ē) the idea that everything is made of small particles

axis (ak" sis) an imaginary line that goes through the center of an object

biosphere (bī" ə sfir) the Earth system that includes all living things

biotic (bī ot" ik) living parts of an ecosystem

carnivore (kär" nə vôr) an animal that eats only other animals, or products of other animals

characteristic (kâr′ ik tə ris″ tik) a trait that can help identify something

chemical change (kem″ ə kəl chānj) a process in which a new kind of matter forms

chemical reaction (kem″ ə kəl rē ak″ shen) the process in which one or more substances change into one or more different substances

chlorophyll (klôr″ ə fil) the green substance in plant cells that absorbs light energy and helps the plant perform photosynthesis.

circulation (sėr′ kyə lā″ shen) a swirling movement

classify (klas″ ə fī) to organize into groups based on a system

comet (kom″ it) chunk of rock, dust, and ice with stretched-out orbits around the sun

community (kə myü″ nə tē) all organisms living in an ecosystem

competition (kəm pə′ tish″ ən) when two or more organisms need the same limited resource to survive

component (kəm pō″ nənt *or* käm pō″ nənt *or* käm″ pō nənt) a part

compound (kom″ pound) a type of matter made of two or more elements

conclude (kən klüd″) to make a statement with data and facts

condensation (kon′ den sā″ shen) the process in which a gas cools and becomes a liquid

conservation (kon′ sər vā″ shen) the protection and care of forests, rivers, and other natural resources

conservation of matter (kon′ sər vā″ shən ov mat″ ər) the scientific law that in any physical or chemical change, the total mass of the matter does not change

constellation (kon′ stə lā″ shən) a group of stars that appear to form a shape or picture

consumer (kən sü″ mər) an organism that needs to eat other organisms to survive

cycle (si″ kəl) a series of events or processes that repeats over and over

decomposer (dē′ kəm pō″ zər) an organism that breaks down the bodies of dead organisms

describe (di skrīb″) to tell about the properties of an object

differentiate (dif′ ə ren″ shē āt) to identify the differences between two or more objects

distinguish (dis ting″ gwish) to clearly show the differences between two objects

distribute (dis trib″ yüt) spread out

Glossary

ecosystem (ē" kō sis′ təm *or* ek" ō sis′ təm) the living things and nonliving things in an area

ectotherm (ek" tə thərm′) an animal that depends on its environment to warm its body

effect (ə fekt") a change that happens because of some kind of action

efficient (ə fish" ənt) able to produce the effect wanted without wasting time or energy

endotherm (en" dō thərm′) an animal that uses energy from their body to keep their body at a steady temperature

establish (e stab" lish) to show an idea

evaporation (i vap′ ə rā" shən) the process in which a substance warms and changes from a liquid into a gas

exert (eg zėrt") to put forth strength or effort

food chain (füd chān) a model that shows how matter and energy flow from one organism to another

food web (füd web) a model of the transfer of energy within a set of interconnected food chains

gas (gas) matter that does not have a definite shape or volume

geosphere (jē" ō sfir′) the Earth system that includes rocks, soil, sediments, and Earth's core and mantle

glacier (glā shər) a slow moving body of ice on land

gravity (grav" ə tē) a force of attraction between two objects

greenhouse effect (grēn" hous′ ə fekt") the process in which heat is trapped in Earth's atmosphere

herbivore (ėr" bə vôr or hėr" bə vor) an animal that eats only plants

hydroelectric energy (hī′ drō l lek" trik en" ər jē) energy produced by moving water

hydrosphere (hī" drə sfir) the Earth system that includes all water

inner planets (in" ər plan" it) the four rocky planets closest to the sun

interact (in tər akt") to affect another organism and be affected by it

interdependent (in′ tər di pen″ dənt) a relationship where different parts depend on each other

liquid (lik″ wid) matter with a definite volume but no definite shape

lithosphere (lith″ ə sfir) a part of the geosphere that contains Earth's crust and outer, rigid part of the mantle

maintain (mān tān″) to keep in the same condition

mass (mas) the amount of matter in an object

measure (mezh″ ər) to compare something to a standard unit

metabolism (mə tab″ ə liz′ əm) the chemical processes animals use to break down or build molecules

microbe (mī″ krōb) an organism that is too small to see

mineral (min″ ər əl) a naturally occurring, nonliving substance

mixture (miks″ chər) a substance where different materials are put together but each keeps its own properties

molecule (mol″ ə kyül) the smallest particle of a compound that has the properties of the compound

moon (mün) a large, round piece of rock and ice that revolves around a planet

natural gas (nach″ ər əl gas) a mixture of methane and other gases formed underground and used for energy

natural resource (nach″ ər əl ri sôrs″ or nach″ ər əl rē″ sôrs) a material supplied by nature that is used by humans and other organisms

nonrenewable resource (non′ ri nü″ ə bəl ri sôrs″ or non′ ri nü″ ə bəl rē″ sôrs) a resource that is replenished at a slower rate than it is used

observe (əb zėrv″) to use your senses to gather information

obtain (əb tān″) to get

omnivore (om″ nə vôr′) an animal that eats both plants and other animals

orbit (ôr″ bit) the curved path of an object around a star, a planet, or a moon

organize (ôr″ gə nīz) to arrange something to make it easier to understand

outer planet (ou″ tər plan″ it) the four large planets farthest from the sun that are made of ice and gases

Glossary

pattern (pat" ərn) objects or events that occur in the same order or manner

photosynthesis (fō′ tō sin" thə sis) the process that plants use to make glucose using carbon dioxide, light, and water and producing oxygen

physical change (fiz" ə kəl chānj) a change in some properties of matter that does not change what the substance is made of

pollution (pə lü" shən) the presence of harmful substances in the environment

precipitation (pri sip′ ə tā" shən) water in the atmosphere that falls to earth as rain, sleet, snow, or hail

primary (pri" mer′ ē) the original or most important

producer (prə dü" sər) an organism that can make its own nutrients, usually with energy from the sun

related (ri lā" tid) connected

renewable resource (ri nü" ə bəl ri sôr" s or ri nü" ə bəl rē" sôrs) material made by nature at least as quickly as people use it

reservoir (rez" ər vwär) a human-made place to collect and store water

revolution (rev′ ə lü" shən) the movement of one object around another object

rock (rok) a natural substance made from one or more minerals

rotation (rō tā" shən) the spinning of an object around its axis

salinity (sə lin" ə tē) the amount of salt dissolved in water

shadow (shad" ō) a dark area or shape made by an object or organism blocking a source of light

solar system (sō" lər sis" təm) the planets, asteroids, and comets that orbit the sun, as well as the planets' moons

solid (sol" id) matter with a definite shape and volume

solubility (sol′ yə bil" ə tē) the property of a substance that tells how well it dissolves in another material

solution (sə lü shən) a mixture in which the substances are evenly spread out and do not settle to the bottom of the container

stable (stā" bəl) steady or unchanging

star (stär) a giant ball of hot, glowing matter

succession (sək sesh" ən) a series of changes in a community of an ecosystem

support (sə pôrt") to back up

system (sis" təm) a group of parts that work together to complete a task

temperature (tem" pər ə chər) a measure of how fast the particles of matter are moving

tide (tīd) pattern of rising and falling water in the ocean caused by gravity

transform (trans fôrm") to change in form

volume (vol" yəm) the amount of space an object takes up

water cycle (wȯ" tər si" kəl) the continuous movement of water on Earth

Index

* Page numbers for charts, graphs, maps, and pictures are printed in *italics*.

Illustrations

Articulate Graphics/IllustrationOnline.com; Aaron Ashley Illustration; Peter Bull Art Studio; Dan Crisp/The Bright Agency; Stuart Holmes/Illustration Inc.; Melissa Manwill/Shannon Associates, LLC; Mapping Specialists, Ltd.; Bojan Orešković; Pronk Media Inc.; Rob Schuster; Geoffrey P. Smith; Jim Steck/Steck Figures; Symmetry Creative Productions; Sam Valentino/Bumblecat Design & Illustration, LLC; Ralph Voltz/IllustrationOnline.com

Photographs

Photo locators denoted as follows: Top (T), Center (C), Bottom (B), Left (L), Right (R), Background (Bkgd)

Covers

Front Cover: Anatol Pietryczuk/Shutterstock;
Back Cover: Marinello/DigitalVision Vectors/Getty Images;

Front Matter

iv: Clari Massimiliano/Shutterstock; vi: Number 76219/Shutterstock; vii: A and N photography/Shutterstock; viii: Opla/iStock/Getty Images; ix: Monkey Business Images/Shutterstock; x: Mark Edward Atkinson/Tracey Lee/Blend Images/Getty Images; xi: Wavebreakmedia/Shutterstock; xii: Kurhan/Fotolia; xiii: Samuel Borges Photography/Shutterstock; xiv: SnowWhiteimages/Shutterstock; xv: Pearson Education; xvi B: Lakov Kalinin/Fotolia; xvi TR: Barry Tuck/Shutterstock; xvii B: Pearson Education; xvii T: Pearson Education

Topic 1

000: Grace Caldwell/EyeEm/Getty Images; 002: Number 76219/Shutterstock; 005 CR: Christophe Launay/Getty Images; 005 R: Tbradford/iStock/Getty Images; 006 B: Adisa/iStock/Getty Images; 006 BL: Matt Grant/Shutterstock; 008: Oktay Ortakcioglu/E+/Getty Images; 009: Richard Megna/Fundamental Photographs; 012 BL: Belchonock/123RF; 012 TL: Indianstockimages/Shutterstock; 013 C: ESB Professional/Shutterstock; 013 CR: Svetlana Foote/Shutterstock; 014: ESB Professional/Shutterstock; 015 B: Syda Productions/Shutterstock; 015 TR: Couperfield/Shutterstock; 016 B: Apiguide/Shutterstock; 016 BR: Mark Baigent Life/Alamy Stock Photo; 018 B: Kinn Deacon/Alamy Stock Photo; 018 BL: Alexey V Smirnov/Shutterstock; 019 BC: ESB Professional/Shutterstock; 019 C: Molekuul/123RF; 022: Photo5963_shutter/Shutterstock; 023 BR: Alexeysun/Shutterstock; 023 T: ESB Professional/Shutterstock; 024 BC: Ociacia/Shutterstock; 024 BR: Baloncici/Shutterstock; 024 CL: 123RF; 026: Schankz/Shutterstock; 027 BCR: Lineartestpilot/Shutterstock; 027 BR: BeatWalk/Shutterstock; 029 BR: Education Images/Universal Images Group North America LLC/Alamy Stock Photo; 029 TR: Goss Images/Alamy Stock Photo; 030: ESB Professional/Shutterstock; 031 CR: Aksenenko Olga/Shutterstock; 031 TR: Dmitr1ch/Fotolia; 032 BR: Viktor1/Shutterstock; 032 T: ESB Professional/Shutterstock; 034: Skodonnell/iStock/Getty Images; 035 B: SasinTipchai/Shutterstock; 035 TR: Suwin/Shutterstock; 037: R. Gino Santa Maria/Shutterstock; 040: Elina Li/Shutterstock

Topic 2

042: Milosz Maslanka/Shutterstock; 044: A and N photography/Shutterstock; 046: Irmun/Shutterstock; 047 CR: U.S. Department of Energy/Science Source; 047 R: Leonid Ikan/Fotolia; 048: Antantarctic/Fotolia; 052 B: Antonina Sotnykova/Shutterstock; 052 BR: Aukarawatcyber/Shutterstock; 052 CL: Tim UR/Shutterstock; 053 BC: A and N photography/Shutterstock; 053 R: Sara Winter/Fotolia; 054: Calek/Shutterstock; 055 TL: A and N photography/Shutterstock; 055 TR: Anne Gilbert/Alamy Stock Photo; 056: Cyran/Shutterstock; 058 CR: A and N photography/Shutterstock; 058 TL: Lersan Moomueansri/123RF; 059 B: Nati Harnik/AP Images; 059 TR: David Taylor/Science Source; 060 B: Santiparp Wattanaporn/Shutterstsock; 060 BL: Foto Images/Fotolia; 060 CL: Kichigin/Shutterstock; 062 B: Tibet Saisema/Shutterstock; 062 TL: A and N photography/Shutterstock; 063 B: Jeff Smith/Alamy Stock Photo; 063 CR: Njnightsky/123RF; 064: Lukas Gojda/Fotolia; 065: Natasha Pankina/Shutterstock; 067 C: galichstudio/Fotolia; 067 CL: galichstudio/Fotolia; 069 BC: A and N photography/Shutterstock; 069 CR: Ahavelaar/Fotolia; 069 TR: Mexrix/Shutterstock; 072 BC: Magnago/Shutterstock; 072 BCL: Ajt/Shutterstock; 072 Bkgrd: Mushy/Fotolia; 072 BL: Lizard/Shutterstock; 072 BR: Daxiao Productions/Shutterstock; 073 TCR: Andrew Kurcan/EyeEm/Getty Images; 073 TR: Steve Carroll/123RF; 074 BCR: Scott Bolster/Shutterstock; 074 BR: Pearson Education; 074 TR: A and N photography/Shutterstock; 075: GlebTv/Shutterstock; 076 BL: Dod/Fotolia; 076 BR: Jay Beaumont/Fotolia; 076 C: Barry Tuck/Shutterstock; 076 CL: RGtimeline/Shutterstock; 078: Joannawnuk/Shutterstock; 080 CL: Hemera Technologies/PhotoObjects.net/Getty Images Plus/Getty Images; 080 TL: Slava_Kovtun/Shutterstock; 081 B: Sergieiev/Shutterstock; 081 BC: A and N photography/Shutterstock; 084: Richard Megna/Fundamental Photographs; 085: Donfiore/Shutterstock; 086 Bkgrd: Severija/Shutterstock; 086 TC: A and N photography/Shutterstock; 088 Bkgrd: Yatra/Shutterstock; 088 TR: A and N photography/Shutterstock; 089 B: JeanMarie Guyon/123RF; 089 CR: Jiri Hera/Fotolia; 089 TR: Nd3000/Fotolia; 091 BCL: Aleksandar Grozdanovski/Shutterstock; 091 BL: Mark Prytherch/Shutterstock; 091 TCL: Gudz Sofiya/Shutterstock; 091 TL: HUANG Zheng/Shutterstock; 095: Nine Homes/Shutterstock

Topic 3

096: Seaphotoart/Shutterstock; 098: Opla/iStock/Getty Images; 100: Rvector/Shutterstock; 101 Bkgrd: Aurora Photos/Alamy Stock Photo; 101 TR: Nick Brundle Photograph/Moment/Getty Images; 102: Oticki/Shutterstock; 104 BL: Jon Manjeot; 104 BR: EpicStockMedia/Shutterstock; 104 TL: Hadot/123RF; 104 TR: Vladimir Mucibabic/Shutterstock; 105 BC: Opla/iStock/Getty Images; 105 Bkgrd: George H.H. Huey/Alamy Stock Photo; 109 B: William Chapman/Alamy Stock Photo; 109 TL: Opla/iStock/Getty Images; 110: Antema/E+/Getty Images; 111: Hchjjl/Shutterstock; 114: Opla/iStock/Getty Images; 115: NASA Archive/Alamy Stock Photo; 116: Opla/iStock/Getty Images; 117: Hadot/123RF; 118 BR: Harald Toepfer/Shutterstock; 118 C: Marcin Rogozinski/Alamy Stock Photo; 118 CL: Boule/Shutterstock; 120: Chris Agnousiotis/EyeEm/Getty Images; 121: Macrovector/Shutterstock; 122: Bridge Community Project/Alamy Stock Photo; 123: Corridor91/iStock/Getty Images; 126 BL: USDA Photo/Alamy Stock

Photography/Shutterstock; 334: Samuel Borges Photography/ Shutterstock; 336 B: Edhar/Shutterstock; 336 BC: Loops7/iStock/ Getty Images; 338: Marlenka/iStock/Getty Images; 340: Bruce MacQuee/123RF; 341 BR: Erikgauger/iStock/Getty Images; 341 CR: Rick & Nora Bowers/Alamy Stock Photo; 342 CR: Samuel Borges Photography/Shutterstock; 342 T: Zahoor Salmi/Moment/ Getty Images; 343: Claudia Paulussen/Shutterstock; 344 BR: Pal Teravagimov/Shutterstock; 344 CR: Panuruangjan/123RF; 344 TL: Samuel Borges Photography/Shutterstock; 344 TR: Mark Herreid/ Shutterstock; 345 B: C.O. Harris/Science Source; 345 TR: Birdiegal/ Shutterstock; 346 Bkgrd: Carlosgaw/E+/Getty Images; 346 TR: Samuel Borges Photography/Shutterstock; 347 B: George Nazmi Bebawi/Shutterstock; 347 TR: Chih Yuan Ronnie Wu/Alamy Stock Photo; 348 BL: Tom Brakefield/DigitalVision/Getty Images; 348 CL: Nattanan726/Shutterstock; 351 TL: Kosam/Shutterstock; 351 TR: Don Mammoser/Shutterstock; 353: Maria Beatrice Missere/EyeEm/ Getty Images

Topic 9

354: Scott Linstead/Science Source; 356: SnowWhiteimages/ Shutterstock; 359 C: Ljupco Smokovski/Shutterstock; 359 R: ChiccoDodiFC/Shutterstock; 360: Oliveromg/Shutterstock; 362 BR: SnowWhiteimages/Shutterstock; 362 CL: Francesco Tomasinelli/ Science Source; 362 L: ImageBROKER/Alamy Stock Photo; 362 TC: Anneka/Shutterstock; 366 CL: Vadym Zaitsev/Shutterstock; 366 T: Vadym Zaitsev/Shutterstock; 367 CR: Jakit17/Shutterstock; 367 TL: SnowWhiteimages/Shutterstock; 367 TR: Gjm123/Shutterstock; 368: Wesley Bocxe/Science Source; 370: Clint Farlinger/Alamy Stock Photo; 371 BR: Jolanda Aalbers/Shutterstock; 371 CR: Candus Camera/Shutterstock; 374 BCL: Scenics & Science/ Alamy Stock Photo; 374 BL: FLPA/Alamy Stock Photo; 374 BR: SnowWhiteimages/Shutterstock; 374 TCL: Naturepix/Alamy Stock Photo; 374 TL: Nature Picture Library/Alamy Stock Photo; 374 TR: Reinhard Dirscherl/Alamy Stock Photo; 375: Ondrej Prosicky/Shutterstock; 376: SnowWhiteimages/Shutterstock; 377 B: James Hobbs/Moment/Getty Images; 377 TR: Edo Schmidt/ Alamy Stock Photo; 378 B: Ruvanboshoff/E+/Getty Images; 378 BL: Chris Alcock/Shutterstock; 379: Marish/Shutterstock; 382 BR: SnowWhiteimages/Shutterstock; 382 CL: Spondylolithesis/iStock/ Getty Images; 383: Kozlik_Mozlik/iStock /Getty Images; 384 BR: Rokopix/Shutterstock; 384 TR: SnowWhiteimages/Shutterstock; 386: Kekyalyaynen/Shutterstock; 387: Bioraven/Shutterstock; 388: Jane Rix/Shutterstock; 389 BCL: Artpixelgraphy Studio/ Shutterstock; 389 BCR: Nevodka/iStock/Getty Images; 389 BR: Tatiana Popova/Shutterstock; 389 TCL: Vasilkovv/123RF; 389 TCR: Horsemen/Shutterstock; 389 TL: Vaclav Volrab/123RF; 392: Rocky33/Shutterstock; 393 TL: SnowWhiteimages/Shutterstock; 393 TR: Merlin D. Tuttle/Science Source; 394 B: Nikitsin. Smugmug/Shutterstock; 394 CR: Caroline Schiff/Blend Images/ Getty Images; 396 Bkgrd: Robyn Mackenzie/Shutterstock; 396 TR: SnowWhiteimages/Shutterstock; 397 B: Herianus/iStock/ Getty Images; 397 TR: Christopher Kimmel/Getty Images; 398 BCR: InterNetwork Media/DigitalVision/Getty Images; 398 BR: CPC Collection/Alamy Stock Photo; 398 C: Roman Khomlyak/ Shutterstock; 398 CL: All Canada Photos/Alamy Stock Photo; 403: Kavram/123RF

End Matter

EM0: Aleksey Stemmer/Shutterstock; EM1: SergeUWPhoto/ Shutterstock; EM2 Bkgrd: Don Paulson/Purestock/Alamy Stock Photo; EM2 BR: Rattiya Thongdumhyu/Shutterstock; EM3: Suzanne Long/Alamy Stock Photo; EM5: National Oceanic and Atmospheric Administration (NOAA), U.S. Department of Commerce.; EM6: Fotosearch/Getty Images; EM7: M. Timothy O'Keefe/Alamy Stock Photo; EM9: Hero Images Inc./Alamy Stock Photo; EM11: CANARAN/Shutterstock; EM12: Vandrage Artist/Shutterstock; EM13: Stephen Barnes/Alamy Stock Photo

My Notes and Designs

Draw, Write, Create

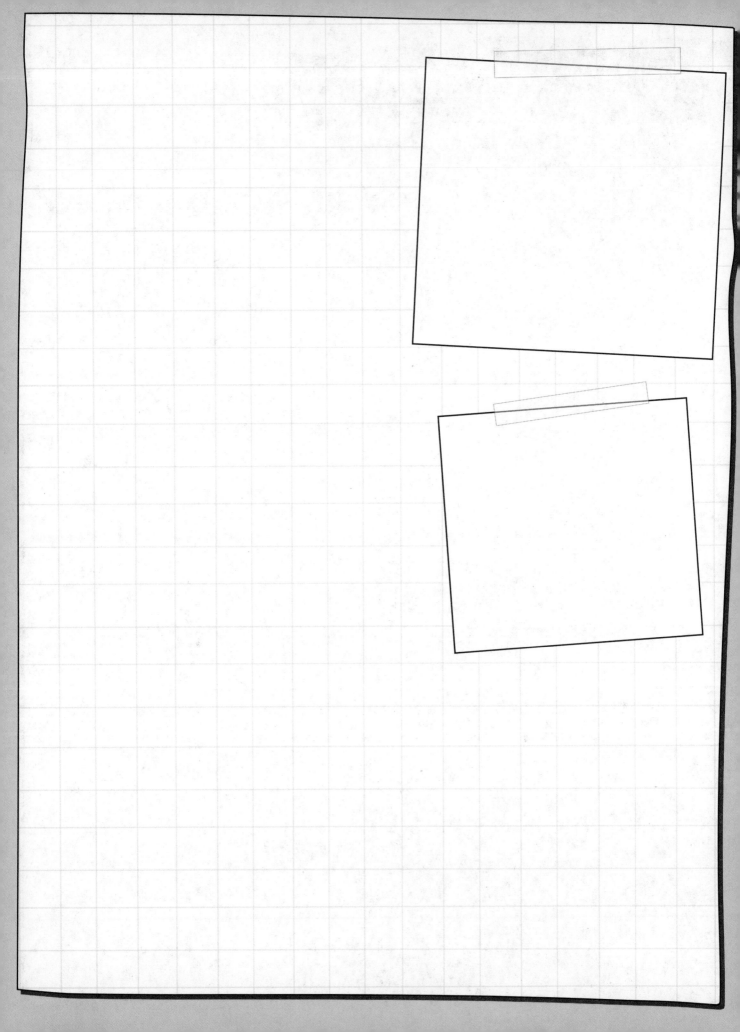

My Notes and Designs

Draw, Write, Create

My Notes and Designs

Draw, Write, Create